Act Your Age!

Critical Social Thought
Edited by Michael W. Apple, University of Wisconsin, Madison

Act Your Age!

a cultural construction of
ADOLESCENCE

Nancy Lesko

ROUTLEDGE FALMER
New York and London

Published in 2001 by
RoutledgeFalmer
29 West 35th Street
New York, NY 10001

Published in Great Britain in 2001 by
RoutledgeFalmer
11 New Fetter Lane
London EC4P 4EE

Figure 1.5 is by T. R. Robertson, New York, NY, who also assisted in image research and
production for this volume.

Library of Congress Cataloging-in-Publication Data

Lesko, Nancy.
Act your age! : a cultural construction of adolescence / Nancy Lesko.
        p.   cm. — (Critical social thought)
    Includes bibliographical references and index.
    ISBN 0-415-92833-8 — ISBN 0-415-92834-6 (pbk.)
      1. Adolescence. I. Title. II. Series.
    HQ796 .L384 2001
    305.235—dc21   00-059260

10 9 8 7 6 5

contents

The rational, the savage, the animal, the human, the degenerate, the normal, all become features of the modern scientific normalization and regulation of children.

— *Valerie Walkerdine, 1984, p. 173*

acknowledgments

I have lived the ideas in this book for a long time, and many people have influenced their substance and form. Several years ago I had responsive audiences to the beginnings of these ideas at the JCT Curriculum Theory and Classroom Practice Conferences, and conference attendees have remained my imaginary supportive readers. Small grants from the Spencer Foundation and from the Marris Profitt Foundation at Indiana University supported this work in its early stages. Readers and supporters whom I wish to thank include: Gary Anderson, Mike Apple, Rene Arcilla, Mimi Bloch, Leslie Bloom, Ellen Brantlinger, John Broughton, Mignonette Chiu, Latoya Connor, Gunilla Dahlberg, Ines Dussel, Lynn Fendler, Deb Garrahy, Jesse Goodman, Maxine Greene, Michelle Haiken, Lisa Hennon, Kathryn Herr, Chris Higgins, Dawn Horton, Kenneth Hultqvist, Michelle Knight, Craig Kridel, Turid Midjo, Mimi Orner, Miguel Parelya, Tom Popkewitz, Sharon Ryan, Alan Sadovnik, Doris Santoro, David Schaafsma, Margie Siegel, Noah Sobe, Ola Stafseng, Fran Stage, Ruth Vinz, Cally Waite, Joyceln Woo, and Christine Yeh. The Wednesday Group in the Department of Curriculum and Instruction at the University of Wisconsin-Madison and the Philosophy Colloquium at Teachers College offered enthusiastic and critical responses.

I am grateful for the support provided by a Spencer Foundation Small grant and a grant from the Marris Proffitt Foundation, Indiana University–Bloomington. Wendy Schwartz provided extraordinarily attentive editing along with humor and political discussions. At Routledge-New York, I thank Heidi Freund for her direction, clarity, and energy from the beginning of this project. I am also grateful to Karita France dos Santos for her careful assistance and continuing support.

I also thank the administrative support personnel at Teachers College, Columbia University, for their competence and good humor: Aimee Fregeau, James Rolling, Kazue Takenaga, Sunny Kim, and Shabiya Wahabodeen.

I am grateful for T. R. Robertson's passionate discussions on youth, vigilant newspaper clipping, original artwork, assistance with image production, and, most importantly, laughter to keep going.

Portions of this book appeared previously in different forms and are used with permission of the editors and the publishers:

Theory Into Practice 33(3), 143–148 (1994).

Youth & Society 28(2), 139–161 (1996).

Educational Theory 46(4), 453–472 (1996).

Books, S. (Ed.). (1998). *Neither seen nor heard: Invisible children in the society and the schools* (pp. 101–131). Mahwah, NJ: Lawrence Erlbaum.

Lesko, N. (Ed.). (2000). *Masculinities at school* (pp. 187–212). Thousand Oaks, CA: Sage.

series editor's introduction

It is a sign of a deeply troubled culture that while we are horrified by the repeated shootings in schools throughout the United States, we are no longer surprised. The very word Columbine has been engraved into our memories as nearly an archetype of the tragedy of adolescence. How could it happen? What is wrong with teenagers today? We are constantly being told that youth have lost their values, have become feral and violent, are oversexed and undereducated. No matter what the lament or explanation, adolescents are now seen as a *problem*. It is not to minimize the horror or the tragedy of events such as Columbine to recognize that there are particular ways in which youth are now seen. These ways of seeing are differential. While many white male middle class youth may be seen as "troubled" or alienated, many black and Latino males are seen as violent and predatory and as apt to be criminals. At the same time, black and Latina young women are sexualized; their bodies are out of control and are, in essence, baby-producing machines.[1] As I show in some of my own work, all of these portrayals have been taken up by powerful conservative forces to attack many of the gains that have been made by dispossessed people.[2]

These differential interpretations have powerful effects. The ways in which adolescents are treated during their teenage years can create tensions that last forever. Class, race, and gender identities are formed in interaction with institutions. If the definitions of youth that we build into our policies and programs in schools and elsewhere are as much a part of the problem as they are a part of a supposed solution, then we risk creating identities that will come back to haunt us for generations to come.

Is all of this new? Are the youth of today and the ways we see them really different than in the past? How do our current ways of talking about "the problem of adolescence" compare to those that dominated past generations? Nancy Lesko's new book provides insights into these issues in a manner unlike any other book I know on these important topics.

Act Your Age! is a form of talking back to dominant interpretations. Rather than seeing adolescents through the usually accepted lenses of "hormones out of control," as delinquents, or as "irrationally subject to peer pressure," it provides an insightful analysis of how these common-sense ways of interpreting adolescence themselves have been and are connected to power relations. It artfully demonstrates how our accepted ways of viewing adolescents were informed by the history of imperialism, masculinity, and racial dynamics. It shows how each of these created and were created by the growth of particular "scientific" approaches that helped cement these interpretations both into popular consciousness and into the schools that were built to house these seemingly "deviant" teenagers.

This book offers a thorough-going deconstruction of our accepted understandings of youth. It causes us to rethink much that has been told to us about developmental psychology, about the history of the very category of adolescence, about masculinity and femininity, and about teenage pregnancy and youth violence. Yet, it does not end there. Nancy Lesko also has a positive program in mind. She rightly argues that we ask not only what youth can learn from us, but also what we can learn from *them*. This is a crucial point. In a time when there has been a rebirth of social activism against the forces of economic globalization, racism, environmental destruction, homophobia, and so many other destructive forces, the growing activism of youth in so many of their local institutions provides a model of how we can learn from them—and connect with them to help create the conditions for more democratic and less alienating and impersonal sets of economic, political, and cultural institutions. That she does this in a manner that demonstrates new methodological approaches for understanding the connections between power and culture adds to her accomplishments in this book.

Michael W. Apple
John Bascom Professor
of Curriculum and Instruction
and Educational Policy Studies
University of Wisconsin-Madison

Introduction

Troubling Teenagers

Consider for a moment some familiar public spaces: your local mall, a cineplex, the outside seating of fast food restaurants, a bowling alley, skateboarding sites, video arcades, or buses around 3 P.M. any Monday through Friday. Ubiquitous in all of those spaces are teenagers—almost always in groups and sporting hair, clothes, piercings, and attitudes that mark them as belonging to "another tribe." Teenagers are so obvious and omnipresent that we seem hardly to notice them unless their peals of laughter cause us to nervously look their way, or they interfere with the expected movement or pace of a common task such as standing in line or shopping for groceries, or they walk too close on the street or in the mall. The ubiquity of teenagers in social spaces beyond households and schools is matched by their prominence in our talk. A little conscious attention finds adolescents in television sitcoms; in social science, psychology, and therapy; and in news-making discussions of public problems. Typically teenagers appear in our cultural talk as synonymous with crazed hormones, as delinquents, deficiencies, or clowns, that is, beings not to be taken too seriously. They are most often spoken of with familiarity, sometimes with affection, and regularly with some hostility or displeasure. In these various venues and with decidedly mixed emotions, we talk about "the trouble with teenagers."

This book takes a close look at these "troubling teenagers" as stock characters in popular narratives, scientific discourses, and educational programs via endlessly repeated stories—clinical and anecdotal—of instability, emotionality, present-centeredness, and irresponsibility. The ubiquitousness of teenagers with problems, their ability to outrage or worry adults, and the certainty about their naturally occurring "nature" beg scrutiny. The ready construction of young people into numerous public problems—most recently, violent Internet-addicted suburbanites, teenage mothers, and urban criminals—suggests that teenagers are complex and malleable accomplishments with broad political and social effects. The overarching aim of this book is to "trouble" these common conceptions of adolescents.

To call the common conceptions of adolescents into question, my inquiry moves back and forth between the present and the past, a method that intentionally violates conventional chronological historical work. Because adolescence is so interwoven with development or growth over time, I needed to work against historical studies that utilized and reflected simple chronological reporting of events consistent with the terms and ideas rampant today. This method is described as a "history of the present," which problematizes the very terms that we use to think of teenagers and their growth, change, and needs in and out of school. This method takes contemporary questions and answers as the starting point for historical research.[1] The orienting questions of this study were:

- What interests and forces effected the creation of adolescence in primarily developmental psychological terms at the turn of the twentieth century?
- What material practices came into being along with new scientific ideas of adolescence?
- Why is the developmental construct so resistant to critique and change?
- What elements of our current ideas must change if we are to be able to think about adolescence differently?

I began by discerning the contemporary "confident characterizations" around adolescence, that is, several grounding assumptions that operate in scholarly and popular talk about teenagers. Although these are not exhaustive, they provided important starting points for my historical work.

CONFIDENT CHARACTERIZATIONS OF ADOLESCENCE

I discuss four "confident characterizations" of adolescents: they "come of age" into adulthood; they are controlled by raging hormones; they are peer-oriented; and they are represented by age.

Adolescents "Come of Age" into Adulthood

Teenagers are "at the threshold" and in "transition to adulthood." These phrases suggest an evolutionary arrival in an enlightened state after a lengthy period of backwardness. These phrases also participate in an "ideology of emergence," which is a belief that teenagers are naturally emerging and outside of social influences. They are autonomous beings who get dropped down into various social and historical contexts. "Coming of age" makes adolescence into a powerful and uncontrollable force, like the arrival of spring that swells tree buds. Finally, "coming of age" and "at the threshold" are also *homiletic*. These terms appear to give adolescence importance but really confer greater authority on the author of the homily. Scientists and educators who proclaim the potentials and problems of the not-yet-of-age are positionally superior.[2] In one or two simple and repetitious phrases we can understand the workings of evolutionary progress, science, and religion. Thus seemingly inconsequential phrases carry weight from different sources and are difficult to maneuver around or to critique. By paying close attention to language we can begin to see the cultural weights that are put on a particular way of understanding adolescence as portentous, uncontrollable, and naturally occurring, and we see how the speakers on adolescents' transitions to adulthood are invested with authority.

Adolescents Are Controlled by Raging Hormones

This characterization of youth points to their physiological growth and its linked emotions and makes us look at their bodies for evidence of raging hormones: height and weight spurts, breasts, deeper voices, facial hair, and broadened hips. The mood swings of adolescence are related to the hormonal rages and to our beliefs that teenagers are emotional, unpredictable, and often confused. Raging hormones also play into ideas of teenagers as rebellious and as natural challengers of authority and limits. This characterization also assumes that adolescence is naturally occurring and locates the source in hormonal changes. It grounds adolescence in biology, and the teenaged body is their destiny. This characterization also emphasizes sexuality, since the hormones are directly linked with male testosterone and with female menstrual cycles; thus it emphasizes the raging sexuality of youth. I think the language of raging hormones emphasizes the uncontrollable force of hormones, links the power to sexuality, and offers these facts as biological and beyond social intervention.[3]

Adolescents Are Peer-Oriented

The third "confident characterization" about adolescents is that they are strongly oriented to peers' ideas and influences. James Coleman's 1961 study, *The Adolescent Society*, began recent decades of sociological studies when he reported that in ten high schools he had studied, being popular was more important than getting good grades. Although Coleman's findings have been critiqued, the sense of adolescents and peer pressure being synonymous has entered the realm of the common sense. To speak of peer orientation is to claim that teenagers are less individuated than adults. Before these traits were attributed to youth, Victorian psychologists demonstrated that women, primitives, and children were more alike, more generic, and more uniform than developed (white, European) men. The attribution of peer orientation also suggests conformity of youth. Adolescents are characterized as succumbing to "peer pressure" and being part of peer cultures that socialize them to peer norms. To be fully under the influence of others implies that adolescents are not fully autonomous, rational, or determining, all of which are valued characteristics for successful, modern adults. Once again, this attribute positions teenagers as immature, as inferior to adults. To demean peer pressure also has the effect of privileging an individualism that is historically associated with middle-class, white males and is largely alien to the experiences of many people of color and women.4

Adolescence Is Signified by Age

This characterization appears to be a tautology, but it needs to be recognized that adolescence is made in and through the passage of time. When I offer "Nathalie is 12" or "Luis is 15," these statements call forth volumes of information and references: developing bodies, strange music, moody distancing, laughter alternating with sullenness, expectations of diffidence, passionate arguments, and talking endlessly on the phone are just a few. Age is a shorthand, a code that evokes what amounts to an "epidemic of signification." As I will demonstrate, age has become the main entry point to thinking within a developmental perspective.

These four confident characterizations of adolescence operate within and across numerous fields, including education, law, medicine, psychology, and social work, as well as in popular culture, such as movies, television, and literature. They declare the nature of youth and they incite us to find instances of their truth in new encounters. In theoretical terms these confident characterizations tell us what adolescents will be like, help us interpret our personal experiences of being teenaged in their light, and inform future observations by telling us what is important and enduring in adolescent lives. We believe that youths are under peer pressure, we understand our own experiences in these terms, and we see new situations in these terms. Thus these characterizations move both into our pasts and into our futures, helping to shape individual subjective experiences but also objective knowledges.

In order to unpack the assumptions and investments of these confident characterizations, I explore the turn of the century, when the problems and potential of adolescence came into popular focus and when numerous organizations, such as the Boy Scouts, the juvenile justice system, the playground movement, and formal secondary education, grew in response. I intersperse the characterizations of youth and emergent specialized institutions and practices at the turn of the twentieth century with chapters on contemporary youth. I purposely juxtapose historically "quaint" ideas and practices with current debates on middle schools, teenage mothers, and violent youths in order to jar readers and to make the familiar ideas about adolescence "strange." My interpretation is historical but it is also thematic and critical, interrogating the present by examining how accepted ideas about adolescence were initially developed, codified, circulated, and popularized. By locating knowledge about teenagers in specific histories and social conflicts, the book intends to interrupt the social relations and politics through which a "natural adolescent" has been accepted, defined as inadequate, and administered to (that is, protected, educated, diagnosed, and/or incarcerated) in various educational, legal, and medical programs.

THE OVERALL ARGUMENT OF THIS BOOK

Although an idea of adolescence had existed for a long time, social and political changes in the late 1800s and early 1900s offered new possibilities for youths and for those who would define and provide for them. As part of the move toward a new modern society, citizens needed to become more self-determining, individualized, and reasoning. Adolescence became a social space in which to talk about the characteristics of people in modernity, to worry about the possibilities of these social changes, and to establish policies and programs that would help create the modern social order and citizenry. Adolescence became a handy and promiscuous social space, that is, a place that people could endlessly worry about, a space that adults everywhere could watch carefully and that could be imagined to have many visible and invisible instabilities. Adolescence became a very useful public problem, and the ways that it was talked about and worried about utilized other cultural materials at hand, that is, other popular preoccupations. I emphasize how three sets of worries at this time merged into how adolescence was defined: (1) worries over racial progress; (2) worries over male dominance; and (3) worries over the building of a nation with unity and power. Adolescent development became a useful way to talk about and strategize for racial progress, male dominance, and national strength and growth. The new experts on adolescence identified particular problems to watch for and offered active, supervised activities, especially team sports, as the prescribed path toward national progress and functional elites.

At the level of material practices, the savers of adolescents emphasized control over precocious development through group sports, building loyalty to others, and the minimizing of reasoning. They emphasized peer connections, believing that peers would oversee each other when adults were not present. Overall, the safest route to development of the race and nation was by watching closely over the small steps of boys toward courageous and loyal citizens and men. Thus close watching over bodies and reading of morality from bodies occurred. This effort was redoubled with girls.

In the contemporary chapters on middle schools and teenage pregnancy, I demonstrate how the material practices of Victorian juvenile justice are reinvented as progressive middle school practices and how the demand for slow, steady development continues and marks school-aged mothers as risks. Finally, I consider how high school athletics, especially football, perpetuate the beliefs that "boys must live out their instincts through active, supervised recreation."[5] My last two chapters take up the violence of life within high schools and how the discourse of adolescence supports it by keeping numerous dynamics and relations unthinkable. I conclude with theoretical and practical ideas that ask adults to take responsibility for their participation in the modern, scientific discourse of adolescence and I pose specific tasks about how to redefine adolescence (no longer as opposite to adults) and yet also advocate for adolescents in different ways.

ASSUMPTIONS AND CONTRIBUTIONS OF THIS STUDY

This interpretation of the construction of adolescence is important for several reasons. First, it offers an alternative theoretical framework to the two dominant understandings of adolescence: the biological view and the sociohistorical view. The natural view of adolescence that grounds most of psychology, medicine, and policy-making assumes that young people between the ages of 12 and 18 have naturally occurring, largely biologically generated characteristics, behaviors, and needs. In this view biology is destiny, in that the adolescent body with hormone-induced growth spurts creates psychological, emotional, and interpersonal problems as young people and those around them respond to the physical and psychological changes. This adolescent is outside society and history, and the important concepts and issues are intraindividual, defined largely by the knowledges of psychology, medicine, and, to a lesser extent, sociology and education. The theoretical perspective is a developmental framework, often discussed as stages of cognitive, psychosocial, or pubertal growth, out of which youths' needs can be determined.[6]

The second approach, a sociohistorical framework, emphasizes how specific contexts of adolescent development, especially economic and educational opportunities, construct youth in distinctive ways. Adolescence was created and democratized (at least in Britain and the United States) when child labor laws, industrialization, and union organizing gutted apprenticeships, which had been the conventional way for youth to move from dependency to independence. This perspective emphasizes the social construction of youth in particular contexts and institutional arrangements and acknowledges the distinctive experiences of youths from different class, race, and gender backgrounds.[7] However, this perspective accepts an economic-based view of the making of adolescence, and it does not inquire into how the naturalized, biologized adolescent was ascendant. Thus, in general, the sociohistorical tradition has not interrogated what I see as the dominant view of adolescence, although it has accounted for the rise of mass compulsory schooling. The conventional historical approach has not challenged the assumptions that adolescents are fundamentally different, developing beings based upon their age. Many historical accounts incorporate ponderous, homiletic language for their titles, such as "coming of age" or "into one's own," which suggest an uncritical acceptance of some assumptions of youth. Overall, constructivist accounts do not consider modern adolescence in relation to broad cultural transformations of time, race, gender, and citizenship.

This interpretation goes quite far beyond conventional historical accounts, although I use many of these works. I offer an alternative theoretical understanding of adolescence that combines poststructuralist, feminist, and postcolonial scholarship to question the knowledge and practices of knowing that created and maintain the modern, scientific adolescence. This *postmodern* approach[8] examines the *reasoning* about adolescence and situates that reasoning within broader social and political crises and scholarly knowledge. I look at the *systems of reasoning* that operate in adolescent theorizing and policy-making at the turn of the century and today. These systems of reasoning can be described and analyzed in various terms: as emblematic of modernity, as colonial, as gendered, and as administrative, among others. While conventional sociohistorical accounts usually focus on particular human agents and actions, to concentrate on processes of reasoning shifts the analysis from person-centered histories. If systems of reasoning, or *discourses*, are the source of action and change, they must also be the focus of inquiry.

In addition to a shift from actor-centered to discourse-centered, this genealogy (or history of the present) calls into question the belief in progress and its place as an unquestioned assumption in the human sciences. Rather than assuming progress toward a better, more rational, efficient, and democratic society, a postmodern approach examines how beliefs in the expansion of freedom may accompany enhanced bureaucracy. This shift is exemplified in Foucault's *Discipline and Punish*, where he analyzes various systems of reasoning about punishment, from torture to the modern penal system with incarceration and rehabilitation. Foucault counters the presumed progress of abandoning torture for incarceration by arguing that far broader controls over humans are executed in the modern, progressive penal approach. Instead of reading penal history as one of progressive enlightenment and more humane practices, Foucault argues that modernity involved ongoing struggles over freedom and autonomy; even in our moments of greatest freedom, power and authority are present. Foucault's work shifts our inquiry to understand how changing ideas of freedom and administration were central to creating a "self-governing, morally directed individual."[9] The social sciences and psychology offered "to make objectivist knowledge the classificatory criteria through which individuals were disciplined and self-regulated."

After abandoning human-centered action and progress, an analysis of systems of reasoning must also be antirealist. If the main goal of the modern historian or sociologist was to objectify all social life in order to explain *how events really happened* via organizing single events or the thoughts of individuals, a postmodern system of reasoning is antirealist. By antirealist, I mean that Foucault's histories are nominalist and focus upon terms, categories, and techniques, not the histories of things. He seeks to dissolve the unity of history and its apparent progress by showing its ruptures, contingencies, and reversals.[10] The attention to terms and categories is apparent in various multidisciplinary studies that shift from, for example, studying *children* to studying *childhood* (that is, the space and time of being a child that is defined, theorized, patrolled, and maintained by adults); similar shifts involve moves from studying whites to whiteness, women to femininity, and freedom to power.

From this postmodern perspective, adolescence can be considered part of a move to a modern nation-state, one in which social sciences and psychology helped make the inner, personal qualities of individuals visible and significant for building a modern society. Modern power operates in the creation of objective knowledge and of subjective realities (for example, we learn that to be successful we must understand and assess our strengths and weaknesses, based on sociological and psychological empirical science). By seeing the ways that the social sciences and psychology were involved with knowing and making modern individuals for a changing nation-state (and how these practices were taken up by modern, rational, self-governing individuals), we can begin to see how adolescence is part of very broad networks of knowledge, policy, and reason. Without postmodern interpretations, adolescence can be seen only as defined by the social sciences and psychology. Because of the theoretical grounding of this work, I can ask: *What are the systems of ideas that "make" possible the adolescence that we see, think, feel, and act upon?* To answer this question, I look at the turn of the century and the fathers of adolescence as well as the systems of ideas today.

A second contribution of this approach is to work against the assumption of progress that undergirds both histories of science and the idea of adolescence itself. To work against progress, that is, to accept a nonrevolutionary trajectory, is often condemned as regressive. However, I believe that the stance of critical detachment and reinvention, when combined with a grounded politics, is necessary if we are not to recapitulate the knowledges of the social sciences, psychology, medicine, and law. Rather than assume that more education is progressive, the postmodern stance instructs us to look closely at our ideas and practices and not to assume improvement across time.

Third, the approach utilized here is vital to reimagining adolescence. Because it is so democratized, so commonsensical, and so trivialized, we often cannot see its regulation and containment of youth. If we want to see adolescence differently, we must first understand the ways we currently see, feel, think, and act toward youth, or we will merely tinker with the reigning practices. My approach believes in the necessity and desirability of different patterns of social relations with youth. But I also believe that we must travel a greater distance toward disengagement and disenchantment with current perspectives than many critical analyses allow. [11]

POLITICS OF THIS INTERPRETATION

In this strategic history of modern, scientific adolescence, white male youths are the central characters, wrestled to center stage by white, middle-class reformers and social scientists, also largely men from small-town backgrounds who feared urbanization, the degenerate masses, and their debilitating effects on society. At first glance this may appear to be a canonical historical interpretation, another one in which white, middle-class males are the central characters. However, postmodern understandings offer a different politics.

Toni Morrison pursues the understanding of dominant white characters in American literature by attending to the flickering yet regularized appearances of African-American characters in the novels' shadows. She argues that the presence of African-American characters, with their presumed less-than-human traits, are necessary to the portrait of fully human, well-developed, white characters. Morrison claims that the realized humanity of the whites relies upon the shadowy blacks, and that the sketchy nature of blacks is developed in relation to the white characters.[12] Thus the meanings of the white characters rely on the opposition and superiority of white over black, on the continuing inseparability of whiteness and blackness, on how the reference to one necessarily relies on its opposite for meaning. White characters require the African-American characters to define them as superior, fully rational individuals.

My argument in *Act Your Age!* draws upon Morrison's. The white, middle-class boys who were centered by the child savers at the turn of the century similarly depended on girls, on working-class youth, and on youth of color, against whom they were defined as masculine, pure, self-disciplined, and courageous. My analysis of the discourse of twentieth-century adolescence highlights this structure of meaning-making, so that the idealized strong, disciplined, white male (toward which the experts were building boys' characters) was literally *unthinkable* without the inferior terms. Similarly, the undeveloped girls and youths of color could not be seen without the ideas of evolutionary stages and their inferiority *vis-à-vis* Western white citizens. In this way, we see and think adolescence as always a technology of whiteness, of masculinity, and of domination, even when boys and girls of color were the ones being developed. This perspective on adolescence was framed, in part, through colonial relations and through sciences such as anthropology that originated in colonial settings, with their racism and sexism.[13]

What does this analysis mean for my interpretation of adolescence? It means that the modern project to develop adolescence was and is simultaneously a construction of whiteness and masculinity as central to the citizen. I make these claims by reading historical accounts *contrapuntally*— as simultaneously describing events and ideas in the West and evoking the colonial relations that made the Western ideas possible. A contrapuntal reading aims for "a simultaneous awareness both of the metropolitan history that is narrated and of those other histories against which (and together with which) the dominating discourse acts."[14] Although I have provided some discussion of programs for girls and for youths of color at the turn of the century, the central focus remains on white middle-class boys because the theory and programs were ostensibly designed to benefit and develop those youths. However, I attempt to portray these ideas contrapuntally with dogged attention to the assumptions and understanding of subordinate peoples that informed and made these worries and efforts possible. Certainly much scholarship has called for an examination of whiteness and of masculinity as criteria of dominance, but other readers may be disappointed that I have not offered more in-depth portraits of those who are the counterpoints. Nevertheless a central part of this book's purpose is to acknowledge and detail a history of adolescence that is neither color-blind nor gender-blind.[15]

I own that this approach is obviously partial; examining how youths from different racial and gender backgrounds lived their adolescent years would provide a different kind of interrogation of the dominant ideas of adolescence. Nevertheless I argue that a dominant set of assumptions and ideas—what I call the "discourse of adolescence"—affects and influences *all* adolescents' lives. All youths become adolescents and are subject to its ideas and expectations. Of course different cultural groups may define adolescence in particular ways, and coming of age in Navaho, Latina/o, and white Southern communities will vary widely.[16] However, I argue that each group and each individual has to come to terms with the modern scientific definition of adolescence and its reverberations in public schooling, therapeutic talk, and expectations for maturity, self-discipline, and well-planned futures. Since adolescence has been defined as *not adult*, this opposition to adults, or at least the assumption that adolescents are distinctive from adults, will influence all cultural and class groups, although these ideas may have different implications and interpretations in particular moments and localities.

I follow Stuart Hall's lead in being conscious of and responsible for the politics of this critical analysis. When critiques take up and use the categories that have been created to administer a particular social order, the political operations are limited. In *Race: The Floating Signifier*, Hall explains how "race" has been constructed across three different time periods and disciplines—from religion to anthropology, to the contemporary sciences of racial differences. To work against these authoritative discourses (sets of language and imagery that produce the "fact" of race as naturally occurring) by relying on those same racial categories—for example, by establishing Afrocentric schooling—will likely reinforce the dominant idea that race is "a fact of existence" rather than a political construction.[17]

I follow Stuart Hall's program in arguing that we cannot operate against adolescent development as a technology and as an inferior position solely by identifying how Asian-American or Native American youths, for example, grow up differently or call the norms into question. Rather, we have to consider how race and gender are intricately woven into the norms for and into the concept of *developmental stage,* or maturity. Offering a different set of developmental steps for a particular subgroup of youth (such as Carol Gilligan describes for girls' development) elides the ways the concept and images of development itself are raced and classed. Racial, gender, and class hierarchies are called from and revivified by the image and theory of development. This must be the focus of critique, not the creation of a different set of steps to adulthood for particular groups of girls or boys. Hall argues for a politics of antiracism that operates without a guarantee of biological racial difference. Similarly, what this analysis recommends is a politics that supports youths and their futures without the biologically based guarantee of "adolescence." Can we work to enhance youths' life conditions without the confident characterization that youths are at a different psychological stage from adults? Can we work to improve youths' life conditions without the hierarchy of adult over youth? Can we consider youth as more than *becoming*? Hall closes by acknowledging that a critical politics against racism "is always a politics of criticism." I have tried to explicate the why and how of my politics of criticism.

LIMITATIONS OF THIS STUDY

This study is, of course, partial. I select certain themes and issues to examine and minimize or ignore others. In addition to acknowledging a general partiality, I want to specifiy some aspects ignored or downplayed.

One limitation of this work is that it emphasizes the events of the turn of the century and the 1980s to 1990s. In doing this, I skip very important decades for cultural developments around youth, such as television, film, and, especially, music. Thus my analysis downplays the making of teenagers through consumption. A second limitation is that in pursuing my three foci of whiteness, masculinity, and citizen as interwoven with the modern, scientific adolescent, I have not been able to discuss youth and families or youth in the workplace. Both of these topics are beyond the specific oeuvre of expertise that I trace here but are certainly important and relevant to understanding the cultural construction of adolescence.

Except for a few references, I have also neglected the topic of heterosexuality, which is also integral to adolescence. In addition to adolescence making whiteness, masculinity, and citizenship, adolescence has been centrally about sexuality and fear of sexuality. The system of reasoning around adolescence has helped to establish a particular interpretation of productive heterosexuality within marriage. It continues to work in that direction, and it is not surprising that researchers regularly document the most rabid homphobia among middle school and high school students.[18]

My emphasis on discourses, or systems of reasoning, downplays the particular understandings and experiences of identifiable, embodied youth. Although I believe that this critical disengagement is necessary, it stands awkwardly by other scholarship that focuses on embodied teenagers. What can only be suggested in this book is how the broader reasoning about adolescence helps produce particular kinds of subjective experiences among youths themselves. Although several chapters raise these issues, overall the analysis leaves underexamined the personal, subjective experiences of various youths.

Although I have tried to demonstrate the ways ideas about youth science and practices crossed the Atlantic Ocean, I have had limited success with that. The study remains more U.S.-centered than I had hoped. Part of my aim in discussing these limitations is to interest other scholars in picking up these pieces.

OVERVIEW OF THE CHAPTERS

Chapter One offers a historical context for the popularization and redefinition of adolescence in the late 1800s by describing the preoccupation with degeneration or progress and its implications for talk of race, gender, and nation. Chapter Two looks directly at the scientists' and policy-makers' new ideas about adolescence and the strategies they implemented for assuring young peoples' development into civilized citizens. Chapter Three takes those turn-of-the-century ideas and strategies and looks at their reinvention in two contemporary reports on young adolescents' emotional and educational needs. Chapter Four examines the close association of teenagers with age and thus with a particular idea of time. This analysis suggests that in order to rethink youth, we will need to reconsider our modern conception of linear, cumulative time. In the fifth chapter I take the idea of proper developmental sequence and order and explore how they are part of the making of the problem of teenage pregnancy, for school-aged mothers have children "before their time." While Chapter Five focuses on a group of problem teenagers, Chapter Six offers a close-up look at one success story—a young man who was a star athlete and good student and who at the time of the study was preparing to coach in high school. The young man's life history portrays the competitive, masculinizing, and privileging dynamics of high school athletics and the likely influences on classroom interactions as well as on school policies. Chapter Seven looks at the origins of violence in high schools, focusing more on the structures of recognition, increasing competition, and sources of humiliation than on a few "crazy kids." The concluding Chapter Eight argues that in the context of fast capital and welfare state down-sizing, we need a new vision of adolescence; if we are to advocate for youth today, the images and reasoning about their slow coming of age are not viable. How can we reformulate adolescents' needs and development within and against the time compression of the global economy and the declining compassion for dependency?

GLOSSARY OF SELECTED TERMS

Because I wish to make this analysis accessible to many readers with different backgrounds, I have kept specialized language at a minimum. However, a history of the present does rely on particular theory and attendant terms, some of which I wanted to use. Therefore, I offer this glossary so that readers who are unfamiliar with postmodernism or Foucault may have a preview of what they are in for and find a friendly guide to some terms that I could not do without.

Discourse

A discourse can be initially identified as knowledge with a specific vocabulary and syntax. Discourses typically rely upon identifiable sets of ideas, metaphors, stories, and feelings that are meaningful, repetitious, and take on the banner of truth or goodness. "Discourses are more than ways of thinking and producing meaning. They constitute the 'nature' of the body, unconscious and conscious mind and emotional life of the subjects which they seek to govern." Discourses, or systems of reasoning, operate across numerous social sites (for example, across the fields and institutions associated with the law, medicine, education, and psychology); this sense of being everywhere confers an aura of naturalness or inevitability to them. Bronwyn Davies ascribes four dimensions to discourses: (1) language, categories, metaphors; (2) the emotional meanings attached to main categories, images, and terms; (3) the narratives in which the social categories and emotions are linked; and (4) the moral frameworks in which the narratives operate to communicate good and evil or desirable and undesirable behavior.[19]

Genealogy

A genealogy is another term for a "history of the present," a method of historical analysis that problematizes the very terms and concepts through which we know and understand a topic. A genealogy starts with questions and issues of the present or categories in present use and interrogates how, where, when, and why they emerged and became popular.

Government and Governmentality

Schools, churches, medical clinics, and juvenile courts are conceived as sites of social administration or *governance*. This perspective focuses on the rules, methods, and especially truths by which social institutions and individuals organize "the conduct of conduct." "Government, here, refers to all endeavours to shape, guide, direct the conduct of others, whether these be the crew of a ship, the members of a household, the employees of a boss, the children of a family or the inhabitants of a territory. And it also embraces the ways in which one might be urged and educated to bridle one's own passions, to control one's own instincts, to govern oneself."[20] In educational studies, to study government is to examine the rules, methods, and truths of students governing themselves as well as teachers' control over children and over themselves as professionals.

Postmodernisms

This term has as many definitions as people who use it, so it is important to acknowledge that it isn't a singular or unitary thing. I find it useful to think about postmodernism as a recognition of several strands or stances: an "incredulity toward metanarratives,[21] or a skepticism toward the "self-evidence of a form of experience, knowledge, or power"[22] that opens up new possibilities for thought or action; attention to language (talk or discourse) as a site of power and conflicts rather than as a neutral medium; a decentering of the subject, that is, the "making the problem of study that of the knowledge that inscribes agents,"[23] rather than a focus upon human beings who make knowledge. Postmodernism offers competing conceptions of knowledge, power, subjectivity, and representation without guarantees grounded in "nature" or Enlightenment "progress."

Poststructuralism

Critics of postmodernism allege that it may result in nihilism, an inability or unwillingness to distinguish among alternative political and ethical practices. In its emphasis on the free play of meanings, adherents' judgments about the consequences of various interpretations may be constrained. Although many scholars use postmodernism and poststructuralism interchangeably, I make a distinction that is important for educators and for addressing this problem of nihilism. Poststructuralism draws from structuralism a recognition that structuring oppositions are basic to mainstream understandings and ways of talking and thinking, such as adult/child, male/female, and modern/primitive. Poststructuralist analysis questions these familiar oppositions and relationships that position, for example, the adult as fundamentally different from and superior to the child. Poststructuralist interpretations aim to provide alternative understandings and ideas about different relationships between adult and child beyond the hierarchical and oppositional one. For example, the conventional opposition of adult and child can also be seen as a form of dependency, in that each term needs the other in order to be defined. Thus, in addition to hierarchy and opposition, we can also discern interdependency. By striving for innovative relations between the terms, poststructuralism offers both an analytical and political strategy to move toward counter-hegemonic meaning.[24]

Subjectivity

Postmodernism works against the liberal humanist belief that human beings have an essential core "self" that is unique and imagined as deeply inside or internal to an individual. The human being of postmodernism is understood as a text, as a composition, as a bricollage, or as a performance without an essential core. The self becomes "subjectivity," which is the effect of material practices, of discourses, rather than a prior unity. Subjectivity is theorized as being constructed along with objective knowledges. Subjectivity assumes that systems of reasoning do not just produce object knowledges, but they also affect how young people or teachers experience and understand themselves.

Technology

Technology is used in postmodernism in a particular way that is much broader than computers and digital productions. A technology refers to a complex of mechanisms through which authorities have sought to shape, normalize, and make productive use of human beings. Technology is an assemblage of heterogeneous elements: knowledges, types of authority, vocabularies, practices of calculation, architectural forms, and human capacities.[25]

Up and Down
the Great Chain of Being

Progress and Degeneration

in Children, Race, and Nation

In 1893, the World's Columbian Exhibition opened in Chicago, with a congressional mandate to be "an exhibition of the progress of civilization in the New World." The focal point of that exhibition was the White City, a complex of beaux arts buildings representing seven aspects of civilization's highest achievements (Manufactures, Mines, Agriculture, Art, Administrations, Machinery, and Electricity) around a central basin named the Court of Honor. The White City was an icon of the superiority of civilized white men and pointed towards the ideal, perfectable future of the race. The White City glorified the masculine worlds by filling the buildings with thousands of enormous engines, warships, trains, machines, and armaments, as well as examples of commerce.[1]

Despite extensive battling by the women's committee to be included in the centerpiece, women's productive labors had been consciously excluded and marginalized to the Woman's Building, which was located between the White City and the Midway Plaisance. The Midway specialized in spectacles of barbarous races, for example, "authentic" villages of Samoans, Egyptians, Turks, Dahomans, and other exotics, with imported "natives." Midway visitors experienced the descent from civilization as they moved from the White City to advanced German and Irish villages, to more barbarous Turkish and Chinese settlements, and finally to savage American Indians. "What an opportunity was here afforded to the scientific mind to descend the spiral of evolution," enthused the *Chicago Tribune*, "tracing humanity in its highest phases almost to its animalistic origins."[2]

The world exhibition can be read as a representation of the established hierarchy of peoples within a long-playing scientific drama. The hierarchy expressed in the architecture and spatial layout of the Columbian Exhibition was widely known as the Great Chain of Being, a rank ordering of species from the least primitive to the most civilized, based on evolutionary theory. The Great Chain of Being located white European men and their societies, norms, and values at the pinnacle of civilization and morality. The Columbian Exhibition materialized the evolutionary, social, hierarchical understandings dominant at the time, as it also tied technical progress to a mythic worldly conquest. White men claimed civilization for themselves; white men stood at the evolutionary pinnacle, with all others on lower rungs. Though still dominant, this societal and individual hierarchy was under siege—both white women and African-Americans had protested the exclusiveness of the White City and its crowning of white men alone as "civilized." And beyond the borders of the Columbian Exhibition, challenges to the dominance of white men were occurring rapidly and regularly.[3]

The social contexts, strident messages, and contested evolutionary ordering enacted in the Columbian Exhibition are the topic of this chap-

Figure 1.1 The White City: Visualizing civilization. Reprinted from Gail Bederman, *Manliness and Civilization*, 1995, University of Chicago Press.

Figure 1.2 The Midway: Descending the evolutionary ladder. Reprinted from Gail Bederman, *Manliness and Civilization*, 1995, University of Chicago Press.

ter, for these were also the contexts and dramas in which the developing and worrisome adolescent won a major role. Although the White City proclaimed and embodied "progress," leaders in the realms of labor, politics, social reform, the new sciences of psychology, anthropology, and criminology worried. In the shadows of the White City, fears of degeneration took up permanent residence. Fears of social decay played in numerous venues, for example, within the problem of race suicide and urban contagion; within the middle-class disease of neurasthenia, or insufficient nerve force; and within scientific proclamations on atavistic youth, criminal types, and immoral races.[4]

In public spectacles, scientific research, popular ideas of health and disease, and political rhetoric, adolescence—defined as "becoming"—became an embodiment of and worry about "progress" and a site to study, specify, diagnose, and enact the modern ideas for personal and social progress. I argue that adolescent development became a space for reformers to talk about their worries and fears and a space for public policy to enact new ideas for creating citizens and a nation that could lead and dominate the particular problems and opportunities of the modern world. This chapter will describe three central preoccupations in which and through which adolescence became an identifiable, important, but ever worrisome modern construct. The preoccupation with progress switched back and forth across racial, gender, and national progress. As I hope to demonstrate, adolescence became a kind of switching station in which talk of racial degeneration could easily be rerouted to issues of nation or gender. This chapter strives to provide an understanding of those discursive contexts and preoccupations that formed the dramas in which adolescence had a major role.

THE GREAT CHAIN OF BEING

Metaphors of progress and gradualism have been among the most pervasive in Western thought. The late 1800s inherited a long and rich set of images and ideas about progress, and the new sciences of physical anthropology, psychology, biology, and medicine offered tools to better understand progress; to rank individuals, groups, and societies as savage, backward, or most advanced; and to diagnose impediments to progress. The Great Chain of Being was a constant reference point in popular and scientific conversations in the late 1800s. The Great Chain of Being refers to the hierarchy of animals, people, and societies that portrayed evolutionary history and a sociological ranking extending from European middle-class males and their republican government on the top, through women to savage tribes, with the lower animals at the bottom. There was also a moral, or spiritual, dimension to this Great Chain of Being, that is, the movement from lower to higher levels also signified the movement from chaos through human law to divine law. Progress was also defined as the "advance from superstition to reason" and "from simplicity to complexity."[5]

With the Darwinian revolution, animals and humans could be located on parallel ascending steps of the Great Chain of Being. Evolutionary rankings of groups were frequently expressed in tree diagrams and in charts, with progress marching from bottom to top. While these illustrations pictured progress, they simultaneously spoke of degeneration, of decadence. These images were pivotal in both popular and scientific thinking, and the diagrams could be consumed "at a glance," which added to their viability. These evolutionary ladders are also central to my analysis of the making of the scientific adolescent.

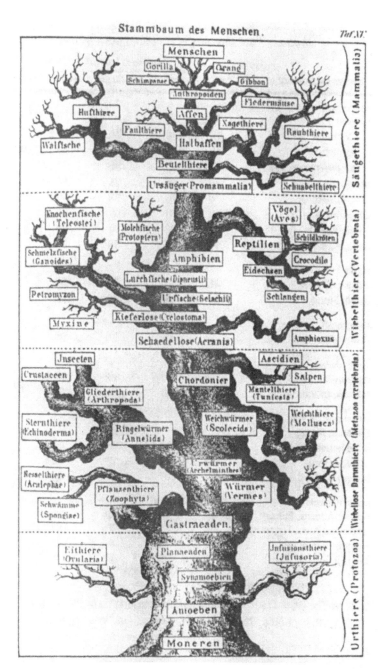

Figure 1.3 The Great Chain of Being figured as a tree. Haeckel's tree reprinted from Stephen Jay Gould, *Ontogeny and Phylogeny*, 1977, Belknap Press.

RACES AND FAMILIES	N	CRANIAL CAPACITY (IN³)			
		LARGEST	SMALLEST	MEAN	MEAN

Morton's final summary of cranial capacity by race

RACES AND FAMILIES	N	LARGEST	SMALLEST	MEAN	MEAN
MODERN CAUCASIAN GROUP					
Teutonic Family					
Germans	18	114	70	90 ⎫	
English	5	105	91	96 ⎬	92
Anglo-Americans	7	97	82	90 ⎭	
Pelasgic Family	10	94	75	84	
Celtic Family	6	97	78	87	
Indostanic Family	32	91	67	80	
Semitic Family	3	98	84	89	
Nilotic Family	17	96	66	80	
ANCIENT CAUCASIAN GROUP					
Pelasgic Family	18	97	74	88	
Nilotic Family	55	96	68	80	
MONGOLIAN GROUP					
Chinese Family	6	91	70	82	
MALAY GROUP					
Malayan Family	20	97	68	86 ⎫	85
Polynesian Family	3	84	82	83 ⎭	
AMERICAN GROUP					
Toltecan Family					
Peruvians	155	101	58	75 ⎫	79
Mexicans	22	92	67	79 ⎭	
Barbarous Tribes	161	104	70	84	
NEGRO GROUP					
Native African Family	62	99	65	83 ⎫	83
American-born Negroes	12	89	73	82 ⎭	
Hottentot Family	3	83	68	75	
Australians	8	83	63	75	

Figure 1.4 The Great Chain of Being charted as cranial capacity. Reprinted from Stephen Jay Gould, *The Mismeasure of Man*, 1981, W. W. Norton.

The concept of progress was inseparable from that of decline, and the fate of societies was similarly linked to that of individuals. "Two binary oppositions dominated sociological discourse in the nineteenth century: *progress/decline* and *social/individual*." As we will see, recapitulation theory, the belief that individuals recapitulated the stages of the development of human races, explicitly linked these two levels of sociological discourse with scientific efforts in biology, medicine, criminology, anthropology, child study, and pedagogy. The explicit race and gender dimensions of the Great Chain of Being and its interwoven fear of decadence are not immediately accessible in the contemporary use of the terms. However, as the White City demonstrated, "civilization," that moral, political, and national state toward which "we" moved, was defined as the exclusive domain of white men. "Civilization" in 1890s America meant "a precise stage in human racial evolution—the one following the more primitive stages of 'savagery' and 'barbarism.' Human races were assumed to evolve from simple savagery, through violent barbarism, to advanced and valuable civilization. But only white races had, as yet, evolved to the civilized stage."[6]

Gender, too was an essential component of civilization, and advanced races clearly identified the sexes. "Savage (that is, nonwhite) men and women were believed to be almost identical, but men and women of the civilized races had evolved pronounced sexual differences." Thus the clearly separate spheres of women and men in the Victorian era "were assumed to be absent in savagery, but to be an intrinsic and necessary aspect of higher civilization."[7]

These race and gender components of civilization were united to a third Christian belief in and need to work toward the Millennium—the vanquishing of evil from the world and the beginning of a thousand-year reign of Christ. "This millennial vision of perfected racial evolution and gender specialization was what people meant when they referred to 'the advancement of civilization.'" Thus the discourse of civilization, with its desire for progress and fear of decadence, drew from and cemented middle class beliefs about race, gender, and millennialism.[8]

The advancement of civilization required strong wills, clear paths of action, and complete courageous involvement. Affect had to be harnessed to the political order and the millennial vision. I understand the strong fear of decline as a central component of the discourse of civilization and its technologies of progress; the multiaccented fears are part of the harnessing of affect, of desire to the political vision. The repetitive graphic representations, as well as verbal discussions within both scientific and popular contexts, indicate the obsessive emphasis on progress and its technologies, among them the productive use of resources, especially human resources. This economistic view emphasizes that enormous social and cultural change required economic, social, and psychological interventions to create a new, modern social order.[9]

Social change, urbanization, and immigration propelled people into contact with others. Central to the idea of degeneration and the thwarting of progress was the idea of *contagion*, which stemmed from Victorian paranoia about boundary order. "The poetics of contagion justified a politics of exclusion and gave social sanction to the middle class fixation with boundary sanitation." Boundary sanitation would become a central task of the new scientists, led by physical anthropology, which inaugurated the sustained scientific effort to measure, record, and rank the differences among human beings in the middle and late nineteenth century. Biology followed, and by the second half of the nineteenth century it was steeped in an atmosphere of evolution, which gave new meaning and a history to the particular facts of anatomy, morphology, and embryology. "Biologists began to study organisms with an eye to their ancestral linkages and to their change and variation over time, as well as to their adaptive fitness in the present." The social sciences similarly became empirically minded and evolutionary in scope: "*models of change and development*, usually though not invariably indebted to Darwin, became the backbone of theory and research." "Historicism" posited that if one wished to understand the true nature of something, one had to understand how it had developed, how it had changed; in this way the ontological view of the Great Chain of Being also provided an epistemology, which can be termed a *development-in-time episteme*.[10]

The new sciences aimed at the pursuit of natural laws, which could be easily translated into social and political policies as well. Science and scientists had not formerly garnered much prestige, but with the weakening of religious belief and the growth of social unrest, scientifically established laws offered a new, viable foundation for social and political action.[11] Foucault's insight that the seeming "salvational" and liberating role of modern social sciences and law have constituted a new regime of truth that provides ever closer surveillance of selves will be helpful as we examine the sciences of the adolescent. For now, the evolutionary ladder of the Great Chain of Being and its incitements to technologies of progress are most important.

SOCIAL CHANGE AND THE GREAT CHAIN OF BEING

The rapidly expanding and industrializing United States of the 1880s and 1890s has been characterized as a nation without a center, without a past, without direction. Historians such as Robert Wiebe and Anthony Platt, for example, argue that the sense of social confusion of that time period cannot be overstated. The Northeast United States was awash in immigrants, with movement of people from rural areas to cities, with changes in middle-class families, and with dramatic changes in work. America was tossed by newness and breaks with traditions and the past, as three revolutions—commercial, transportation, and industrial—affected every realm of life. By way of illustration, the years 1890 to 1910 witnessed:

> the introduction of the safety bicycle, then the automobile, and then the airplane; an increase of 1500 percent in the number of telephones and 1000 percent in the number of commercial ice plants; the revolution in the physical sciences which followed the work of Planck, Einstein, and the Curies; a 50 percent rise in population, in part the result of the largest influx of immigrants in the country's history (13 million); the introduction and distribution of motion pictures and the advent of modernism as an artistic movement; the most violent labor unrest in American history and the establishment of national labor unions; the "closing" of the continental frontier and the beginnings of overseas empire; the quadrupling of the number of married women in the work force; the incorporation of major industries and a vast increase in the governmental regulation of business and social life; the emergence of modern advertising and consumerism; a rise from an average of six hundred books of fiction published annually to an average of twenty-three hundred; a 100 percent increase in the number of cities with a population over one hundred thousand.[12]

These profound social and cultural shifts were akin to tidal waves that made the economy and many institutions almost unrecognizable. Changed as well were many less tangible dimensions of U.S. social life, such as: "the experience of time and space, the functions, structure, and internal dynamics of the family, [and] gender and generational relations." Kathy Peiss, for example, details the growing world of leisure for young, single, working-class women as they moved from domestic labor into restaurants, factories, department stores, and offices with shorter workweeks. The heterosocial world of dancing, silent movies, trips to Coney Island, and gossiping with fellow workers was seen as dangerous by both their immigrant families and middle-class women reformers. The speed and relentlessness of the changes left the newly emerging bourgeoisie grabbing at straws for social cohesion. "Within this unknown and evolving world, few could be certain where they would find either places of power or zones of safety." But the new middle class struggled to impose order on the social, economic, and domestic chaos. They created new voluntary organizations that aimed to reform society and legitimate their perspectives and values. Many became preoccupied with self-determination and with purity and unity.[13]

In the South, the perils of the new century for the white middle class were largely attributed to the demise of slavery and the evils of Reconstruction. Segregation of blacks and whites was understood as necessary to preserve order and hierarchy, and Jim Crow laws swept the Southern landscape and crept into the North as well. The evidence of challenges to white-dominated order can be read from the increase in lynchings, the increase in race riots, and the movement of blacks from the rural South to Northern cities. Although lynching declined in absolute terms after 1892, blacks became the target of 91 percent of the lynchings in the 1910s, up from 68 percent, and the killings were also increasingly brutal and sadistic. "During the decade 1898–1908, serious race riots broke out in Wilmington, NC; New York; New Orleans; Atlanta; and Springfield, IL." In the 1910s, African Americans took over Harlem, with its spacious apartments, ample businesses, and cultural entertainments. The mix of black and white in the cultural expressions of the early 1900s, including music, theater, and dance, provided ample evidence of hybridity, which many fearfully read as contagion. The first mass public demonstration by African Americans, the Silent Protest Parade, occurred in 1917 in New York City as a protest of the July massacre of blacks by whites in East St. Louis.[14]

In addition to gender and racial challenges, class warfare seemed inevitable. Between 1881 and 1905 there were nearly 37,000 strikes, often violent, involving 7 million workers, out of a total workforce of 29 million in 1900. The strength of socialist and anarchist movements reinforced these fears. Middle-class white men seemed to be losing the power to wield civic authority, to control strife and unrest, and to shape the future of the nation. Thus they were losing control of the advance of civilization—losing personal power and abandoning their Christian mission.[15]

Across these changes that pulled distinctive groups in different directions, T. Jackson Lears emphasizes a drive for the rationalization of work lives and the human psyche. For him the modern era was defined by technical rationality moving into high gear; put simply, the drive for maximum profits through the adoption of the most efficient forms of organization led to the use of scientific principles to maximize personal and organizational resources, especially time and space. Frederick Winslow Taylor's time-and-motion studies rationalized the labor process; John Harvey Kellogg's personal regimen for manliness sought to eliminate all sensual self-indulgence in food, in sleep, and above all, in sex. Discipline, close study, and controlled regimens of actions and thoughts would lead to fully productive, civilized lives. These ideas were largely articulated by whites, but some blacks also championed these values too. Booker T. Washington and others who argued for African-American "self-help" rather than agitation for social change also spoke of self-discipline and hard work; some of the black schools in the South were notable for their strict adherence to these ideals. Although there were, of course, substantial differences between Kellogg's and Washington's political and educational agendas, one commonality was the emphasis on the moral and economic productivity of a strict and pure bodily regimen.[16]

One particular disease was associated with the stresses of modern life and the impenetrability of the future: neurasthenia, a disease that struck middle-class white "brain workers" but no other kind of laborer. According to the national expert on neurasthenia, George M. Beard, M.D., who authored *American Nervousness* in 1881, social and cultural changes were the underlying problems that led to neurasthenic diagnoses. The diagnosis of neurasthenia rested upon certain assumptions, for example, that people have only a certain amount of "nerve force" or nervous energy and, like any limited commodity, when the "supply of nerve force was too heavily taxed by the demands upon it, or when the available nerve force was not properly reinvested, nervous bankruptcy, or nervousness, was the result." If neurasthenia was a sign of modern life, medicine drew on traditional gendered social expectations for the remedy, which was either the female rest cure or the male exercise cure. Productive work and procreation were understood as positive reinvestments of nervous energy that led to both peace and spiritual contentment. However, wasting the nerve force, through masturbation, gambling, or illicit forms of sexual activity, among others, was a drain and led to decadence:

The idea of "dissipation" thus is based on a notion of dispersed rather than directed nerve force, spent without any possible return on the investment. Dissipation eventually led to "decadence," the death and decay of nerve centers in the individual, and the death and decay of civilization at the social level. *The links between medical thinking and economics, and the links to morality, were constantly apparent to both doctors and patients.*[17]

Medicine was only one among many new sciences that accumulated status as specialized knowledge about others, civilized and uncivilized, threatening and comforting; medicine and its investments in diagnosing and remedying potential failures of modern expectations of citizens helped produce modernity.

In addition to incitements to pay careful attention to the body regimen for usefulness and morality, many Americans also experienced the momentous economic, industrial, and social changes in terms of the most immediate and concrete in their lives: *family structures and generational relations*. In generational terms it often seemed that young men stood alone—facing the future without the aid of fathers, for their fathers' understandings were unlikely to provide guidance for the unknowable future. Women and girls were drawn into the public world via institutions of reform, education, and philanthropy, although science amassed further evidence of their inferiority. The problems of bringing along the next generation of girls and boys to face still-to-be-defined challenges in the future was one of the paths by which scientists and reformers became united in a focus on adolescence. Boys facing the future alone became the central work of scientific reformers who labored in psychology and education as well as in organizations such as the YMCA, Boy Scouts, and the juvenile justice system. As the next section demonstrates, the racial sciences played an important part in understanding children and youth and in theoretical and practical efforts across racial and child development.[18]

SCIENTIFIC KNOWING OF CHILDREN AND YOUTH

"The most formidable ally of economic and political control had long been the business of 'knowing' other peoples," and science replaced religion as the primary font of expert knowledge, although many of its categories, symbols, metaphors, and narratives were continuous with evangelical religious understandings and beliefs. During the late 1800s in the United States and in other countries, science emerged and became consolidated as "the dominant mode of cognition of industrial society" and as *the* nonpolitical, unbiased arena of knowledge. Science also acquired its "modern epistemological, institutional, and cultural forms." The move toward a new, internalized moral authority was led by the scientific expertise of medical men, public educators, and social reformers. Although middle-class parents had a well-established precedent to consult the clergy when their children were wayward, parents of anorexic girls in late nineteenth-century United States and Britain sought help from physicians rather than from men of the cloth when their daughters would not eat, which is one particular example of the gradual transfer of cultural leadership from the clergy to "men of science, particularly professional medical men." [19]

These young sciences appeared within social hierarchies, particular preoccupations, and popular discourses. A "common context" for social thought and the biological sciences existed in the nineteenth century, which was a debate over "man's place in nature" that engaged readers from popular magazines to specialized journals in psychology, brain research, biology, geology, and political economy. "New ideas were not fragmented into academic disciplines but were viewed as part of a common set of themes for a common culture. Great issues hung on them: the basis for morality and responsibility; the relations between 'races' and between humans and other species; hopes for the future of society and for an afterlife."[20]

Scientists were moving into a privileged domain of knowledge-building and policy-making. Scientists diagnosed modern ills and prescribed remedies for individuals and groups. Progressives' belief in science and technical rationality became the foundation for efficient organizational and public policies. The articulation of public problems was in turn connected to the discourse on progress and degeneration. Recapitulation theory was a central part of most scientists' understandings during the late 1800s and early 1900s in the United States, Britain, and France and was part and parcel of the ways children and adolescence were described, diagnosed, and theorized.[21]

Recapitulation Theory

Classical recapitulation theory, which was widely held among scientists and the general public until the early 1900s, stated that each individual child's growth recapitulated the development of humankind. German zoologist Ernst Haeckel originated the catchphrase "ontogeny recapitulates phylogeny" to capture the ideas that the ancestral lineage of the human species could be read off the stages of a child's growth. "Every child rehearses in organic miniature the ancestral progress of the race. The theory of recapitulation thus depicted the child as a type of social bonsai, a miniature family [or race] tree." The theory that each individual child reenacts the evolutionary climb from primitive to savage group and finally to civilized society offered an irresistible way to rank people from every social class, race, and gender. Recapitulationists said that every child walked the same path from the most barbarous origins at the end of the Columbian Exposition's Midway toward the White City; however, many travelers were waylaid or "arrested" on their paths and never became fully civilized. This equating of boys and savage tribes was used everywhere and by everyone, especially to scientifically compare white male children with "other living races and groups to rank their level of evolutionary inferiority." Recapitulation theory appeared to offer an "absolute biological criterion not only for racial but also for sexual and class ranking." The white boy could be compared with Semites, Hottentots, or the Irish to offer certain observations about their degree of sophistication, that is, these groups' degree of resemblance to white middle-class men.[22]

Scholars of colonial discourses in Africa, Asia, and the Americas have regularly noted that racialized others have been invariably equated with

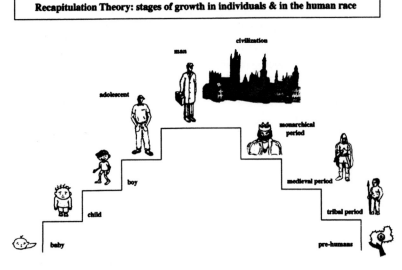

Recapitulation Theory: stages of growth in individuals & in the human race

Figure 1.5 Relationships between primitives and children established in recapitulation theory.

and compared to children: "a representation that conveniently provided a moral justification for imperial policies of tutelage, discipline and specific paternalistic and maternalistic strategies of custodial control." Indians or Brazilians or Indonesians became like children who needed to be dependent on adults/Westerners. The widespread acceptance of recapitulationist perspectives reaffirmed the dominant image of the Great Chain of Being and made a comparative methodology desirable, such that sociologists drew upon biomedical studies of children and students of child development borrowed from anthropologists, criminologists, and biologists, among others. Children and youth, like primates, were important for what they could reveal about the past and the future of the races. During the reign of recapitulation theory, child study glowed with the promise of yielding key information on the progress of the white race and of the white boy toward civilization.[23]

Putting the Primitive-as-Child and Child-as-Primitive to Work

Recapitulation theory established a threefold parallelism across animals, savages, and children: children were like savages, savages were like animals, and animals were like children. This theory "formed the thematic core of anthropology, psychology, and child study" and was enormously popular. Stephen Jay Gould describes the worldwide reach of this theory: "Recapitulation intruded itself into every subject that offered even the remotest possibility of a connection between children of 'higher' races and the persistent habits of adult 'savages.'"[24]

Recapitulation theory was incredibly malleable and useful for colonial and racist endeavors abroad as well as for urban reform at home. The description of the "primitive-as-child" "stood second to none in the arsenal of racist arguments supplied by science to justify slavery and imperialism. . . . If adults of other races are like white children, then they must be treated as such—subdued, disciplined, and managed (or in the paternalistic tradition, educated but equally subdued)." Anne McClintock also assesses the scope of recapitulation theory: "*A host of 'inferior' groups could now be mapped, measured and ranked against the 'universal standard' of the white male child—within the organic embrace of the family metaphor and the Enlightenment regime of 'rational' measurement as an optics of truth.*"[25]

Modern conceptions of children and youth are not usually located in historical frameworks that include colonial relations. However, recapitulation theory explicitly linked the understanding of the growth of children and adolescents with primitives, who were known via travel writers, government officials, entrepreneurs, and anthropologists, the science most intimately associated with and dependent upon colonial rule.[26] Thus ideas about adolescence and childhood must be considered in the light of colonialism and its legacy of exploitation and brutality despite supposedly rational and humane control.

The equation of children and primitive, of children and colonized savage, was operative in overt colonialist discourse but also in child-rearing manuals, children's literature, travel writing, popular culture, and racial science. In child-rearing manuals, children are compared to lower-order beings: "they are animal-like, lack civility, discipline, and sexual restraint; their instincts are base, they are too close to nature, they are, like racialized others, not fully human beings." Stoler links the primitivism of children, which I extrapolate to youth, as a significant location for the making of the white, bourgeois self; that is, a mature, developed adult must become nonchildlike, nonprimitive. I quote her conclusion at length because it is central to understanding the construction of modern adolescence:

> If we are looking to trace the embeddedness of race in the cultivation of the bourgeois self, it may be that this prescriptive discourse on child rearing is a place to turn. . . . *For becoming adult and bourgeois meant distinguishing oneself from that which was uncivilized, lower-class, and non-European. . . . In rehearsing repeatedly what a child must shed to become an adult, these verbal and written injunctions also rehearsed a social hierarchy and racial taxonomy of libidinal desire and uncivilized habits that bourgeois children would have to shed to become fully human, adult, and European.*[27]

In this way recapitulation's analogy of primitives and children set up basic ways of knowing, labeling, and ranking that were endlessly repeated in child rearing but also in psychological knowledges and public policies about adolescence. Adolescent development similarly invokes and repeats social hierarchies and racial taxonomies of being, knowing, and desiring. Adolescence was singled out as a crucial point at which an individual (and a race) leaped to a developed, superior, Western selfhood or remained arrested in a savage state. Adolescence marked the race and gender divide to be crossed by each boy-man if he were to come civilized and if he were to help the advancement of civilization. Within such understandings, primitive races could be discussed as "adolescent," for example: "[T]he Ethiopian race has stopped at the beginning of Caucasian adolescence . . . and the Mongolian race at [Caucasian] adolescence itself.[28]

Within the framework of recapitulation theory, adolescence was deemed a crucial divide between rational, autonomous, moral, white, bourgeois men and emotional, conforming, sentimental, or mythical others, namely primitives, animals, women, lower classes, and children. Adolescence became a social space in which progress or degeneration was visualized, embodied, measured, and affirmed. In this way adolescence was a technology of "civilization" and progress and of white, male, bourgeois supremacy. The centrality of recapitulation theory in the history of the ideas of the modern adolescent alerts us to several important understandings: First, the modern concepts of child and adolescent development have a color and a gender. Second, recapitulation theory links ideas about developing children and adolescents to a paternalistic and exploitative colonial system, which endlessly reiterated the inadequacies of the natives and the need for Western rule. Finally, recapitulation theory's intimacy with colonialism suggests that knowledge will provide a continuing gloss of and cover for the exercise of subordinating power that speaks of immaturity, emotionality, conformity, and irrationality.

COLONIALISM AND RACIAL SCIENCES

As exploration and imperialism spurred increased contact between Westerners and native peoples around the planet, the new sciences took up race and gender as the two great themes of the nineteenth century. George Stocking has characterized the discipline of anthropology in the 1800s as obsessed with race and racial difference and dubbed it the "the century of 'race'": "Contact with native peoples aroused interest not merely in race but in sex, since it revealed sexual customs, cultural beliefs, and labor patterns quite at variance with European expectations." Because of abolitionist movements, race was also a burning issue in England and America. The Seneca Falls Convention of 1848 marked the beginning of the movement for women's rights, which similarly touched deep social nerves, as did attempts to organize working-class laborers. In this atmosphere, science became a tool or weapon that legitimated or undermined claims of black people, the working classes, and women to political and social inequality. Anne McClintock links racial science with the contradictions of imperialism abroad and middle-class domesticity at home and the challenges to those interrelated social orders from the poor and women.[29]

Pioneering work in comparative anatomy emphasized the relationships between different physical structures and competencies—skull size and intelligence continued in one important and resilient relationship. Inevitably, such a comparative anatomy had a large subjective, or semiotic, element that was "a judgment of equivocal signs which revealed something of the inward nature of the signifying animal and [relied] upon measurements which included in their very construction the evaluation they were designed to make." Thus comparative anatomy involved the scientific glossing of aesthetic, moral, and imaginative judgments. The new biology suggested that the traditional hierarchy from European man to Negro based on European ethnocentricity was now "proved" by modern science. A scale of human races, for example, allotted apes an intelligence index of 30 degrees; Negroes were empirically placed at 70 degrees and Europeans at 80 degrees. With the restoration of polygenesis, the belief that human races evolved from separate races (not from one original race), "certain races in certain places were seen to be originally, naturally, and inevitably degenerate."[30]

Again and again the details of the body provided a map of the character and psyche of the race:

> To the earlier criterion of cranial capacity as the primary measure of racial and sexual ranking was now added a welter of new "scientific" criteria: the length and shape of the head, protrusion of the jaw, the distance between the peak of the head and brow, flatheadedness, a "snouty" profile, a long forearm (the characteristic of apes), underdeveloped calves (also apelike), a simplified and lobeless ear (considered a stigma of sexual excess notable in prostitutes), the placing of the hole at the base of the skull, the straightness of the hair, the length of the nasal cartilage, the flatness of the nose, prehensile feet, low foreheads, excessive wrinkles and facial hair.[31]

As noted above, recapitulation theory supported all manners of comparisons: for example, English slums were compared to slave ships and the East London poor were compared with the Polynesian savage. Female brain size was compared to that of the gorilla, and women were "closer to savages than to an adult, civilized man." At the same time the rhetoric of gender and class was used to make fine distinctions among different races: the white race was figured as the male of the species and the black race as the female and the Zulu male was regarded as the "gentleman" of the black race. Within the racial sciences, race, class, and gender were interchangeable and regularly stood in for each other.[32]

The manifold uses of recapitulation theory and the evolutionary ladder of the Great Chain of Being merged into a "triangulated, switchboard analogy" among racial, class, and gender deviance. The modern, imperial imagination switched effortlessly from gender perversions to race suicide and unwholesome family life. The "degenerate classes were metaphorically bound in a regime of surveillance, collectively figured by images of sexual pathology and racial aberration as atavistic throwbacks to a primitive moment in human prehistory." These human throwbacks survived in the interstices of the White City and threatened its continued power.[33]

Racial sciences, born of encounters with savages in colonial settings and "lower-class peoples" at home (e.g., immigrants, working-class women, prostitutes, poor urban youth), swelled with nationalistic fears of immanent disorder and desires for benevolent progress and harmony. Disorderly groups threatened social stability through labor organization but also through gender and race transgressions and through unproductive urban lives, as the next sections detail. In defining and desiring civilized bourgeois selves, others shared irrationality and excessive sexuality and were a threat to civilized society because they were innately different and could not become self-governing. The new sciences drew upon colonial discourse and images and in turn contributed to them and fortified the scientifically established racial differences.

"NERVOUS MASCULINITY" AND SOCIAL CHANGE

Challenges by women to the traditional gender order were another prominent feature of turn-of-the-century U.S. life. The "nervous masculinity" (Macleod, 1983) that historians have used to characterize the period was an effect of the questioning of social arrangements in which white men held advantaged places. By the 1870s the new bourgeois woman had emerged; she was "confident and independent" and, in working for herself and other women, "she had begun to demand equality in education, in employment, and in wages." In order to implement her social plans more effectively, the new woman worked for the vote, too. [34]

These matrons were followed by their daughters, the New Women, who made further changes in gender arrangements. In 1870, 21 percent of all enrolled college students were women; by 1890, 36 percent were women, and by 1920, over 47 percent were female, with women receiving one third of all graduate degrees. The female percentage of the workforce also increased: from 16 percent in 1890 to 20 percent in 1900 to 25 percent in 1910. By 1930, women comprised nearly 50 percent of the workforce. With so many women in schools and in workplaces, traditional notions of masculinity as synonymous with autonomy and self-control were no longer tenable. Urbanization and the growth of bureaucratic workplaces meant that men could not control their own work lives nor be autonomous in them. Fewer men owned their own shops, controlled their own labor, owned their own farms; increasingly men were economically dependent and subject to the time clock. Between 1870 and 1910, the proportion of middle-class men who were self-employed dropped from 67 to 37 percent. [35]

Given women's and men's equal presence in waged work, masculinity was harder-pressed to define itself in traditional, exclusive terms. "American manhood had earlier been grounded upon the exclusion of blacks and women, the non-native-born (immigrants), and the genuinely native-born Indians, each on the premise that they weren't 'real' Americans and couldn't, by definition, be real men." These lower social beings, whom the Great Chain of Being and social Darwinism proclaimed to be inferior, now jostled the superior white men everywhere—on city streets, in workplaces, and in leisure pursuits. Both Native Americans and black men were seen as especially threatening to white male autonomy and control. Michael Kimmel argues that the growth of the Ku Klux Klan was a response to masculinity under attack, since Klan rhetoric was "saturated with images of heroic and chivalrous Southern manhood."[36]

The emergence of homosexuals on the social scene further aroused concern for heterosexual masculinity. George Chauncey documents "an organized, multilayered, and self-conscious gay subculture" in New York at the turn of the century. Although for a period of time straight men coexisted easily with gay males, slowly the sense that straight men were under siege grew into sexual antagonism. Jonathan Ned Katz represents these changes in these words: "In the first quarter of the twentieth century the heterosexual came out, a public, self-affirming debut the homosexual would duplicate near the century's end." Rather than just a conflict between groups of men and forms of sexuality, Katz emphasizes the building of the institution of heterosexuality, which became normal and then normative, with Freud and Freudians as the major boosters. As heterosexuality became normative, homosexuality became deviant. Freud defined homosexuality as "fixated" and an "immature" stage of development: "inferior, because less evolved, less civilized, closer to the natural, roaming, "polymorphous perverse" sexuality of the unsocialized child and primitive savage."[37] Here again we see difference, here sexual difference, as synonymous with children and savages and as indicating a less-developed or mature self.

No realm of human experience is as closely tied to the concept of degeneration as that of sexuality: "The concepts of human sexuality and degeneracy are inseparable within nineteenth century thought." Since science had reconfirmed that "civilization was a result of masculine vigor and intelligence," race progress and national strength were threatened by women who behaved in the public sphere like men and by men who in their self-absorption and inaction behaved like women. Each inversion forecast dire consequences for civilization.[38]

Feminist advances in the workplace, in social reform, and in schooling incurred new pathologizing of women in the sciences, specifically in medicine, psychology, and psychiatry. "Victorian men generally and the male medical profession in particular focused some of their earliest legislative efforts at sexually regulating and socially controlling these seditious female figures." The New Woman easily devolved into the hysterical woman, and Smith-Rosenberg sees gender conflicts as the ground upon which new professional knowledges were created and utilized. Scientific questions and answers were heavily weighted with gendered and sexualized symbols of national danger and decay. When scientists pathologized the New Woman and the new decadent for deviancy, they simultaneously made masturbation, homosexuality, birth control, and abortion into symbols of national danger and decay. "Black men and immigrants were seen simultaneously as less manly than native-born whites and as *more* manly, especially as more sexually voracious and potent." The Great Chain of Being cut two ways, establishing the social superiority of white males but worrying about the sexual vigor of "primitives."[39]

Homosexuality and effeminacy were added to the repertoire of men's anxieties, and gay-bashing was legitimated by appeals to nation, normalcy, and masculine upholding of purity. Elizabeth Young-Bruehl notes that adolescents and homosexuals shared the limelight as two newly defined populations in the turn-of-the-century United States. Both these populations were tropes that in one sense promoted the importance of normalized bourgeois selves. Thus, the sallow, self-abusive, undisciplined, urban hooligan joined the homosexual, the New Woman, and the uppity African-American as problematic groups for new professionals to describe, diagnose, and redeem. These deviants were also crisp, immoral figures against whom upright, Christian, middle-class, white men could and should stand.⁴⁰

The fears and dangers of the New Woman and the new decadents made it increasingly important to be masculine, to perform masculinity, to look masculine, to be *read* as masculine. "Men felt themselves on display at virtually all times; and the intensity of the need for such [masculine] display was increasing." On the U.S. domestic front, the Boy Scouts, athletics, and even the new home "den" with masculine furniture bolstered gender differences. Imperialist projects near and far provided many opportunities for development of and display of masculinity: Hawaii, the Philippine Islands, Puerto Rico, and Guam were all annexed in 1898; the Samoan Islands were divided with the Germans in 1899; the Boxer Rebellion was suppressed in 1900; and the Spanish-American War began in 1898. At the same time, virulent racism provided opportunities to protect white women and tradition. Howard Zinn calculates that between 1889 and 1903, "on the average, every week, two Negroes were lynched by mobs—hanged, burned, mutilated." Constant performances of masculinity thus took many forms.⁴¹ This incitement to perform masculinity was a central feature of the need to make boys strong, courageous, loyal, and patriotic.

MAKING NATIONS, BOYS, AND DESIRES

There is no automatic or immediately understood connection between nations, nationalism, and conceptions of adolescence. However, nation-making was an overriding issue and concern at the turn of the century and contributed important aspects to the emerging ideas of adolescence and the future.

In stating this I need to explain several linked ideas. First, I adopt Benedict Anderson's idea that nations are imagined communities and that national history and culture are invented—the past and its traditions and distinguishing characteristics are imagined back onto previous times as well as forward into the future. Imagined nations might have little significance if they remained primarily as abstract ideas; nationhood becomes aligned with particular interests and values, say, economic imperialism, that produce particular policies and positions *vis-à-vis* other nations. How is it that people of a particular nation come to take up some sense of their nationality? This is where youth have enormous significance, which is unrecognized because it is so commonsensical. Adolescence became significant to nation-making through the linking of affect with a political order, that is, adolescence became viewed as a time when emotional connections with gangs, scout troops, crime rings, or football teams could be established, with good or evil results. In my view, adolescence was strategized as the right age to get boys to imagine and *desire* a particular national and international order. In *desiring* a particular nationalism, boys would likely become willing to struggle and sacrifice for this national identity. In their *desiring*, boys would be shaped in particular ways.[42] In Chapter Two I will discuss how team sports and team loyalty became fixed components of proper coming of age, but here I want to describe some historically specific interests for boys to become good citizens.

This language of *desire* was not used by turn-of-the-century reformers, who spoke, rather, of manliness, Christian duty, courage, loyalty, and patriotism. Dependable, patriotic men developed through disciplined efforts, team loyalty, and the acceptance of authority. Breaking wills, the previously accepted approach to raising boys (and girls), became passé because reformers feared that boys might become effeminate or conformist. If a nation needed tough, courageous, and patriotic young men to broaden its reach, then new scientific methods were necessary to raise both strongly willful and team-oriented citizens. The next chapter details some of the specific methods deemed valuable to create future male leaders.[43] In this section I describe some elements of nation-making contexts in England and in the United States and the position of boys in those national fortifications.

By the 1890s in the United States, increasing support for imperialism was heard among politicians, business leaders, and military men, and the "ideology of expansion" swept up "even some of the leaders of farmers' movements who thought foreign markets would help them." Embodying this fervor, Senator Henry Cabot Lodge of Massachusetts wrote that "Americans must now begin to look outward." In advocating for international expansion, he claimed that the United States must keep up with other great nations who are planning ahead for their "future expansion." But, he added, the United States also had a duty to participate in "a movement which makes for civilization and the advancement of the race. As one of the great nations of the world the United States must not fall out of the line of march."

Theodore Roosevelt's expansionist views appeared to be supported by both his own political ambitions and a sturdy contempt of races and nations he considered inferior. When the United States failed to annex Hawaii in 1893, after the missionary and pineapple interests of the Dole family set up their own government, Roosevelt termed this decision "a crime against white civilization," a conclusion interwoven with a strategic knowledge of markets and profits. The expansionist rhetoric, the images of national and racial superiority, and the material payoffs for businessmen were unbeatable. Between 1875 and 1895 new investments by American capitalists overseas reached a billion dollars, including steel, oil, and surplus agricultural products. Lafeber summarizes the accomplishments of the expansionists: "By 1893, American trade exceeded that of every country in the world except England." But he also notes that certain categories of the U.S. economy, for example, farm products, especially tobacco, cotton, and wheat, had long depended heavily on international markets for their prosperity. Thus the *scope* of international trade was new, as was the rationale of bringing civilizing government and business to the lesser peoples of the world.[44]

However, the dominant mode of U.S. expansion was an "open door," not the traditional empire-building of Europe. This "informal empire" relied on America's economic strength to dominate all underdeveloped areas of the world once the door had been opened. The Spanish-American War showed the limits of the informal empire approach. President McKinley did not want war, but wanted what war would bring, which was: "The disappearance of the terrible uncertainty in American political and economic life, and a solid basis from which to resume the building of the new American commercial empire." Several years later, the period was assessed by the chief of the Bureau of Foreign Commerce of the Department of Commerce: "The Spanish-American War was but an incident of a general movement of expansion which had its roots in the changed environment of an industrial capacity far beyond our domestic powers of consumption. *It was seen to be necessary for us not only to find foreign purchasers for our goods, but to provide the means of making access to foreign markets easy, economical and safe.*"[45]

The Case of England

The expansion of the United States under the banners of civilizing and saving others, preparing for the national future, and creating markets for domestic businesses in the late 1800s appears to be almost a mirror image of Britain's decline at that same time. England's diminishing colonial grip triggered rhetorically similar concerns about the problem of lost boys, manliness, leadership, and dominance. The Boer War (1899–1902), a struggle between British and Afrikaaners over the political control of

South Africa, threw Britain's imperial power into doubt. The poor performance in many situations of the British troops in the Boer War flowed into sustained concern around working class boys, "since many army recruits had to be rejected as unfit and many even of those accepted performed badly." New social-scientific methods of surveying populations provided detailed examinations of the "squalor of lower-class life and triggered a spate of books warning of national deterioration beginning in boyhood."[46]

It is important to note how *surveys*—quantified numbers that became statistics—increased in significance after the Boer War. Here we glimpse the dynamic of the creation of ways of governing citizens through the development of "normal" behavior and "normal" families. Surveys produced "the concept of a calculated, known population." Surveys became an important technique in documenting, diagnosing, prescribing, and implementing practices in law, social welfare, medicine, schooling, and the military, among others. The author of a 1904 U.S. *Bulletin on Age Statistics* wrote: "For the purpose of a scientific study of the population, the classification by age is only less important and fundamental than that based on sex." Age data provided crucial information about military strength, size of the electorate, economic potential for the workforce, and characteristics of the coming generation and facilitated predictions about crime, pauperism, literacy, and mortality. The crisis of empire contributed to the value placed on knowing and managing a national population; adolescent boys in particular were important raw materials for nation-building. My broader point is summed up by Koven: "*Control over boy nature was the key to the future of nation and empire*. 'Boy life' became a convenient shorthand for the assumption that working-class, adolescent, urban male behavior was necessarily a social problem."[47]

In 1901, a book edited by C. F. G. Masterman, *The Heart of the Empire*, powerfully "illustrated interconnections between national culture and nationalism, social reform and hooliganism, race degeneration and imperialism, masculine identity and the state." Unlike manly youths just a decade earlier, the town dweller was "stunted, narrow-chested, easily wearied; yet voluble, excitable, with little ballast, stamina, or endurance." Masterman diagnosed city dwellers as suffering from the absence of the healthful and virility-supporting life of the country. "The new city race was effeminate, 'bloodless' and incapable of performing the manly tasks of ruling Britain and her empire."[48]

In Britain, the aftermath of the Boer War and the national report on physical deterioration led to the beginnings of an interventionist state, a decidedly "manly state" that would order and care for various social groups, including children and their female caregivers. "*[T]he image [of degeneration] fostered a sense of the legitimacy and urgency of state intervention*, not only in public life but also in the most intimate domestic arrangements of metropolis and colony." A new British nation-state was begun, one that posed "as neutral arbiter between the competing interests of citizens." Koven asserts that this neutral, manly state has proven to be an "enduring and powerful 'imagined community' on which to build a nation." Koven also believes that historians of modern, national welfare states have missed the relationship between masculinity and national identity stemming from the crisis of the Boer War and the ways that those panics supported a paternalistic policy approach: "Fears about the conditions of life of the urban poor, the strength of the empire and the degeneration of male soldiers/citizens antedated the onset of the Boer War. However, the heightened tensions of war brought into stark relief the extent of these problems and *suggested underlying connections between nationalism, sexuality, and social welfare*." The masculinity-empire connection was a central element in the ways in which reformers imagined the state and the shape of interventions they encouraged. If Koven's analysis is accurate, the British hooligan—the white, working-class, urban boy—became a foundational image to the modern welfare state formation.[49]

Koven links the discourse of English nation-and-empire at the turn of the century as grounding a newly imagined nation with an interventionist state. A major part of the rationale for the new forms of government policy of such an interventionist state (e.g., legislation controlling and protecting children and their female caregivers) was the "hooligan"—the urban, working-class boy beyond the grasp of self-discipline, patriotism, and empire. In his view, the furor over wayward boys in the context of a weakening empire eased England toward a new national identity, with ideas of empire still alive and well. Heightened concern about masculine identity during and after the Boer War was accompanied by a loss of confidence in previous ideas of the nation and young men, and British social reformers "reimagine[d] fundamental relationships between men, women and children, families, the state and the nation." Domestic state intervention, threats to empire, and a normalizing of male youth were closely intertwined. The English example illustrates how the progress of white boys was the measure of nation and empire-making. Although these pieces were organized differently in the United States, the significance of a normative boyhood was also evident. On the future of white boys the civilized nations would rise or fall.[50]

Historian George Mosse's work has documented the broader processes of building nationalisms upon respectability; and respectability has had everything to do with being properly masculine and feminine as well as self-controlled—that is with a particular libidinal economy. Mosse sees sexuality as: "vital to the concept of respectability, indeed, to the very existence of bourgeois society." Mosse makes respectability and particular economic activities synonymous with bourgeois life. The middle classes in England and Germany perceived their way of life as grounded upon: "frugality, devotion to duty, and restraint of the passions, [and] as superior to that of the 'lazy' lower classes and the profligate aristocracy." Thus "family values" of frugality, devotion to duty, and restraint of passions were foundational to the imagined communities of these two nations. Following Koven, I have positioned boys and adolescence within this nation-forming emphasis on respectability and self-control; in and through the adolescent body, the fears and hopes of race, sexuality, gender, and empire could be visualized, openly desired, politically strategized, and measured. In the United States, reformers focused more on middle-class white boys as future leaders, and their problem became one of inventing a theory and a method: How could young men learn to *desire* nations, discipline, and order without being diverted into unhealthy and unproductive longings and practices or being arrested in a female stage of conformity? The "boyologists" took up this multifaceted problem, which is the topic of Chapter Two.

SUMMARY

In the late 1800s and early 1900s, concerns over progress and degeneration framed every discussion about the future of U.S. and European societies. Revolutions in commerce, industry, and transportation; labor strife; family relationships; generational understandings and expectations; ideas of the child and education, among many others, were regularly interpreted as indicators of glorious or problematic futures. These understandings were always in relation to, in fear of, numerous others who threatened tradition and the continuation of an evolving and proper social order. I have read this turn-of-the-century period, marked by enormous conflict, transformation, and reaction, as the sociohistorical soup within which adolescence, as a profoundly multileveled entity, was formulated.

Specifically, my interpretation emphasizes three strongly accented groundings for adolescence: race, gender, and nation. I have described how racial hierarchy and racial comparisons were carried in discussions of the Great Chain of Being, on which children and races were plotted. Scientific studies in anthropology, physiology, criminology, and child study informed each other as scientists tried to understand present social groups in the context of past and future, that is, in terms of their development. When I state that adolescence was *raced*, I mean that it carried ideas of proper and mature human beings that stemmed directly from middle-class white perspectives. Thus adolescence was a technology of whiteness that supported white boys and white men as superior but also echoed the rightness of racialized dominance at home and abroad.

Men and women, heterosexuals and homosexuals were also mapped and evaluated for how they contributed to the development of the race, to the progress of the civilizing and superior races. When I argue that adolescence was *gendered*, I mean that emerging ideas of teenagers and their proper growth centered on masculine characteristics as desired and necessary for the progress of individuals and societies. Boys were most worried over, and their proper advancement was the core of adolescence. What came to be defined as valued and normative adolescent behaviors were grounded upon white middle-class male lives, needs, and perspectives. Just as adolescence was inscribed by whiteness, so was it constructed as synonymous with virile masculinity.

Crises of nation and empire in England and the United States suggest that *nationalism* was also woven into concerns for white boys and their progress. National renewal was to rest upon an interventionist state, one of whose priorities was raising proper boys. This nation-making context for the modern scientific adolescent suggests that at the heart of the adolescent problem and potential is a sense of citizenship, and that proper development is meant to produce well-socialized, productive citizens who will bolster the nation's policies, both domestically and abroad. Working for the larger good, being willing to sacrifice for a larger entity, and obeying laws, for example, are themes from nation-making, but so are learning to govern oneself through proper sexual and gender identities. When crime or the preparedness of armies or the proper mother are discussed along with teenagers, they are indications of the nation-making level. This chapter has offered an overview of the contexts in which adolescence came to be defined as a social problem as well as a social resource. Both as problem and possibility, adolescence was racialized, gendered, and nationalized.

The active identification, diagnosis, and segregation of degenerate groups was coupled with equally active constructions of progress and civilized people, and through respectability the middle classes established themselves as superior. Sexual restraint, self-control, productive use of human energy, and traditional gender roles were valorized and came to define proper adolescence; thus adolescence was an active part of class, racial, and gender conflicts over what and who could count as mature, responsible, and powerful.

I have introduced the modern, scientific adolescent as a social creation that mobilized fears and prejudices, desires, love, and domesticating passions. Like other national fantasies, the modern adolescent embodied "sense and sensibility, productivity and passion." Science colluded with sensibility to imagine an interventionist state that could build empires by creating and applying professional expertise with *identifiable populations*. If the male adolescent was "the symbol of both the vitality and the problems inherent in these massive social changes," then white boys were marked as a target population for scientific nation-building. The next chapter portrays adolescence being defined via new technologies of statistics and record-keeping, with information on sex, religion, race, age, physical anomalies, leisure pursuits, and attitude.[51]

In the gender, race, and generational upheavals of the turn of the century, the adolescent was newly made as a multilayered object, a "multi-accented," polysemic being. The adolescent was an object that could be discussed, diagnosed, scientized, differentiated, and familiarized in terms of unsettled race relations, economic prospects, emerging manliness, purity, and future preparedness as citizen and soldier. In these ways, the modern adolescent was always promiscuous, always ready to indicate and exemplify national crises, and a perfect trope for worry, study, and action-taking that also met the coming-of-age interests of white middle-class professionals.[52]

Making Adolescence at the Turn of the Century

2

Romancing and Administering Youth

At the turn of the twentieth century, adolescence was a character in multiple stories: the city as jungle, family upheaval, nation-building, political reforms, immigration, economic tumult, and international imperialism, among others. The adolescent was enormously plastic, even promiscuous, and was eagerly and regularly invoked in discussions about the threats to nation and empire, the erosion of Anglo Protestant values and morals in urban areas, and fear of racial suicide. This chapter describes the "boy problem" and dominant responses in child study, character-building, and play reform. Although white middle-class boys were the focus of salvation efforts, their central positions were articulated and meaningful against the shadows of uncivilized others: working-class boys, girls, and primitives. I seek to portray not only the reasoning of the reformers, but also the material arrangements used to identify problems, offer recommendations, and implement strategies. This materialist analysis is important because when we combine ideas and concrete practices, "peculiar activists" of another time begin to resemble ourselves. I look at the constructions of the problems and the solutions in ways that highlight the continuing influences of these reformers.

In a time of national uncertainty, massive cultural change, and nervous masculinity, the adolescent came to occupy a highly visible and recognizable place, as a being who was defined as "becoming," as nascent, unfinished, in peril—in today's terms, "at risk." Adolescents were identified as having great potential but also as being liable to go astray, imagined as ships without stable moorings or rudders,[1] sexually charged beings who needed to develop character, responsibility, manliness, and focus. The

adolescent was a trope for turn-of-the-century worries about unknown
futures, about ability to succeed and dominate in changing circumstances,
about maintenance of gender and class hierarchy in changing social and
cultural landscapes. Adolescence was also a standard, a flag, around which
reformers rallied in largely Progressive-inspired reordering of social institutions, including the educational and juvenile justice systems. At the same
time adolescence was a social fact produced through a set of practices,
including emphasis on and control of sexuality, segregation of girls' and
boys' curricular areas in increasing years of compulsory schooling, separate
justice facilities for juvenile delinquents, and unrelenting emphasis on
youths' futures. In this light, adolescence can be glimpsed as a *technology* to
produce certain kinds of persons within particular social arrangements. In
considering adolescence as a technology, I will examine the chains of reasoning and feeling that called reformers to take up the problems of youth.[2]

Put in different terms, adolescents, like the primates of Donna Haraway's work, took up positions in *border zones* between the imagined end
points of adult and child, male and female, sexual and asexual, rational and
emotional, civilized and savage, and productive and unproductive. The
stakes in being able to define proper sexuality and reason, for example,
were and are high. From this perspective, the categories and processes
involved in adolescents' identities are simultaneously sites of broader cultural debates about knowledge, identity, representation, and power. In
other words, adolescent bodies became a terrain in which struggles over
what would count as an adult, a woman, a man, rationality, proper sexuality, and orderly development were staged. Adolescence today continues to
be defined within the doubled tensions of its history: the mixing of fear
and desire, emotions and reason, sexuality and purity, black and white,
and masculine and feminine.[3]

In discussing the specifics of the emerging discourse of adolescence in
the late 1890s and early 1900s, I turn first to G. Stanley Hall, dubbed "the
father of adolescence," who popularized adolescent storm and stress and
utilized a romantic idea of youth potential and problems that mandated
increasing supervision of young lives. The correct form and amount of
that control was tricky, because modern society demanded energetic,
manly, and strong citizens, not docile or cautious boys. Both the problems
of boys and their potentials provided unlimited work for newly minted
experts in psychology, pedagogy, playgrounds, and juvenile justice. Thus
my interpretation of modern adolescence is as a site to worry over and on
which to work on new citizens for a new social order.[4]

ROMANCING YOUTH: PERFECTABILITY AND PROTECTION

G. Stanley Hall, Adolescence, and Race Progress

Granville Stanley Hall was born in 1844 in a small farming village in western Massachusetts, and his upbringing was modest, conservative, and puritan. He would produce over 400 books and articles and become the first president of Clark University; he was best known for his public speaking, in which he connected with popular, albeit mostly middle-class, concerns; he tapped into fears and hopes of a society in transition and combined conservative and progressive language and ideas.[5] Although he wears the mantel of the "father of adolescence," his ideas were largely imported from Germany. While Dorothy Ross, Hall's biographer, does not specifically document his contact with the German Youth Movement, he had made three trips to the country by 1880 and his romantic view of youth seemed strongly influenced by it and other German manifestations of youthful idealism in the arts and in progressive schooling. Certainly Hall would have been influenced by what flourished in the late 1800s in Europe as a "culture of adolescence:" a turning toward youth in art and literature, spurred by a broad critique of cultural decline, a belief in the free expression of emotions, reconnections with nature, and a new brand of patriotism.[6]

The German Youth Movement protested "the lack of vitality, warmth, emotion, and ideals" in German society. Ola Stafseng suggests that Thomas Mann's *Buddenbrooks* captures the stifling formality that the German Youth Movement protested. The middle-class youth who joined the Youth Movement ranks wanted "above all to be integrated human beings" and decried the alienating character of their lives, which included factory-like schooling to produce exact replicas of their professional elders, very strict discipline, classical studies, and girls and boys in separate spheres. Despite such wide-ranging criticism, the *Wandervogel* (wandering birds) solutions focused mostly on human relations. Members espoused the German tradition of *romanticism*, which included eschewing materialism via the adoption of the simple life, the rediscovery of old folk songs and folklore, and the reintroduction of medieval names and custom. Members of the Youth Movement were known for long walks through the German countryside, and "this education by rambling was to produce a new German who had a better, more rounded picture of his country, and whose identification with and love of that country was deeply rooted in his personal experience."[7]

The German Youth Movement spoke loudly and powerfully to an entire generation of middle-class, Protestant, and largely urban youth, ages twelve to nineteen, about defining one's way of life. Leaders of the movement identified youth as the age for getting to know oneself; before the pressures and stresses of adult life arrived, "young people needed to withdraw into the wilderness, as Christ withdrew into the desert, to acquire inner knowledge." Peers were understood as able to demand an inner discipline and comradeship from each member, something neither schools nor parents could do. This emphasis on peers as the primary source of values and discipline would become a foundational element of modern adolescence in the United States.[8]

Although the German Youth Movement officially maintained an apolitical stance, its policies and activities contained elements of anti-Semitism, sexism, racial superiority, homophobia, and right-wing nationalism, attitudes that intensified within later youth organizations, most notably the Hitler Youth. In a society that educated boys and girls separately, girls' participation in the *Wandervogel* was delayed until 1907. Some of the images of German Youth Movement publications illustrate the romantic portrayal of strong, young, Aryan men united against imagined others; these images powerfully link youthful, virile, heterosexual, white men with the future of the German nation, connections which George Mosse has elaborated in his work on nationalism and sexuality. Although overall conservative and nationalistic, many *Wandervogel* alumni established themselves as progressive, even radical, educators, activists, and thinkers.[9]

As a young man in his mid-twenties, G. Stanley Hall's critiques of American staidness, which he "fairly loathed and hated so much," echoed those of the *Wandervogel* on middle-class German society. In his autobiography, Hall catalogued these failings: "The narrow inflexible orthodoxy, the settled lifeless mores, the Puritan eviction of the joy that comes from amusements from life, the provincialism of our interests, our prejudice against continental ways of living and thinking, the crudeness of our school system, [and] the elementary character of the education imparted in our higher institutions of learning."

Hall's "youthful spirit of revolt" was intense in the liberal atmosphere of German cities, and he went to bars, danced, and dated, all of which were strictly forbidden at home. Fundamentally, Germany allowed Hall emotional expression. When he returned to the United States, he took up studying Darwin's work and moved toward an evolutionary perspective,

Figure 2.1 Romantic portraits of young men and women with nationalistic feelings, from the German Youth Movement publication, *Hohe Wacht*. Reprinted from Walter Z. Laqueur, *Young Germany*, 1962, Basic Books.

which restored his optimism in "the progress of knowledge to restore meaning and purpose to the natural world." But Hall believed his radical ideas would have jeopardized an academic career, so he stuck to his motto, "Safety First," and later recalled that "it was most fortunate that these deeply stirred instincts of revolt were never openly expressed and my rank heresies and socialistic leanings unknown." Despite this and other evidence

Adolescent feared?

of traditional viewpoints, Hall's early interest in and support of Freud, including his sponsorship of Freud's first lectures in the United States, for example, confirms that this scholar and man defied simple categories.[10]

According to Bederman, "a Christian millennialist interpretation of human progress had been rooted in American culture for centuries" and decreed that "human history had one cosmic purpose: the millennial fight against evil." This aim of perfectability was approached by Hall and his scientific colleagues via evolutionary theory cobbled together with millennialist visions and called "civilization." Civilization, as Chapter One detailed, included a vision of human perfectability through evolution of the species. That millennial vision of civilization would be achieved through further development of the superior race with its white, middle-class, male leadership. Hall carried this civilizing fervor into all of his lectures and writings and developed a scientific concentration on children and adolescence.[11]

With the publication of "The Contents of Children's Minds," Hall established himself as the leader of the "child study" movement, which aimed to utilize scientific findings on what children know and when they learn it to understand the history of human life. That is, Hall pushed an ambitious program of child study because, given recapitulation theory, studying children and youth would help provide a history of humankind. "By correlating the results of observations of children with those of anthropological investigations, Hall hoped that genetic psychology and anthropology would each throw light on the other, eventually producing 'a true natural history of the soul.'"[12] Thus Hall partook of the German Youth Movement's emphasis on emotional expression, on connection with nature as a corrective to modern urban life, and on an untempered optimism, but rejected the emphasis on sexual freedom. His pursuit of human perfectability accepted mainstream ideas of racial evolution, to which he applied an empirical, scientific method.

Recapitulation Theory and Adolescence

Chapter One presented the structuring image of the Great Chain of Being, the hierarchy of animals, people, and societies, with European middle-class males and their republican governments on the top and savage tribes merging with animals at the bottom. Youth were important for what they could tell scientists, imperialists, and politicians about the past and the future of the races, since recapitulation theory stated that each individual moved through the same stages of development as the race.

Hall idealized adolescence as the apex of human development—the period "before the decline of the highest powers of the soul in maturity and age," and this romanticized view found widespread popular resonance. Cole reads Hall's celebration of adolescence as linked both to his own emotional struggles and to a broader cultural shift from a religious standard of being to what Max Weber called "hygienically oriented utilitarianism." In the rural New England of Hall's youth, religiously sanctioned virtues of independence, self-denial, and work constituted the path to salvation and to male power, which was wielded in civic authority, in control of strife and unrest, and in shaping the future of the nation. However, this manly ethos of self-restraint, interwoven with self-employment, was becoming unprofitable due to economic changes and depressions that had made small-scale, competitive capitalism an anachronism by 1910. In a society slowly giving way to a culture of health, self-fulfillment, and consumption, Hall, like William James and Theodore Roosevelt, suffered from a sense of exhaustion and confinement that plagued many late nineteenth-century intellectuals. Searching for a source of regeneration and a unified worldview, Hall turned to the theory of evolution for a biologically based ideal of human development whose optimum condition was health. In *adolescence* he counterposed the purity and vigor of youth (drawn from the barbarian stage of development) to the fragmented, deadening, and routinized qualities of urban industrial life. Hall had plenty of company in this positive, hybrid view of youth, since that was what the European "culture of adolescence" promoted.[13]

Others joined with Hall and deemed adolescence a crucial point at which an individual (and a society) jumped to a developed, superior, Western selfhood or remained arrested in a savage state. Adolescence became the dividing line between rational, autonomous, and moral white bourgeois men, those civilized men who would continue the evolution of the race, and emotional, conforming, sentimental or mythical others, namely primitives, women, and children. Hall, who drew from Darwin's work in biology and Spencer's in social applications of Darwinism, touted adolescence as "not just an exciting and stressful time of rapid change: it represents the phyletic transition from preconscious animality to conscious humanity."[14]

Hall's gospel of the special potential and pitfalls of adolescence resonated with worries about manhood and dominance, coded as civilization or the future of the race. The composite portrait of urban laggards—sullen, nonvirile youth who smoked cigarettes, masturbated, and lived in unhealthy conditions—threatened the further evolution of the race and the material growth of the nation. Furthermore, in the Northeast of the United States at this time, the actual number of white, middle-class boys was low. These population figures likely augmented fears of social decay without enough manly Christian leaders. Hall's response involved an idealization of adolescence as the beginning of a new life, and a scientific claim that this new life could contribute to the evolution of the race, if it were properly administered. [15]

Muscular Education

Hall explained some of his concerns on education for health in an editorial in one journal he founded, *The Pedagogical Seminary*:

> Health is the condition of all success and nothing can atone for its loss. The art of keeping our bodies always to the very top of their condition is thus the art of arts in which so many sciences culminate. . . . The muscles are the only organs of the will, and have done all the work man has accomplished in the world. . . . All exercises that strengthen and enlarge muscles strengthen and enlarge the nerve and brain fibres or cells.

Here Hall addressed the intersection of morals, physical health, and economic productivity, which has been termed "muscular Christianity" and was popular among the reformers who started the YMCA, Boy Scouts, and other character-building organizations. Hall lent scientific support to the muscular Christian approach to education. In addition to muscular health, Hall argued that man [*sic*] must learn to know his limits and "not attempt tasks too arduous for his powers, or open problems he cannot solve. This atonement *is physiological economy; it is rest, health, strength.*" Here Hall advocates for an economistic logic of human health in which the nerve force of humans is limited, and one must not dissipate it in masturbation or other wasteful sexual activities. Thus health involves a rational inventory and investment of limited energies in profitable activities.[16]

Further, Hall recommended school arrangements that mixed Rousseau's emphasis on covert control of male pupils with a strict social-efficiency attachment to education for future lives and roles. Hall argued against coeducation and promoted girls' schooling as preparation for marriage and motherhood, while boys' education was to emphasize the development of strength and virility. Hall's colleagues in the Boy Scouts and YMCA youth programs all sought to get older boys into the hands of men in order to make them strong, courageous, honest, and disciplined. This could only be done by getting them away from women, both mothers and teachers, and the soft, feminizing, emotional influences. This fear of feminization rose along with the proportion of female teachers: between 1870 and 1920, the percentage of women teachers moved from 59 to 86 percent. The boys' character-builders displayed extreme concern for sex differences, aggressiveness, and energy in "lavish amounts." Although Hall taught at Antioch College in Ohio for four years (before his second trip to Germany), he faulted coeducation for promoting a "strong feminine element [which] dominated the college sentiment" and led to a lamentable absence of an "active boy student life" that characterized single-sex colleges.[17] → masculinity essential for the

Hall's educational prescriptions for adolescents deserve close scrutiny *addescent* for their continuing influence on commonsense practices. Six central ideas *male?* that Hall advocated were:

1. Differentiated curricula for students with different futures, that is, an efficient curriculum, including an education for girls that emphasized preparation for marriage and motherhood; → *Appleyard College*
2. The development of manhood through close supervision of the body, emphasizing exercise and team sports and minimizing draining academic study;
3. An education that drew upon and utilized the expression of (boy-stage) emotions through emphases on loyalty, patriotism, and service;
4. A school program against precocity that kept boys as boys;
5. A curriculum sequence informed by recapitulation theory, or cultural epochs curriculum (i.e., a curriculum that looked to the past and future to educate present youth);
6. An administrative gaze that was longing, desirous, and erotic.

1. *Differentiated Curricula.* Although Hall expressed ambivalence about pedagogy, he embraced and promoted education as a way to develop a broad audience for his applied psychological work. Hall recalled his first lectures on pedagogy in this way:

[Harvard President Eliot] stated that Harvard had never been much impressed by pedagogy but I [Hall] was a young man who had studied it abroad and this course had been instituted as an experiment. In concluding he invited the audience to decide whether Harvard was right in ignoring it or I was right in advocating it.[18]

Hall subsequently poured his legendary energy into elevating the status of pedagogy, as well as firm ideas on curriculum in and out of school.

Hall promoted a social efficiency perspective on curriculum; he believed that a common curriculum was wasteful and that schools should prepare children and youth for the distinctive social roles that they would assume. Although he taught in coeducational settings (e.g., Antioch College) and in African-American colleges (e.g., Wilberforce University in Ohio) and supported female and black students, Hall nevertheless staunchly adhered to the gender and racial hierarchy despite romantic, even mystical, sentiments about women and the desire to invest wifehood and motherhood with reverence and honor. Historian Merle Curti believed that Hall was well aware of the increasing pressure for the emancipation of women; nevertheless, he struggled to "convince both sexes of what he believed was the true social position of women, a position derived from their biological and psychological status." Hall similarly advocated the educational ideas of Booker T. Washington, who prescribed a course of study for blacks that prepared them at best for manual labor, deeming any attention to classical subjects as wasteful.[19]

Hall believed that only an elite could ever hope to live the life of the mind, and demanded that "gifted children" be given more attention. For average children, Hall prescribed schooling that would call into play their muscles, emotions, and will more than their intelligence, and he warned that taking pity on less talented children "interfere[d] with the process of wholesome natural selection by which all that is best has hitherto been developed." Certainly, Hall's perspective was supported by the recapitulation view of children and youth, women, the working class, and people of color as phyletically savage; when one was interested in avoiding the degeneration of the race, greater attention had to be given to those seen as able to excel.[20]

Hall's recommendations for school curriculum and pedagogy echoed Rousseau's in *Émile*, which emphasized a preparation for engagement in the world by being removed from it (so as not to be corrupted too early in life), close supervision by a tutor who discerned/shaped Émile's natural interests, and a subtle manipulation of pupils' interests to the greater good, which the tutor alone discerned. Of course, Rousseau segregated the sexes and limited girls' education to preparation for marriage and motherhood.[21] Overall, Hall stressed the careful education of middle-class white boys and a curriculum differentiated by future social-economic role.

2. *Developing Manhood: Restricting the Body, Emphasizing Exercise and Team Sports, and Minimizing Academic Study.* Urban life was seen as over-stimulating and thus likely to deplete male nerve force. Educators and boy workers alike catalogued the dangers of the city, which was a shorthand for unsettling social changes. Although contemporary U.S. urban life was obviously the most highly evolved, it seemed to sap white men's strength, and boys needed to be sheltered from its seductions and distractions. Thus fears of youthful immorality mingled freely with idealized images of small town boys' lives; the forest would save the boys from the city. Scouting, outdoor education, bountiful physical exercise, and visits to farms and countryside were all part of the repertoire of boys' education that directed their energies toward proper manliness and race-enhancing growth.[22]

The boyologists faced a paradox as educators of boys. Their mission was to produce young, manly Christians who were strong and responsible for their positions in society, but they knew, often from personal experience, that too much adult control over young men could break their wills and drain precious life-force resources. How could they carefully sculpt strong-willed boys without creating weak-willed, effeminate youth? The boyologists' quite brilliant answer was to follow boys' lead and utilize their "naturally occurring" interests in sports, camping, and physical activities. The cataloging of boys' interests, spontaneous ideas, and activities furthered the dominance of adults and made young people ever more dependent on adult experts, all in the name of developing young males' strong powers and firm wills.

The belief that the human body had limited resources and that male energy must be protected and wisely invested underlay the boyologists' focus on endless exercise. A central piece of this neo-Victorian approach was the battle against masturbation, which was widely viewed as both a waste of manly energy and the gateway to degeneration. "Hall loathed masturbation, believing that reabsorbed semen gave one strength. Starbuck, Hall, and the YMCA's Luther Gulick all asserted that a boy's sexual nature opened the door to conversion. Thus a boy who abused his sexuality [i.e., masturbated] cut the taproot of faith." Much of the character-building regimen started with the implicit (but sometimes explicit) need to prevent masturbation. Nonstop activities, specifically team sports but also camping and woodcrafts, were deemed central to boys' distraction. Of course, segregation of boys from girls, mothers, and women teachers was already a stock preventative to other kinds of sexual arousal. In these prescriptives, the American boyologists borrowed the British public school model of single-sex schools, with its mania for games, teams, and hyperloyalty.[23]

Urban life, masturbation, and effeminacy were joined by numerous other threats to the development of manly Christians. In a letter to G. Stanley Hall in 1899, Theodore Roosevelt warned that too much civilization turned men to mush:

> I must write you to thank you for your sound common sense, decency and manliness in what you advocate for the education of children. Over-sentimentality, over-softness, in fact, washiness [sic] and mushiness are the great dangers of this age and of this people. *Unless we keep the barbarian virtues, gaining the civilized ones will be of little avail.* I am particularly glad that you emphasize the probable selfishness of a milksop [i.e., sissy]. My experience has been that weak and effeminate men are quite as apt to have undesirable qualities as strong and vigorous men. I thoroughly believe in cleanliness and decency, and I utterly disbelieve in brutality and cruelty, but I feel we cannot too strongly insist upon the need of the rough, manly virtues.[24]

Roosevelt linked manliness with barbarian virtues of strength and roughness, and felt that effeminate men were selfish and unlikely to uphold the manly Christian model of service to others. Roosevelt's letter also testifies to Hall's national reputation and the broad impact of his ideas.

Another threat to manliness was excessive intellectualism, a problem that manifested itself in the disease of neurasthenia—a lack of sufficient nerve force in middle-class adults who overused their brains. Hall was a good friend of Dr. Beard, the foremost U.S. expert. "Neurasthenia resulted when a highly evolved person seriously overtaxed his body's finite supply of nerve force—the same nerve force that masturbation squandered." Beard identified the source of the disease as *modern civilization*. Beard prescribed gendered cures: a rest cure for women and a vigorous exercise regimen for men. Theodore Roosevelt was a stunning example of the success of the exercise cure; after being diagnosed as a neurasthenic, he moved to the American West and remade himself as a hybrid woodsman, cowboy, and, above all, virile man. Of course, he also restarted his political career. Beard's gendered cures reverberated in schooling for adolescent boys and girls.[25]

[margin handwritten note: Good quote on interpolating Adolescence]

3. *Primitive Emotions and Education for Progress of the Race.* In addition to a physical regimen of outdoor exercise and team sports, Hall emphasized education through the emotions. Surveying the course of the development of the race, Hall trivialized reason as a determinant of behavior and doubted the intellectual capabilities of the average man. "Instincts, feelings, emotions, and sentiments are vastly older and more all-determining than the intellect," Hall wrote. He called for an educational program that stressed the development of a sound body and sound emotions rather than the cultivation of intellectual abilities. Hall's view of emotions was a complex mixture of various definitions of emotions. I think Hall utilized diverse influences in his emphasis on education through emotions. He seemed to draw from Herbartianism, with its mixture of German philosophy, psychology, and pedagogy; from a loosely interpreted Freundianism; and from evangelical Protestantism. Hall followed this view of Herbartianism:

> According to psychology there are three distinct activities of the mind,—
> knowing, feeling, and willing. These three powers are related to one
> another as coordinates, and yet the will should become the monarch of
> the mind. . . . For strong character resides in the will. Strength of charac-
> ter depends upon the mastery which the will has acquired over the life;
> and the formation of character, as shown in a strong moral will, is the
> highest aim of education.[26]

The will was synonymous with strong character and with control over the intellect and the emotions. A man with a broken will did not have the ambition, drive, and desire to achieve in the emerging corporate capitalism nor the character to promote further racial evolution. It seems likely that Hall also drew upon the centrality of emotions in youthful religious conversions, a standard stage of the life course in evangelical Protestant communities. The dominant plot of conversion narratives began when young women and men were overcome with intense emotion that they interpreted as religious fervor and that led them to commit themselves to a deeply religious life; this conversion was a form of transition to adulthood, for afterward the newly religious person took up his or her place as an adult in the congregation. This normative, intensely emotional conversion was probably known to Hall and could have provided part of his view of the usefulness of proper emotional expression. As president of

Clark University, Hall sponsored Freud's visit to the United States in 1909 and undoubtedly also accepted Freud's ideas about sexuality and motivation and the problems of repression. However, Hall also believed that freely expressed sexuality would too often lead to debauchery, so the sexualized energies of boys needed to be promoted yet protected, managed, and channeled.[27]

Hall believed that the promotion and expression of emotions could be developed through competitive sports, patriotic endeavors, and service. Emotions such as loyalty and a sense of responsibility were promoted and rewarded in team sports. Patriotism was another positive avenue for the expression of strong emotions, as was service to others. Other character-builders such as Lord Baden-Powell, who started the Boy Scouts, joined William James and Theodore Roosevelt in recommending war to build patriotic feelings, courage, and a sense of serving others. Hall's pedagogical recommendation was an immersion of boys in activities that stimulated the expression of loyalty, competition, patriotism, and service to others.[28]

Feminist scholarship has recognized a prominent tradition of associating reason with men and emotionality with women, and my description of Hall and other boyologists appears to be somewhat at odds with that. Raising white boys to become leaders was especially treacherous if one believed in recapitulation theory, because to become reasoning adults, white boys had to proceed through lower stages, that is, through emotionality and other savage and/or feminine states. Anyone could be arrested in the emotional, or primitive, stages of development and remain there permanently. Because Hall thought developmentally and located boys in the emotional stages, he believed educators had to recognize and use emotion in order to move boys toward civilization. But only certain emotions were promoted as educational—uplifting emotions such as team loyalty, patriotism, and altruistic service were highly valued for their ability to move boys toward a form of muscular Christianity. It was Hall's developmental (or evolutionary) perspective that put emotion and reason into a different relation.[29]

4. *Working Against Precocity: Keeping Boys as Boys.* Given the dominant image of the Great Chain of Being and the urgency to promote the civilized leap of adolescent boys, preparation for the adolescent transition became paramount. A protected and controlled adolescence "promised vigor in later life, whereas precocity aroused fears of debility." *Recapitulation theory promised that the boisterous, unprecocious lad could draw upon lavish*

stores of ancestral energy. Boys' play came to be invested with virtue and inter-preted as ancestrally inherited "work." By precocity adults meant "any adult-like behavior or proclivity, especially passion or self-assertiveness." Turn-of-the-century adolescence was often marked by "overpressure and an acceleration of experiences." Prolonging boyhood into the teens became an acknowledged aim of organizations such as the Boy Scouts, and was three-pronged: keep boys unintellectual, dependent, and asexual. *Slow development* became the ideal, most likely achieved by middle-class boys who were sheltered from the streets. David Macleod suggests that these fears of precocity occurred while the biological "facts" of puberty were also in transition. Menarche moved downward (some scholars esti-mate a drop of three to four months per decade), and both boys and girls were physically larger and developed at younger ages. For example, between 1880 and 1920 North American boys on average gained two inches in height and fifteen pounds in weight. These changes, along with the greater contact of adults with boys and girls of different classes and races in urban neighborhoods, likely contributed to the sense of more quickly maturing youth and their threatening presences on city streets. Many factors contributed to the equation: precocity equals pathology.[30]

More generally, early independence of all sorts came to be seen as dan-gerous, so efforts to keep boys dependent accompanied those to keep them pure. Even quick religious conversions could provoke a hysterical response, so the emphasis moved toward a *"mild and steady socialization of children and teenagers."* Teenagers were everywhere demoted, for example, from having been Sunday school teachers to being merely pupils, and "by 1900 it was a rare dissenter who objected that adolescents should not be kept 'in the children's place.'" Adolescence became reformed as a *"perpet-ual becoming."* Age grading in religious pedagogy "fostered a sense of progress while in fact prolonging dependency," and youth were mired in functionless "endeavor"—pledge-taking, literary meetings, worship ser-vices, and other kinds of busywork.[31]

Prolonged stays in secular schools followed the lead of religious educa-tion, growing first more intensive and then longer. Part-time school atten-dance (to allow seasonal work) was no longer acceptable, so full-time attendance became mandatory. Certified credentials became the accepted requirement for entrance into jobs in bureaucratized corporations and civil service systems. Middle-class white parents wanted their sons to remain in school to gain the credentials; education became a screening system that differentiated class and race via preparation for careers rather than dead-end jobs. "Nationwide, public high school enrollment shot up from 110,000 in 1880 to 519,000 in 1900 and 2,200,000 by 1920. By 1900, although some worthwhile blue-collar opportunities remained, most boys of fourteen or fifteen who quit school ended up in 'dead-end' jobs."[32]

Dependency and more time in school supported age grading "by making differences in age stand out as mileposts in an otherwise featureless landscape by preventing the intrusion of responsibilities demanding sudden maturity." David Macleod links age grading with the bureaucratic school working to eliminate retardation, the inefficient failure of students to progress through the grades. *Advancing on schedule*, neither too fast nor too slow, came to be a major preoccupation of both the schools and age peers, who likewise developed narrow, finicky standards for associates' ages and activities. "By the early 1900s, two or three years' difference in age effectively divided boys." "Pervasive age grading had reoriented the issue between adults and boys; instead of a few convulsive struggles for autonomy, *there were endless little tests along a finely calibrated course.*" Laws prohibiting child labor, though not effecting many changes before 1910, provided another kind of support for children and youth defined as needing protection and nurture, not responsibility. Other Progressive Era reforms such as curfew ordinances and laws against smoking, enforced by the new juvenile justice system, provided the platform for careful scrutiny of working-class and middle-class youth.[33]

5. *Cultural-Epochs Curriculum.* (That is, a curriculum that looks to the past and the future to administer present youth.) If adolescence was the key to the evolution of the race, "a second birth," evolutionary history likewise became the foundation for curricular decisions. Although a believer in genetic endowment, Hall incorporated Lamarckian views that new characteristics could become inheritable, thus opening youth to cultural influences too. Child study, informed by anthropology and cultural history, would provide the informed educator with the understandings of what children know and do not know and what the curriculum needed to include for children to evolve. For example, children's eagerness to "throw, run, dodge, hit, chase, wrestle, box, fish, and hunt were all lingering vestiges of ancient times when these activities were necessary to survival." In this way, Hall pushed a familiar yet unique unity across anthropology, child study, and curriculum:

> The notion that youngsters resemble culturally the adults of earlier societies was not new with Hall; German educators had previously applied it

to curriculum design. But Hall posited an actual, biologically inherited link between the child and past cultures, resting his argument upon reports that the human fetus develops in sequence the physical traits of long extinct ancestors. From Ernst Haeckel, Hall got the idea that the process continues after birth; he concluded that children recapitulate as instinctual drives those mental traits which proved useful for survival during each successive epoch of the past. Since anthropologists believed that cultures advance through a fixed series of stages, Hall expected that sequence to provide a normative guide to child development.[34]

Dr. Charles Van Liew of Illinois State Normal University provided a lengthy explanation of Cultural Epochs as an educational theory, utilizing evolutionary theory, anthropology, and cultural history to determine the proper succession of materials and activities in the grade school curriculum. As already noted, child interest was paramount for educators who drew from Herbartian ideas, and cultural epochs theory informed teachers on children's successive interests. Van Liew emphasized a Herbartian emphasis on emotions in education. "*Large, entire* and *connected* portions of a subject are alone able to arouse a sufficiently deep interest and sympathy in the youthful mind, to keep it permanently on the alert and thus to affect the formation of character," wrote Van Liew and continued with a quote from Herbart, "Great moral energy is the effect of great scenes and entire unbroken thought masses." Thus a cultural-epochs curriculum emphasized study through the "great scenes": the sequenced study of sacred and profane myths and history, from folklore and fairy tales to Robinson Crusoe and Bible studies, and ending with St. Paul and Luther and the powerful stories of Reformation and nationalization. This curriculum moved through the stages believed to have been key developmental points of the race: from the mythical and heroic mind to state-building and the historic mind to the modern scientific and philosophic mind. Stories of great men would be used throughout to draw boys into the tales and to build on their natural interest. Van Liew subscribed to the idea that the latter emphasis on national development would contribute "directly to the true national feeling and national spirit." Here nationalism became a central part of the curriculum, seen as linked to character education and effective in promoting desirable social attitudes. Further linkages between nation and boys' character are developed below in the discussion of the Boy Scouts.[35]

Dewey criticized Cultural Epochs as the basis for curricula because he saw no necessary overlap between the literature and myths of other eras and children's psychical orientations, which had to be the ground upon which child-centered education proceeded. So his criticism was not with the idea that children's development might follow the outlines of the development of the race, but with its educational implications. Dewey demanded that cultural-epochs curricula pay attention to the changing psychological interests of children, which might or might not be engaged with medieval myths or Robinson Crusoe at the age of six or eight:

> It does not seem to me that the upholders of the theory have clearly recognized that if the correspondence [between the development of the race and the development of the human being] is not exact, *the standard, educationally* [that is, for making curricular decisions], *is the sequence in the child, not in the race*. It is a question of psychology, of child study, not of race history. To study first the race side, and finding certain epochs then to conclude to the same in the child is unjustifiable.[36]

Hall and other cultural epochs supporters looked to the racial past and to the racial future to identify the proper curriculum and its sequencing. The *present* interests and understandings of the child, as Dewey noted, were absent or minimized. This tendency to look backward and forward and away from the present is part of the racially romanticized legacy of Hall, and it is simultaneously part of imperialism and nationalism, which I describe in the Boy Scouts section below.[37]

6. *An Administrative Gaze That Is Longing, Desirous, and Erotic*. It is important to consider the passions of these builders of modern selves through adolescence. As they were keeping youth away from passion, their own desires filled their science and pedagogy. The character-builders evinced a "hunger for perpetual early boyhood." The boyologists may be imagined as desiring an escape from the responsibilities of modern manhood, with its bureaucratic contexts, social demands for conformity, and lack of autonomy. Boyhood, defined as a savage stage of active play, became an idealized antidote to the modern. Thus this longing is suggestive of loss. While adolescence was clearly a technology of change in social and political conditions, the hunger for boyhood was simultaneously "a melancholy fix on a golden time that we all slip away from."[38]

But I want to suggest another desiring process—one that works upon the exoticness of the other. As adolescence was increasingly defined as a separate identifiable stage, easily and necessarily distinct from adults, the adolescent took up qualities of other Others, that is, of savage races and women. Anthropologists had already provided accounts of promiscuous savages to whom recapitulation theory linked youth over time. The association of adolescents with primitive traits of conformity, emotionality, and sensuality pathologized them but simultaneously provided boyologists with endless incitements and opportunities to identify, detail, recount, worry, and reiterate their *every minute characteristic*. As I have read and reread the words of Hall and Baden-Powell and other boyologists, it is impossible to discount the erotic charge that heightens the truths of adolescent perils and possibilities. Frantz Fanon observed that when the look makes a person other, *there is always desire in the look*. Hall's insistent, careful, and controlling attention via biblical-laden, ponderous language can be "tripped up" by transfiguring it from moralistic melodrama to spunky boy-play; the boyologists can be refigured as pranksters who made every adolescent movement dangerous and necessary to watch (scientifically, of course). Every game became the site of multiple glimpses of titillating adolescent bodies.[39]

Hall's particular configuration of adolescence as sexual, idealistic, and emotional and his excessive "rhetorical bullying" on the facts of adolescent turmoil, its significance, and society's necessary responses are especially accessible to an interpretation of racial and sexual longing that James Kincaid argues was a strong part of "child-loving" in the Victorian era. This (homo)eroticization of others is visible in cultural figures as distinct as Theodore Roosevelt and the Tarzan of Edgar Rice Burroughs's imagination. Theodore Roosevelt was a primary emblem of the connections between white masculinity, patriotic nationalism, and imperialism and its affinity for savage energies:

> The fin de siècle mission to thwart feminization and revirilize boyhood—and by extension, manhood—reached its symbolic apotheosis in Theodore Roosevelt. TR "epitomized manly zest for the new imperial nation in part because of his jaunty energy, but also because *his image brought together both aspects of the new myth: the top rung of the ladder of social aspiration and the gladiatorial animal arena sensed at the bottom.*"[40]

Here we have the Great Chain of Being again, with a cultural and political hero drawing from the top and the bottom, an approach to hybridity that also occurred in G. Stanley Hall's developmental psychology. This merging of top and bottom serves to give legitimacy to all social hierarchies and to titillate by its evoking of the desire/fear for the "gladiatorial animal arena." Harry Stecopoulos provides a useful and related reading of *Tarzan of the Apes*, a blockbuster of 1912; in his view Tarzan, really Lord Greystoke, combined the aristocratic Englishman with the virile, black, animal body. Tarzan/Lord Greystoke was a perfect manly hybrid of Western rationality and brutish strength, the same characteristics that Roosevelt promoted and Hall struggled to comingle in adolescence.[41]

In this simultaneous distancing and desiring, the denunciation and affirming of sexual energy, the problematizing and idealizing of young men, the discourse of Hall and other boyologists was double-voiced, double-accented, desirous of that which it shunned. Adolescence today utilizes similar doubled tensions: the mixing of fear/desire, black/white, savage/civilized, emotional/rational, male/female, and adult/child. In this doubling—scientists and presidents proclaiming that we needed the dark virility *and* the white, Christian purity—we have one powerful source of the continuing interest in and commodification of youth. Adolescence as always "becoming," as constantly "budding," evokes physicality and sexual charge. The white, manly purity depended upon the movement through the lower stages; *development* simultaneously recognizes the claims of civilized strength and social order, the need for adolescents to become mature, as it recognizes, with pleasure and danger, the tensions of controlling desire. Thus through its sexual valence and its emphasis on avoiding *precocity*, the discourse of adolescence speaks about race and class. In this way, adolescence is a discourse about making middle-class whiteness, in which the threats to maturity—sexuality and physicality of budding teens—are historically associated with primitive races and women.[42]

ROMANCING THE STATE AND CULTIVATING AN ADMINISTRATIVE GAZE

Hall advocated that the raising of children and youth not be left to tradition or neglect; he became convinced that *"laissez-faire* individualism would no longer answer the needs of a complex, civilized society," and he saw Germany as leading the way toward "an educational state, governed by an elite and dedicated to the cultural perfection of mankind." Such an approach involved a strong "distrust of reason, individualism, and democratic egalitarianism." Stephen Jay Gould apprises Hall's use of recapitulation to orchestrate a sweeping construction and maintenance of an educational state; Hall aimed "to reconstruct the grammar-school course: scientifically, so that school-hours, curricula, exercise, buildings, etc. shall all be . . . in accordance with child-nature, the true norm."[43]

But Hall and his fellow reformers were really making a new society as well as a new school. Hall's argument for an educational state contributed to the movement toward a watchful state that would oversee health and development. For Hall and other middle-class professional men and women, turn-of-the-century life seemed to demand domination of new situations, and its possibilities for degeneration (i.e., failure) cried out for direction from the empirical findings of social and educational scientists. Child nature became the standard by which all social practices could be judged—as supporting or undermining it and its representation of race progress. Thus in making the modern developing adolescent, a new society was being envisioned and effected. Child study and schooling took a place with other emerging knowledges, such as criminal anthropology:

> The object of this and other sciences of the social (sociology, social medicine, social hygiene) was no longer the society envisaged by liberalism: a collection of autonomous individuals, each equipped with free will, and responsible for his or her own actions. Rather, *it was a social body, with its own laws, regularities, and pathologies, which had to be known by new sciences and managed according to new rationalities of government. In this sense, criminal anthropology was linked to the emergence of what Foucault called "governmentality," modern forms of power and knowledge concerned with the management of risk and the promotion of the health and welfare of the biological population.*[44]

The following section further examines the *new rationalities of governing* the young through a description of a range of concrete material practices in and out of schools, many of which were legitimated through association with Hall's conceptual framework. Thus I turn more fully to the technologies of adolescence, that is, the techniques of naming, studying, diagnosing, predicting, and administering an identifiable adolescent population at the turn of the century. These developments were especially marked in England with the problem of "hooligans" and the popularity of the Boys Brigades and Boy Scouts, among others, to save them.

Baden-Powell, the Boy Scouts, and a New State

Great Britain at the turn of the century illustrates how boys and boy organizations were part of a broader reconfiguration of the state and its more active administration of particular populations in relation to national aims. When the British Army, which had subdued so much of the globe, was nearly defeated by Dutch farmers in the South African Boer War, the problems of "external security," "domestic health," and boys were fused. The South African struggle demonstrated that the British Empire was not inviolable, and the empire's weakness lay in the bad physical condition of working-class army recruits, many of whom were rejected as unfit. Poor health was readily interpreted to mean a deteriorated moral condition, which easily flowed into degeneracy and decadence, inflammatory words in England as in the United States. It is difficult to appreciate the full-blown panic among the upper classes after the Boer War. We must try to understand "degeneration theory," which linked the perceived increase in internal ailments—diseases such as tuberculosis and syphilis, alcoholism, or crime with national health. "This mode of thinking encouraged the appraisal of social problems from the point of view of national interest, thrusting, as it were, the issues of domestic health and external security into an identical frame of analysis."[45]

A nationwide debate on the sources of imperial power emerged in England, and "a decade-long crusade began that sought to regenerate the 'national efficiency' of the Victorian era." Increasing economic and social uncertainty characterized the years 1880 to 1910 in Britain, with threats to national power not only from the Boers but also from the German Navy and U.S. businesses. Prices and profits declined. Socialists presented internal threats, and for many middle-class Britons the importance of "cementing national unity" became paramount. Youth became a focal point, in part because up through 1881, 46 percent of the population of England and Wales consisted of youth under twenty years of age. Youth became a symbol of and a population whose manliness, religious beliefs, education, patriotism, and physical fitness were a social site for new adult supervisors and reformers to prepare for a secure and known future; the dynamics appear to be very close to those in the United States, although nationalism and militarism may have been more explicit. Springhall concludes that: "youth movements ensured the continuity of certain broadly conservative, conformist attitudes toward the British Empire." My argument is that the making of adolescents as problems/possibilities was part of a shift toward a new society with new science and administrative needs; thus, although conservative ideology might have seemed familiar, truths about state policies and practices were being refigured.[46]

Improving the national efficiency was the standard taken up by various reformers, academics, eugenicists, and educators at this time, many of whom were directly and strongly influenced by G. Stanley Hall's version of recapitulation theory. The obsession with adolescence as part of the social problem of turn-of-the-century Britain influenced both the rising rates of arrest for "nonindictable juvenile crime" and the creation of various youth organizations to take the "problem" off the streets. In 1910, Winston Churchill gave nationalism and youth issues a familiar liberal spin:

Are they not being exploited? Are they not being demoralised? Are they not being thrown away? Whereas the youth of the wealthier class is all kept under strict discipline until eighteen or nineteen, the mass of the nation runs wild after fourteen years of age. . . . [N]o boy or girl ought to be treated merely as cheap labour. . . . [I]t is there you will find the seeds of Imperial ruin and national decay—the unnatural gap between rich and poor, the divorce of the people from the land, the want of proper discipline and training in our youth, the exploitation of boy labour, the physical degeneration which seems to follow so swiftly upon civilised poverty.

Churchill's statement provides a map of the reformers' efforts: better education (a uniform school-leaving age of 14 was established in 1918), greater surveillance of youth, better discipline and training, and better physical health and development. Sexual excesses played less of an explicit role in the British disciplining of youth via turn-of-the century reforms than in the United States.[47]

There had been both a romanticizing of working-class lads and a distinctive homoerotic component to male social welfare reformers in pre–Boer War London. University-educated reformers reverenced the rough lads' refusal to bow to the stultifying conformity of Victorian and Edwardian respectability and pedestaled them as representatives of an "aboriginal boyhood uncorrupted by an emasculating civilizing process." However, as England's domestic ill-health continued, upper-class male reformers moved from an eroticized admiration for "spirited and manly" working-class lads to wariness: "[T]he independence, ingenuity and loyalty reformers treasured in rough lads were unbecoming in future wives and domestic servants. And such attributes were dangerous in future trade unionists and potential members of the emerging Independent Labour Party." This sea change in relationships occurred after the Oscar Wilde trials, a time when the easy blurring of homosocial and homosexual was halted in Britain as in the United States.[48]

"Control over boy nature was the key to the future of the nation and empire. 'Boy life' became a convenient shorthand for the assumption that working-class, adolescent, urban male behavior was necessarily a social problem." Reformers who had previously viewed the rough lads through rose-colored glasses now used Darwinian imagery to shock readers about the "emergence of a new degenerate race festering at the very heart of the empire." As Hall, Theodore Roosevelt, and other boyologists did in the United States, C. F. G. Masterman and Baden-Powell gained prominence through their articulations of "the interconnections between national culture and nationalism, social reform and hooliganism, race degeneration and imperialism, masculine identity and the state." Degenerate boys were imagined to be staking out territories in the interior wilderness of cities, as enemies of the British Empire had so recently done in South Africa, a "counternationalism."[49]

The "enemy within" must be placed under the "guidance and control of the few wise." What was being rationalized and envisioned was "a manly state that actively intervened in the lives of its citizens." But the state was glossed as a nuclear family, so that every child would have "in the State a social father who more and more controls and trains him, and in Society a social mother who daily seeks to love and tend him more truly." Thus a British welfare state began to work through various organizations for boys as a father and a mother, operating, of course, on upper class ideas of proper education, gender differentiations, and civilizing influences. Around the boy problem reformers imagined and began to create a new male community of fathers, sons, and the "social father," the interventionist state. The active administration of youths' lives became as commonplace as the belief in their unlimited potential. "Modern, home-based, institutionalised adolescents" would become the "democratized" norm for all youth, and the Boy Scouts was the preeminent boys organization of the new paternalistic state.[50]

Boy Scouts

Fittingly, a hero of the Boer War, General Robert S. S. Baden-Powell, led the efforts to reform boy and nation. Baden-Powell made it his mission to develop fit soldiers by marketing a mix of public school traditions and conventional boy-play into the Boy Scouts. Scouting sought less to instill any genuine fighting capability than to cultivate obedience and unswerving devotion to duty, which was fundamental to a military organization. Scouting philosophy and laws drew from British public schools at the time, whose overriding trait was to inculcate an all-consuming loyalty to institution, class, and country. Baden-Powell proposed to make boys

Figure 2.2 The relationship between the Boy Scouts and British nationalism. Reprinted from John Springhall, *Youth, Empire, and Society*, 1977, London, Croom Helm.

"personally responsible" for their own health and strength through games and badge work. Scouts appeared in England as soldiers who would save the country from young men who were "pale, narrow-chested, hunched-up . . . smoking endless cigarettes." The scrawny physiques of lower-class young men were understood as representing their flimsy characters, and they were the "problems" to which scouting proposed an answer. The perceived national malaise allowed Baden-Powell and his scoutmasters and scouts to participate in a broadly-based surge in patriotism, in which vigorous, disciplined young male bodies represented the body politic.[51]

Organizing Boys in the United States

In the United States, the origins of scouting were in the Woodcraft Movement articulated by naturalist Ernest Thompson Seton. He aimed to create men and critiqued Baden-Powell's organization, first, for stealing his ideas, and second, for wanting to produce soldiers. Seton's aim was to make men in the image of the Shawnee chief Tecumseh, a great athlete, hunter, and leader. But Seton clearly articulated an urban critique and argued that boys became bad in the sordid city surroundings, which he termed "city rot." Cities promoted flabby muscles and indolence, especially through spectator sports added onto the passivity of church and school. Seton wanted to break with the values of industrial America, whereas Baden-Powell's "ideal Boy Scout went out to serve the British Empire and never cut his ties to the society he left behind." But the Anglophile Boy Scouts were better organized than the Woodcraft Movement and they appropriated symbols of American nationhood, for example, by having the scout uniform closely resemble the army's. Between 1914 and 1922 membership in the Boy Scouts of America grew from 103,395 to 432,995. David Macleod explains the enormous success of the Boy Scouts in the United States over the Woodcraft Movement in this way:

> Baden-Powell's efforts to socialize boys for a stable social role went over better in Progressive Era America than anachronistic yearnings for frontier liberty. Given the urgent striving for mastery that marked American notions of masculinity, Seton's rejection of dominance over nature, of white superiority over Indians, and to some degree of rigidly conventional morality was too extreme for a mass movement.[52]

Thus character-building organizations like the Boy Scouts shored up conventional masculinity, support for national expansionism, and white superiority. The next section looks closer at the strategies utilized to achieve those ends.

Organizing Play

Today we worry over youths' free time and whether their leisure pursuits are wholesome, productive, and protective. These were exactly the concerns of the reformers who focused on play and playgrounds and who recommended expanding the role of peers as supervisors since adults could not be around all the time. The boyologists identified play as central to creating young men who had disciplined spirit and would obey superiors. Play came to be revered for making children and adolescents moral and strong via direct and efficient processes, unlike the passive, unfocused, and feminized school curriculum. Cognitive approaches to civilized behavior were associated with schooling and were deemed unsatisfactory. Play invoked muscles directly, and muscles were believed to be the location of automatic, instinctual morality. Courage in war, it was reasoned, must be an instantaneous response, since there was no time for thought and moral reasoning. Muscles, if properly prepared, carried civilized morality, ever at the ready. Expertly organized play would promote discipline and control, qualities sorely lacking in the largely immigrant children who were the play reformers' targets.

Although playground reformers first concentrated on young children and brought "sand gardens" from Germany to Boston in 1886, adolescents eventually gained in attention. The Playground Association of America (PAA) was founded in 1906; its ranks included Theodore Roosevelt as honorary president and Luther Gulick as the first director, as well as Jane Addams, Jacob Riis, and Henry Curtis. The PAA's statement of purpose emphasized that play produces moral behavior, efficient citizens, and democracy:

> Delinquency is reduced by providing a wholesome outlet for youthful energy. Industrial efficiency is increased by giving individuals a play life which will develop greater resourcefulness and adaptability. Good citizenship is promoted by forming habits of co-operation in play.

Gulick believed that the PAA had to convince Americans that organizing leisure was just as important as organizing industrial production and just as technical. One play curriculum for teenagers included 30 minutes of patriotic songs, 30 minutes of supervised "free play," 30 minutes of track and field events, and 90 minutes of team sports, vocational training, or dancing. Competitions, festivals, and pageants were all highly thought-of for their positive political socialization effects.[53]

The funding of play reforms was originally provided by private foundations such as the Russell Sage Foundation in New York City; but reformers lobbied for local and national government support, and across the first four decades of the twentieth century children's and youth's play was increasingly supervised by the state. The state, it was argued, needed to fill in for hopelessly inadequate immigrant parents who were deemed incapable of preparing their children for the stresses, challenges, and prospects of the New World.[54] *The play reformers, like the Boy Scouts and other similar organizations, consciously nurtured peer relations to replace unsatisfactory families and extended expert influence by promoting boys watching over other boys.*

Reformers utilized statistics to argue for playgrounds and for their effectiveness. Rowland Haynes, a PAA field director in Milwaukee, developed a survey method to gather information about the city's most congested "foreign colonies," how younger and older children used their spare time, as well as how much street space was available for play. His marshalling of statistics and survey information put the PAA far ahead of any public or private group in knowledge about recreation and in its ability to sway opinions. Haynes also formulated three standards to evaluate recreation: (1) Did it make people more fit for their regular lives? (2) Was the recreation educational? (3) Was the recreation promoting morality? Haynes's concerns sound decidedly contemporary: "[D]oes the given form of recreation build up habits of quick thinking, of initiative in dealing with new situations, of self control, of ability to work with others in the give and take of group activities?"[55]

Statistics were used not just to argue for the need for playgrounds but also to demonstrate their effectiveness. Juvenile crime on Chicago's South Side declined by an average of 44 percent in wards with supervised playgrounds, and Cincinnati claimed a 50 percent decrease in youth offenses. Although these specific effects may be questioned, the populational reasoning around "immigrant youth," "ethnic youth," and state intervention that utilized scientific methods was not questioned and became the accepted ways to make arguments and public policy. Thinking about and talking about youth took on modern administrative trappings with the use of statistics and identifiable subgroups.

Team Play

Since the team player was the ideal American citizen of the early twentieth century, team sports were canonized as the perfect pedagogical approach to civilizing boys. According to play organizers and the Great Chain of Being, a *team* was a form of association rooted in the heritage of the Anglo-Saxon "race." So team play came naturally to Anglo-Saxon youth but could uplift others if they were educated to it:

Teamwork required both obedience to the rules of the game and specific attitudes on the part of the players. The player should obey the rules, but he must also be loyal to teammates, willingly sacrifice personal glory to the common cause, graciously accept defeat, perceive victory as a group rather than an individual achievement, and obey the team captain.[56]

Thus team play had a racial tradition that was extremely relevant to modern life, but expert coordination was needed for the benefits to be gained. Scientifically designed and well-equipped playgrounds were necessary, and *laissez-faire* team play, like *laissez-faire* capitalism, was likely to lead to moral anarchy.

Scientifically organized team play generated a greater consciousness via rhythmic muscular movements (as in football or basketball) which created "an almost mystical sense of oneness among the players" and a loss of individual consciousness as the player merged with the group. Group loyalty, a necessary transcendence of individual identity, followed such experiences of oneness. Group loyalty was the "moral fulcrum" of personal morality and social order, and supervised athletic team participation offered one of the best hopes for the creation of a generation of loyal young people. Some reformers admitted the political utility of sports as well: a 1899 French sport almanac praised football as "a veritable little war, with its necessary discipline and its way of getting participants used to danger and to blows."[57]

Besides aiming for muscular morality and loyalty, which could be employed in imperialist pursuits, playground reformers also sought to make the peer group an extension of adult supervision; if the reformers' techniques were sufficiently sophisticated, boys would eventually supervise other boys when adults were absent. The peer group, expertly guided, could replace the inadequate ethnic family as primary socializer. Thus the playground reformers, like the scouts, sought to emphasize and extend peer conformity as a new form of regulation that included patriotic nationalism, acceptance of a given position in the social order, and a muscular Christian morality. The PAA gathered information about the political, social, and ethnic contours of American cities that allowed statistics (individual cases devoid of context) to identify, describe, and diagnose ills; predict ill-health, delinquency, and moral decay; and prescribe remedies or punishment. The playground reforms contributed to the new form of governmentality that "massified" the individual as a statistic, the contours of which could be plotted, analyzed, and made predictable for future management. The play organizers' insistence on peer conformity ("loyalty"), youth as an identifiable and calculable population, and the administrative need to create the next generation solidified ideas and practices in which youth still come of age.[58]

CIVILIZED SEXUAL DIFFERENCES, OR WHERE THE GIRLS WERE

The bulk of this chapter has described the boyologists' discourse on adolescence that obviously concentrated on males. Apparently absent, girls were, in fact, always present—hauntingly present. Like the shadowy black figures in Toni Morrison's reading of American literature, girls were *necessary* to define manliness by virtue of their difference from and distance from manliness. *Fin-de-siècle* masculinity came to depend upon femininity (as well as on children and savages) to define itself. This section examines the multileveled absence/presence of girls in reformers' ideas and theories and in progressive programs and policies for girls.

Given the dominant imagery of the Great Chain of Being in the emerging discourse on adolescents, girls were always below boys on the phylogenetic map. Taking recapitulation theory seriously meant that white middle-class boys had to pass through a *female stage* before they moved on to a higher position. For reformers who were ferociously defining and performing manly masculinity, as described in Chapter One, the female stage had to produce theoretical and personal trembling. Thus within the very schema of adolescence as a *developmental stage*, femaleness loomed as an obstacle that had to be navigated and surpassed; we can say that femininity haunted the modern developing adolescent. We have already seen numerous ways that boys were segregated and protected by men to guard their emergent masculinity and superiority. One beacon of civilization was a clear, marked differentiation between the sexes; advanced societies sported greater differences between men's and women's appearances, social positions, characteristics, and, of course, education and training. At the 1903 National Education Association (NEA) conference, G. Stanley Hall asserted:

> in savagery women and men are more alike in their physical structure and in their occupations, but with real progress the sexes diverge and draw apart, and the diversities always present are multiplied and accentuated.

Hall encouraged educators to aim for more manly boys and more womanly girls, advice that was widely heeded. For example, the mission statement of St. Louis high schools called for an education to "develop manhood and womanhood with strength of character and trained intelligence." Given the cultural preoccupation with promoting civilization and avoiding degeneracy, this rhetoric was likely quite meaningful, and it soothed those nervous about disorderly women, because preparing for adulthood would follow the adult norms for separate male and female spheres.[59]

Segregation promotes Civilization ↓ Avoids degeneracy.

Creating Separate Spheres in England and the United States

In England, the Boer War and fears of national decline also produced a panic around working-class girls and their education. As noted above, many of the army volunteers for the war had been rejected; in Manchester, for example, 8,000 out of 11,000 volunteers were unfit to serve. The national report on young men's physical deterioration laid the responsibility in part on mothers' insufficient knowledge about "household affairs, hygiene and nutrition." The report recommended an emphasis on domestic education for girls in state-supported elementary schools, which would teach female students, for example, how to cook cheap, nutritious meals. Lessons on child care and infant management also came into being because the infant mortality rate remained high, another eugenic concern for the future of the British Empire. In secondary schools *domestic science* elevated the preparation for future positions as wives and mothers through a scientific mantle, and girls were routinely encouraged to substitute domestic science for natural science studies. Overall, girls needed fewer lessons in academics and more shaping into "efficient women citizens, good home-keepers and mothers."[60]

Feminist scholars record similar processes in the United States at the turn of the century. In response to an enrollment of 60 percent girls, Los Angeles educators' "fear of feminization" fueled curricular reforms such as manual training and domestic science, higher salaries for male teachers, and a "thorough masculinization of interscholastic sports and student government." Despite the fact that the girls' basketball team had winning seasons between 1902 and 1907, by 1910, all interscholastic female teams at Los Angeles High had been disbanded and only intramural girls' sports continued. To coax boys to stay in school, high school administrators offered a well-organized, competitive sports program run by rugged men, and channeled girls into cheerleading. The shift of girls from participants to supporters was repeated in other activities at Los Angeles High, such as in the movement from female-dominated literary clubs to male-dominated student government organizations. "Extracurricular clubs and sports were a key part of the educators' effort to give high schools an active, virile, masculine image and thereby persuade boys to stay in school." Manual training programs designed "not to turn out mechanics but to make men," a night school program for male truants, and more male teachers all aimed to keep boys in school. To recruit and keep more male teachers, despite no evidence that male teachers kept male students in school, their salaries were boosted; between 1890 and 1905, the gap between male and female teachers' salaries quadrupled.[61]

Karen Graves's study of St. Louis high school curricula in the early 1900s demonstrates that social efficiency perspectives masculinized the courses of study by demoting and weakening the classical curriculum (academic study for its own worth rather than for vocational ends), which became seen as feminine. Science and commercial courses of study became the most valued and most popular tracks, which Graves links to a decline in the number of courses needed for graduation. We see several things occurring simultaneously: the decline of academics-for-themselves, the rise of preparation for citizenship and work, lowered requirements for high school graduation, and a masculinization of secondary schools that is linked to vocational education and extracurriculars. Girls' presence in secondary schools needed to be carefully managed, for their dominance of a high school population produced a frightening image: "If the boy quits school to go to work before he reaches the eighth grade, while the girl goes forward to the high school, intelligence itself is pretty sure to smack of femininity."[62] If male supremacy was to be preserved, high schools could contribute by keeping boys in school, offering practical courses of study and emphasizing the value of extracurriculars, especially sports. As the cartoon in Figure 2.3 demonstrates, male dominance in the curriculum also involved the ascent of a sporting, muscular, practical man over effeminate, intellectual men.

Parallelling the domestication of girls' education during the "progressive" era, separate scouting programs for girls also developed. In England, Baden-Powell turned over the direction of the Girl Guides (emphatically not "scouts") first to his sister Agnes and then to his wife Olave. Agnes feminized the organization, for example, by abandoning the masculine patrol names of Wildcats, Foxes, and so on that had been chosen by the girls themselves, and instituting names like Roses and Cornflowers instead. The object of the girls' program came into line with the woman's sphere, to make "better mothers and guides to the next generation."[63]

A cartoonist's view of the competition between the liberal, classical tradition and emerging utilitarianism in education.

Figure 2.3 Masculinizing the school curriculum: virile commercial studies over-power the effeminate and elitist traditional, academic coursework. Reprinted from G. Joncich, *The Sane Positivist: A Biography of Edward L. Thorndike*, 1968, Middletown, CT: Wesleyan University Press.

A large body of advice literature for women and girls appeared in the early 1900s in Britain, "characterised by a strident, imperialist vocabulary, urging women to regard the preservation of their own health as a moral duty, a duty they owed to 'the Empire and the Race.'" Health became a moral and patriotic duty and extended to untidy dress, the lagging step, and the dull eye and heavy countenance. Empire and Race demanded good posture, a brisk pace, and a bright, cheerful face.[64]

Fears of precocity overshadowed every discussion of girls and their organizations. Girls, like boys, were dangerous when they resisted the correct steps and slow pace of socialization to their future status.[65] For girls, too much independence, early paid work, or experiences without school or family oversight made precocity imminent. Sexual precocity was most feared, and state intervention in the United States around adolescent girls was generally around sexuality.

Juvenile Justice as a Technology of Gendered Sexuality

The conventional marking of the beginning of the juvenile justice system is Cook County, Chicago, in 1899—a centerpiece of the making of adolescence as a social fact, as well as the making of state intervention in adolescent lives. The primary aim of juvenile courts was not to decide guilt or innocence but to "assess the conditions in a youth's life that had led to delinquency." In the gendered and sexualized practices of juvenile justice from its inception, we see an additional aspect of adolescence as a technology of self- and population-making. Although the "boy problem" dominated public consciousness and private and public efforts, and boys committed more serious crimes, by the late 1800s the "girl problem" came into its own. Private civic groups, such as settlement houses, women's clubs, the YWCA, and the Girl Scouts inaugurated efforts, and governments followed with a proliferation of reformatories for girls. Girls were brought to court almost exclusively for alleged early sexual exploration and received harsher punishments than did boys. In part, their disproportionate share of "justice" was justified as *preventive intervention* into the lives of antisocial girls, who were depicted as especially vulnerable to temptations and immoral forces.[66]

Massachusetts had inaugurated female juvenile justice in 1856 with the first reform school for girls, but campaigns for the moral protection of young women were not new. What was new in the late 1800s and early 1900s was

> the broadened scope of the campaigns and the mounting demands for state regulation of the problem. Public anxiety about the morality of young women greatly intensified and spread to all regions of the country during this period of rapid urban and industrial growth. Instead of the religious and voluntary efforts pursued earlier, moral reformers now began to insist on a forceful response from the state.[67]

Widespread fears of immigrants and of the poor were also reflected in disproportionate representation in the juvenile courts. Promiscuous girls called forth all the concerns and prejudices against racial, ethnic, and lower-class others (given recapitulation theory and adolescence as a cultural switching station). Girls were mostly charged with noncriminal activities, generally "immorality," which might be actual sexual acts but was often showing the "signs" in their appearance or conversation that they had had intercourse in the past or *"might do so in the near future."*[68] Since immigrants were, like other groups on the lower rungs of the Great Chain of Being, instinctively emotional and lacking in self-restraint, their daughters were read in the same way. Thus language and demeanor that were insufficiently demure and repentant were interpreted as evidence of "immorality." Whenever a girl used vile language, masturbated, or indulged in lascivious thoughts, the court intervened.

Court Intervention

Alleged girl delinquents in Milwaukee, for example, were subject to close questioning about their private lives and *"every girl who appeared in court was subjected to a vaginal examination."* Even if an intact hymen indicated a girl was a virgin, doctors could diagnose "self-abuse" through masturbation and make a case for the necessity of state supervision. Thus female delinquency was primarily precocious sexuality judged by Victorian standards of women's moral passiveness in this area and necessary preparation for marriage and motherhood. Courts wanted the *performance of docile femininity*; if a girl would not "feign repentance" and if her parents "would not at least feign shock," the court responded punitively.[69]

Extreme

State interventions regularly involved isolation of delinquent girls from males, preferably in rural settings like those that G. Stanley Hall saw as the essence of healthfulness. *"The mere act of isolating delinquent girls came to be seen as a rehabilitative tool.* As such it served an important, latent, economic function by rationalizing a minimal public investment in other, more positive methods of treatment."[70] This same logic of isolation appears in many contemporary discussions of single-sex schooling, where the segregation of girls is the major and sufficient intervention.

Prevention took numerous forms.[71] First, legislation worked to sanitize dance halls and local hotels by prohibiting the sale of alcohol and "tough dancing," prostitution, and pandering. Second, girls were recruited to engage in moral self-defense by joining "protective leagues" that investigated and reported immoral conditions at dance halls, amusement parks, and moving picture theaters and encouraged other girls toward "right thinking." Third, reformers brought working girls into contact with educated and ethical women through girls clubs sponsored by settlement houses, the YWCA, and many churches:

The clubs gave adolescent girls opportunities to hold public dances in "wholesome" settings, attend concerts and museums, participate in literary debates, study dramatics, meet with labor leaders and consumer activists, engage in homemaking and handicraft projects, and take part in community service, charitable, and fund-raising activities.

The National Urban League and other black organizations and churches organized comparable religious, educational, and recreational activities for African-American girls.[72]

A fourth prong of the prevention response to the girl problem was sex education, especially for girls from poor or working-class families. Although complete repression of sexual feelings was no longer considered best, experts warned girls against "coquetting" and "leading on," because men's passions could not be reined in. One expert told teenage girls that it was wrong to "play with love." Social service agencies and female police officers participated in delinquency prevention and intervention, trying to understand an individual girl's circumstances and tailoring schooling, vocational training, employment, and recreation to suit her needs. Finally, reformatories and probation officers took over when prevention failed.[73] The same reformers who urged prevention also supported using the state for surveillance, legal prosecution, detention, and institutionalization of girls and young women who engaged in suspect behavior.

In calling for state regulation of female sexuality, middle-class women reformers envisioned the creation of a "maternal state" that would become as near as possible a "real mother" to the girls. In order to achieve this maternal state, women needed to be appointed as police officers, juvenile court judges, probation officers, and heads of correctional facilities, all of whom would combine their natural maternal understanding with "scientific" methods of diagnosis and treatment. Of course, this vision of the maternal state also created many new professional opportunities for educated, middle-class women.[74]

Love and Juvenile Delinquents

The juvenile justice system that was produced during the Progressive Era institutionalized new ideas and practices, as it also mixed new legal ideas with traditional approaches to rearing children. The enlightened juvenile courts, reformatories, and probation policies contributed significant elements to the emerging discourse on adolescence. Victorian justice for youth had thrown accused juveniles into detention facilities that warehoused all kinds of adult criminals; those convicted of crimes were sent to large prison facilities that sought to control every moment of the prisoners' lives.[75]

The U.S. juvenile justice system drew on model penal developments in Germany and France, which believed that "family reform schools" were more effective. This model emphasized smaller cottages or houses with perhaps three dozen offenders and one or two adults (obviously a *large* family). The new architecture broke down the familiar single behemoth building into more humane cottages. The family reform school attempted to "make personal contact and communication the essence of the rehabilitative effort." These modernists saw children's natural capacity to love and to be loved as the key to moral regeneration and strove to evoke and manipulate emotional resources. The Massachusetts Industrial School for Girls was an early model of this approach to reforming delinquents:

> It is to be a *home*. Each house is to be a *family*, under the sole direction and control of the matron, who is to be the *mother* of the family. . . . [This organization will make the "scholars" feel] that there is one affectionate, motherly ear, into which they can whisper their wants and afflictions, with confidence and sympathy; one heart which beats in union with their own, and to which they can appeal for kindness, for guidance and support, and around which their affections may cluster, with the assurance of a kind and affectionate response. It is to educate, to teach them, industry, self-reliance, morality and religion, and prepare them to go forth qualified to become useful and respectable members of society. All this is to be done, without stone walls, bars or bolts, but by the more sure and effective restraining power—*the cords of love*.

This *romancing* of the state reformatory as loving mother initiated the use of motivational techniques of persuasion, kindness, and empathy into an "affectional discipline" that included shame, guilt, but above all, love. Moses Barnett, the superintendent of the Wisconsin State Reform School, believed that his institution needed to "appeal to the emotions" of delinquents to be effective. In his reformatory each night he gathered the inmates, his wife, and two teenaged daughters for a "family" conference which intermingled "prayer, confession, ethical instruction, and, most importantly, sympathetic listening."[76]

```
Name                              Western House of Refuge for Women

Heart lesions  none               Deformities Lordosis.

Gonorrhoea  Negative.  Syphilis  Wass.positive. Other diseases
                                               Diphtheria.
                                               Pertussis.
                                               Measles,
Social and moral traits                        Typhoid in childhood.
                                               Nasal obstruction.

Judgment  some.                   Temper controlled.

Industry . good worker.           Moral sense  fair.


Mental traits

Concentration  is good.           Reasoning -yes

Association of ideas  good.

Memory,  Auditory  normal         Visual good,

Motor coordination  balanced.     Muscular strength  reduced.


Summary     Normal mentality.

Physical     Her physical condition is below par and syphilis is also
             present. Was not well as a child. Respiratory system is de-
             fective.

Mental       Physical age: 21 7/12.  Mental age:XIV.
             This gives her a normal intelligence quotient.  Reasons
             to some extent. Able to initiate and carry out a plan. A
             good case for reformation as she has normal mentality.is
             attentive and adaptable.

Delinquencies
        Sex.




Diagnosis        Feeble-Minded      Imbecile    Moron

Normal           Subnormal          Psychopathic

Insane           Hysterical         Epileptic

Prostitute       Alcoholic          Criminalistic .
```

Figure 2.4 A record of a young woman's psychological examination at the Western House of Refuge, Albion, NY, circa 1915. Reprinted from Ruth M. Alexander, *The "Girl Problem": Female Sexual Delinquency in New York, 1900–1930*, 1995, Ithaca and London, Cornell University Press.

In addition to the evocation and manipulation of youths' emotions, juvenile justice also emphasized probation, and the reform of juveniles within their own homes, and gave probation officers, dubbed "family tutors," broad powers of surveillance and intervention. This reasoning about probation, used disproportionately with boys, focused the expert gaze of juvenile justice on the youth and the family together. Although the boyologists moved toward the separation of boys from the feminizing influences of the family and women teachers, juvenile justice workers place youths, especially boys, back into a family setting—if not their family of origin, then the reform school family. Boyologists retreated from the cult of domesticity, and justice reformers utilized it to diagnose family and youth ills.[77]

Despite these differences, common across these efforts was an insistence on *prevention* and *diagnosis*. The broad surveillance that was usual can be gauged by examining the record of intake examination at the Western House of Refuge, a women's reformatory in Albion, New York, shown in Figure 2.4. The form assesses physical, temperamental, moral, and mental traits. At the bottom of the report is the diagnosis—from normal to feebleminded, alcoholic, or hysteric. The progressive juvenile justice of prevention launched a surveillance of every aspect of juveniles' (especially girls') bodies and souls.

The turn-of-the-century focus on girls also invoked racial, gender, and national concerns. Civilized societies evidenced strict separation of men and women, and precocious girls would contribute to social degeneration, racial suicide, and imperial decline. Girls' formal and informal upbringing needed to safeguard their purity and docility and prepare them for useful roles of wife and mother. Outside schools, cultural programs enhanced their wifely potential. Within schools, domestic science often replaced natural science, and girls were enjoined to become supporters of male-centered activities rather than participants and leaders in sports and clubs. The infant juvenile justice system watched girls closely for any nuance of possible impurity. Under the guise of protection, they removed girls to reformatories and utilized a pedagogy of love to influence them. The juvenile justice system demonstrated the significant place of expert diagnosis and prevention supported by the state in defining and solving girls' and boys' problems.

SUMMARY

This chapter looked closely at various producers of new truths of adolescence at the beginning of the twentieth century. Modern facts of adolescence emerged within worries over the futures of the white race, the nation, and masculinity, which raised the problems of degeneracy/progress to a frenzy. Adolescence became a way to connect with this set of worries and to establish new professionals who diagnosed problems in order to prevent further degeneracy. Adolescence became a way to prepare individuals for a new social order yet maintain the social hierarchy. Public schools, private philanthropic endeavors, Boy Scouts, Girl Guides, and juvenile courts all participated in an enlarged and intensified discourse about adolescence, a discourse that is still vital and powerful.

Although adolescence had been demarcated before the late 1800s, the line between youth and adult became sharper, more intently watched, and democratically applied to all youth. Hall emphasized adolescence as a new birth, a new opportunity to move upward or downward on the Great Chain of Being. He and his colleagues also issued "pedagogical imperatives," that is, disciplinary and instructional techniques that were essential for each stage of boyhood and adolescence. Thus laissez-faire approaches to youth were deemed likely to lead to moral anarchy, and the administrative gaze of teachers, parents, psychologists, play reformers, scouting leaders, and juvenile justice workers was everywhere cultivated. Precocity had to be prevented. This was the banner under which state and private interventions were orchestrated.

I have also sketched some of the specific administrative responses that became part of the truths and repertoire of adolescent experts. Across the various reformers, emotions were utilized to manipulate and educate youth. Boyologists and protectors of girls uniformly recommended close monitoring of their bodies to protect against precocity; boys' regimens mandated team sports and the building of strong bodies, while girls' programs were directed toward high culture and domestic skills. Separate curricula were consciously bolstered, because recapitulation theory proclaimed that highly civilized groups had greater differentiation between men and women. Working against youthful precocity enhanced economic dependency as well as the removal of any adultlike responsibilities. These prescriptions segregated youth from the world and from the pressures of adulthood but gave them *leisure*, which became the most highly surveilled and contested portion of their lives. A slow, steady coming-of-age was prescribed. Same-sex peers became increasingly significant as boyologists, especially, consciously developed peers as surrogate-adult-managers who could operate when adults were absent. Thus there was a strong emphasis on the positive role of peers—when expertly guided, of course.

I have offered a playful consideration of the erotics of boy- and girl-watching. Controlling sexuality was the centerpiece of evolutionary progress, and adolescence was the time when sexuality and sexualized bodies became disturbingly visible. The "budding girl" included a romanticized vision of the next generation of "angels in the house," but the focus on girls' maturing bodies was simultaneously titillating and voyeuristic.[78] The idea of adolescence as always becoming (and not really existing in the present) fostered a hide-and-seek of knowing, watching, and cataloguing maturing bodies, for *prevention* necessitated unlimited scientific looking. The adolescent body, endlessly divided and described— as strong-muscled or sunken-chested, chaste or self-abused—was the site of diagnosis, prescription, and action.

This discursive analysis of adolescence is a strategic one aimed at demonstrating how "truths" of adolescence participated in and contributed to new ways of making selves and making society at the turn of the century. This new form of governmentality emphasized the manipulation of emotions, keeping youth asexual, unintellectual, dependent, and watched by peers; all of these practices extended over more years. Laissez-faire approaches to youth were insufficient; in both public and private settings experts organized recreation, school, scouting, and, above all, love. We will see contemporary reiterations of these beliefs and practices in later chapters on model middle schools, teenage pregnancy, and the dominance of boys' sports in high schools.

I have also tried to highlight how descriptions of adolescents in general came to be understood as essential characteristics of each and every adolescent. Adolescents were massified, and then the massed populational characteristics were applied as naturally occurring characteristics of individuals. A concrete social situation in which certain youth played particular kinds of games, for example, became a statistic (for example, a percentage of all immigrant youth) and eventually an inherent trait of youth in general.[79]

I have characterized the boyologists' approach as romancing youth and romancing the administrative apparatuses (state and private institutions) they helped ordain and design. By this I emphasize what Madeleine Grumet calls a "sentimentalization," a tendency to see through rose-colored glasses, eschewing power and authority, and to dwell upon idealistic aspects. There is strong desire in such romantic visions and a technique of naturalizing.[80]

A common evaluation of Hall's work is that he was left in the dust, discredited and outdated, specifically when recapitulation theory was abandoned. The analysis of this chapter offers another interpretation. As modern, scientific producers of truths and technologies, Hall and his colleagues continue to exert enormous influence; they define adolescents as natural and thus beyond social change or critique, and structure what can count as truths about adolescence. Furthermore, the boyologists' emphasis on interpreting adolescent actions and ideas phyletically, as invoking another time, another stage of human development, is one of the strongest aspects of this discourse. This discursive strategy that we have inherited reads an individual's characteristics—sunken-chested, weak-willed, smoking, masturbating—in terms of future effects and looks everywhere but in the present social relations for the explanation. It empties the present and lets the adults and scientists off the hook; like the discourse on nationalism that it mimics, it looks toward the past and the future. This temporal dimension of adolescence will be further examined in Chapter Four.[81]

The shapers of the modern, scientific adolescent made adolescent bodies and sexuality the primary foci. Following Foucault, I do not view such unceasing talk about sexuality as liberation but rather as *compulsion*. But this compulsion was shaped by neo-Victorian progressive traditions with a white middle-class base and simultaneously identified working-class, ethnic immigrant, African-American, and Native American youth as deviant. At a time when movie theaters, beaches, dance halls, and other new urban pleasures beckoned, it is unsurprising that juvenile justice was built largely on *misuse of leisure time* and that worries over and attempts to control peer group influences catapulted youth ever more firmly into their peers' company.

Back to the Future

Model Middle Schools Recirculate

Fin-de-Siècle Ideas

3

The progressive beginnings of social science and policy attention on adolescents established a network of private and public institutions that supported research and programs for youth, a tradition that has continued. In this chapter I focus on the ideas about adolescents of a major foundation, the Carnegie Council on Adolescent Development, which is an arm of the Carnegie Corporation of New York. The Carnegie Council on Adolescent Development existed for ten years and concentrated on supporting policy-directed research. I examine the council's first and last reports as a window into contemporary ideas on adolescents and their education. The first report, *Turning Points: Preparing American Youth for the 21st Century*, appeared in 1986 and offered programmatic recommendations for model middle schools, which were subsequently implemented with Carnegie Corporation money in 15 states, involving about 100 schools in the United States and Puerto Rico. The council's final report, *Great Transitions: Preparing Adolescents for a New Century*, appeared in 1995 and concluded the council's work. While these reports offer a partial view of contemporary reasoning around adolescents, the efforts of the council form some of the most visible and influential work on youth in the United States in that decade. They offer snapshots of the contemporary discourse on adolescence.

Supporters of the remaking of junior high schools into middle schools have argued that young adolescents have special needs that differently organized schools must address. The middle school movement has claimed to understand the special needs of 10- to 15-year-olds and has offered curricula and programs to help this special age group succeed. In this chapter I explore the definitions of the needs of young adolescents and administrative responses. Thus this chapter follows up on the latter part of Chapter Two in examining how administrative practices make youth in concrete ways. A second aim of this chapter is to demonstrate the hardiness of Progressive Era youth practices, which are regularly reinvented and heralded as "new." Finally, I describe the regulation and normalization that occur through schooling practices that rhetorically connect with freedom and democracy.

TURNING POINTS: PREPARING AMERICAN YOUTH FOR THE TWENTY-FIRST CENTURY

I find *Turning Points* to be a slippery document, simultaneously flat and overflowing with meanings. To understand its complexity, I believe the report must be examined intertextually, along with other ideas and documents. My intertextual reading focuses upon young adolescents as a way of talking in the late 1980s of the economic and social future. This analysis foregrounds the report's discussion of youth and schooling in relation to goals to make the nation "economically competitive and socially cohesive," to avoid "a divided society: one affluent and well-educated, the other poorer and ill-educated . . . an America at odds with itself." At first glance the report commands respect, which rests upon its seeming comprehensiveness and generalizability to all young adolescents, its mixture of current pedagogical thinking and the economic bottom line, and the power and status of the members of the task force.[1]

Turning Points was part of the work of the Task Force on the Education of Young Adolescents, whose members were noteworthy for their high visibility in recognized institutions. In alphabetical order the members were (with their positions in 1989): Bill Clinton, Governor of Arkansas; James Comer, Professor of Psychiatry at Yale; Alonzo Crim, Professor of Urban Educational Leadership at Georgia State University; Jacquelynne Eccles, Professor of Psychology at the University of Colorado; Lawrence Green, Vice-President of the Kaiser Family Foundation; Fred Hechinger, President of the New York Times Foundation; David Hornbeck (Chair), lawyer and Professor of Education and Public Policy at Johns Hopkins University; Renee Jenkins, Professor of Pediatrics at Howard University School of Medicine; Nancy Kassebaum, U.S. Senator from Kansas; Herman LaFontaine, Superintendent of Hartford, Connecticut, schools; Deborah Meier, Principal of Central Park East Secondary School, New York City; Amado Padilla, Professor of Education at Stanford; Anne

Petersen, Dean of the College of Health and Human Development at Pennsylvania State University; Jane Quinn, Director of Programs for Girls Clubs of America; Mary Budd Rowe, Professor of Science Education at the University of Florida; Roberta Simmons, Professor of Psychiatry and Sociology at the University of Pittsburgh; and Marshall Smith, Dean of the School of Education at Stanford. This is a distinguished list of participants that includes a (future) U.S. president and academics with specialties in medicine, psychiatry, and psychology that have applications to schooling. The task force members and their broad connections across science, government, and public policy echo the positions and backgrounds of speakers on adolescence at the turn of the twentieth century described in Chapter Two.

I examine three aspects of the *Turning Points* report: recommendations for school organization, curriculum, and underlying conceptions of the young adolescent. The report articulates recommendations for changing middle-grades education through changes in organization and curriculum. Grounding these principles for reforming middle schools is a particular conception of youth; that is, the report and its recommendations allow young adolescents with certain characteristics to emerge and be discussed. Ultimately I am interested in ferreting out the young adolescent being who "demands," makes reasonable, and legitimates these reformed middle school practices by explicating implicit assumptions, interests, and values.

The "Problem of Young Adolescents"

The report opens with familiar images of young adolescents as "youth adrift," tossed on seas of sexuality, drug and alcohol use, and peer pressure: disequilibrated and needing to be guided into responsibility and productivity. The imagery that is intended to take our youth into the twenty-first century is identical to G. Stanley Hall's a century ago. He saw adolescents as ships without mooring, tossed on tempestuous seas of sexuality. Hall also emphasized adolescence as an evolutionary turning point, where youth and the species could move forward or stand still. His popularizing of adolescence reiterated it as a crucial era in social and individual life—heavy with opportunity and potential disaster. This 1986 quote on the adolescent "turning point" echoes Hall's ideas:

> For many youth 10 to 15 years old, early adolescence offers opportunities to choose a path toward a productive and fulfilling life. For many others, it represents their last best chance to avoid a diminished future.[2]

One difference between *Turning Points* and Hall's rhetoric is the emphasis on young adolescents, beginning with 10-year-olds. The younger age is more visible in *Great Transitions* because of black-and-white photographs of young adolescents throughout, but both reports urge a look at the youngest of teenagers. This emphasis on younger teenagers is in keeping with the shifting market attention to younger children, especially girls, in popular culture, advertising, and pornography. In order to catch attention and produce new desires, younger and younger children represent commodities from jeans to breakfast cereals.[3] To keep up with the merchandising of younger adolescents in other dimensions of social life, policy and social science research also look at younger teenagers.

Turning Points identifies schools as the powerful force to recapture youth adrift.[4] However, the organization and curriculum of middle-grades schools and the intellectual and emotional needs of young adolescents are "mismatched." This mismatched metaphor identifies the contemporary period as being substantially different from other times and suggests that the speaker is enlightened and benevolent. The mismatched idea cannot discern the adolescent as a creation of the same society that institutionalized schools. Finally, the disconnect between schools and youth results in disengagement, increasing alienation, truancy, and dropping out. The mismatch occurs because of the erosion of traditional moorings (close-knit families, stable neighborhoods, plentiful low-skilled jobs), which places youth at risk of not becoming adults who are able to "meet the requirements of the workplace, the commitments of relationships in families and with friends, and the responsibilities of participation in a democratic society." Here we have a clear statement of the fear of youth adrift in relation to the future of the economy, families, and democracy. If youth are to have a chance at responsible adulthood, middle schools' organization and curricula must change. Medical, psychological, and political experts, with a few educators, are the ones to reform middle schools.

Middle School Organization

The emerging adolescent is caught in turbulence, a fascinated but perplexed observer of the biological, psychological, and social changes swirling all around. In groping for a solid path toward a worthwhile adult life, *adolescents can grasp the middle grade school as the crucial and reliable handle.*[5]

In this quote the report puts forth a view of adolescence identical to that of G. Stanley Hall and the boyologists: the language—*emerging, turbulent, perplexed, swirling changes*—is most effective in suggesting chaos and disorder. The second sentence offers assistance: *solid path, worthwhile adult life, grasp, reliable handle*. School architecture in the 1920s tried to create "cathedrals of learning" that would uplift the students, many of whom were from poor and recent immigrants.

What kind of "reliable handle" is the proposed middle grade school? The report articulates eight principles for transforming middle schools, which will improve the education of all students and will be especially beneficial for students "at risk of being left behind."[6] I focus, first, on the single principle that pertains to the organization of middle schools and then on the three principles of middle school curriculum, omitting the recommendations that address teachers, administrators, and school-family-community relationships.[7]

- Large middle-grade schools are divided into smaller communities for learning.
- Middle-grade schools transmit a core of common knowledge to all students.
- Middle-grade schools are organized to ensure success for all students.
- Schools promote good health; the education and health of young adolescents are inextricably linked.[8]

Smaller Communities for Learning

The first principle responds to the widespread criticism that secondary schools are large, impersonal bureaucracies in which many students are alienated and neglected. The report recommends small "houses" or teams for youth who face "unprecedented choices and pressures."

> School should be a place where close, trusting relationships with adults and peers create a climate for personal growth and intellectual development.

The report advocates school-communities, and smaller units of teachers and students are variously labeled schools-within-schools, houses, teams, or families. The school-community idea recommends that in these settings adults can coordinate learning to be meaningful and challenging, and each student is known well enough by at least one adult that discussions of "academic matters, personal problems, and the importance of performing well in middle grade school" can occur. In addition to building personal connections, teaming allows better coordination and integration across subjects and across individual teachers and students. The aim of these organizational changes is to cultivate "close, personal relations between students and teacher," but, importantly, classroom discipline problems are also "dramatically reduced through teaming."[9]

Contexts for school-communities. My analysis of practices from other historical periods draws upon a contemporary understanding of the flexibility of language so that "terms are by no means guaranteed their meanings, and . . . these meanings can be appropriated and redefined for different purposes, different contexts, and, more importantly, different causes." As this quote from Andrew Ross indicates, the purposes and meanings of an idea like small school-communities are maleable. Small school-communities can involve a renewed emphasis on control of students, intense efforts to ensure student progress and a sense of belonging, and many things in between. Two main contexts of the *Turning Points* report were the lowered confidence in the American economy and the wave of foreign youth into U.S. schools and society, and these contexts pushed many school-communities to be primarily about *management* of youth.[10]

The late 1980s were dominated by concerns about economic viability. John Akers, chairman of IBM, stated: "Education isn't just a social concern, it's a major economic concern. If our students can't compete today, how will our companies compete tomorrow?"[11] Historian Larry Cuban characterizes the "group think" of the corporate and political leaders of both parties about education in this way:

> America's competitiveness in the international economy has eroded. The shrinking buying power of the dollar, declining work productivity rates, and rising unemployment have combined to make the economy a major national problem. A primary cause of that problem is that students coming out of the public schools possess inadequate knowledge, limited skills, and poor attitudes toward work.[12]

Cuban disagrees with placing the blame on schools for economic problems and with using schools to solve economic issues.

The second important context for the *Turning Points* report is the seeming "invasion" of students who come from mother-only families, poor families, families with English as a second language, and nonwhite families. The special issue of *Education Week* in May 1986 was entitled "Here They Come, Ready or Not" and proclaimed the crisis for schools and society of a population without a white middle-class majority. Other manifestations of the same fear of invasion by foreigners appear in literature against multicultural curricula, such as books by Arthur Schlesinger and E. D. Hirsch. The specter of alien youth in our schools connects with economic worries to produce escalating fear of and resistance to these "others." According to historian Kate Rousmaniere, when U.S. immigration was at its previous peak in the early 1900s, public schools initially adopted a curriculum that coupled academic knowledge with education for a healthy lifestyle, the productive use of leisure time, and worthy home membership.[13]

Although the *Turning Points* report incorporates humanistic psychology in its attention to young adolescents' "needs" for intimacy and autonomy, economic and social utility concerns dominate the document. This is most visible in the use of well-established imagery and organizational and pedagogical responses stemming from the great waves of immigration and economic woes of the late 1800s and early 1900s. Barry Franklin examined the theme of community-building among U.S. curriculum workers and social scientists during this earlier period of change and argued that *community* was a trope for social control, that is, the basis for order, stability, and progress. The new class of intellectuals and professionals, for example, the psychologist E. L. Thorndike, as well as G. Stanley Hall, had grown up in small towns in the Midwest and the Northeast and believed that

> stability, order, and progress were ultimately dependent on the degree to which beliefs and attitudes were shared. . . . [I]f American society was to be both orderly and progressive, a homogeneous culture and a spirit of like-mindedness and cooperation had to exist within its population.

The language of the *Turning Points* report evidences a clear aim to educate urban youth away from the dangers of city streets and "toward civic and social cohesion."[14]

This historical comparison is further borne out in the report's discussion of school communities. The description is strongly reminiscent of the "affectional discipline" popular among Victorians and Progressives, which utilized love, guilt, and shame to manipulate and control children's behavior. Stephen Schlossman documented the use of *love* as control in progressive juvenile justice in the form of the "family reform school," which emphasized

> persuasion and manipulation of children's native emotional resources, especially their capacity to receive and reciprocate affection; strong maternal influence; close, frequent and informal relationships between youngsters and exemplary authority figures; isolated settings in order to avoid perverse worldly pleasures.[15]

The *Turning Points* image of a good middle school emphasizes affectional ties among adults and youth who participate in close, personal communities for learning. Such relationships may seem unequivocally good to white, middle class professionals, but they are historical creations that use emotional connections to shape behavior and thinking; women are the usual providers of such caring. I believe it is important to acknowledge the particular kinds of interpersonal power orchestrated in such settings rather than to pretend that authority and control are dissipated or absent in schools with *good feelings*. Even though school practices feel good and appear nonauthoritarian, all social arrangements involve power. Harmonious feelings within a school involve power as much as do conflictual feelings.[16]

Another echo of the affective discipline of the Progressive Era reformers is the current attention to *emotional intelligence*. Emotional intelligence is defined as impulse control, so that the individual can always be optimistic and empathic even in the face of obstacles. Megan Boler elaborates on connections among management of one's own emotions, those of others, and the global workplace. Emotional intelligence becomes a set of skills—such as knowing your own feelings and learning to negotiate—that are assumed to be without cultural or gender differences. In this way, emotional literacy curriculum echoes the social efficiency emphases on becoming a good worker, learning to contribute from one's social position, and using one's leisure time productively. However, the aim of contemporary emotional literacies is to utilize the seemingly invisible power of *self-control* to accomplish what the social reformers of other decades asked teachers to do.[17]

Middle School Curriculum

The three principles for transforming the middle school curriculum focus upon the transmission of "a core of common knowledge to all students" an assurance of "success for all students" and promotion of "good health."[18] In the section detailing the knowledge core, the authors state:

> Every student in the middle grades should learn to think critically through mastery of an appropriate body of knowledge, lead a healthy life, behave ethically and lawfully, and assume the responsibilities of citizenship in a pluralistic society.[19]

The section on critical thinking emphasizes a multidisciplinary, inquiry approach to learning, which diverse scholars and practitioners endorse. But if we examine the lengthy example of a *good* curriculum, there appears to be a stronger emphasis on learning factual knowledge and behavioral controls. Given the legacy of trivialized, factual knowledge in schools, changing to knowledge in depth is a major challenge.[20]

The "comprehensive life sciences curriculum" is a centerpiece of the report.[21] The course of study integrates the biological and behavioral sciences in its focus upon the nature of adolescent development, health education, and health promotion; it moves from the "biological under-pinnings and social responses to puberty" and then "directly to sexuality: the reproductive system, sexual behavior, and maintaining health." These biological and sexuality topics occupy the first semester of the two-year curriculum; the second semester deals with culture, including marriage and the family in comparative perspective. The second year concentrates on "the physiology of body systems, their behavioral associations, implications for good health, and societal consequences." This two-year course of study illustrates an interdisciplinary curriculum that is directly *relevant* and allegedly of high interest to most youth and is a vehicle for teaching correct behavior. This curriculum seems to be a dream come true: a mix of disciplinary knowledge, relevance, and "behavioral science."[22]

Science curricula in the 1920s also linked academics with social issues to influence behavior. Biology was deemed especially salient for those youth disadvantaged by poor, urban lives because it presented natural phenomena to those who lived in the unnatural city, but also because it taught the values of organic unity to youth who lived among chaos, the principles of adaptation to immigrant youth who had been transplanted, and basic principles of healthy living in an unhealthy city environment. Biology taught students about the natural order and hierarchy of life, as well as how to value cleanliness, to develop healthy (and restrained) attitudes about sex, to respect and value nature, and to believe in natural progress.[23]

The natural order of the biological world would transform urban adolescents.

Although the comprehensive life sciences curriculum to teach healthy behavior purports to utilize critical thinking throughout, when healthy behavior for young adolescents is defined as abstaining from sex, drugs, and alcohol, the curriculum leans toward indoctrination and persuasion to "just say no." The authors of the report never articulate the dilemmas of teaching critical thinking alongside prescriptive health "don'ts." This omission contributes to the conclusion that critical thinking goes only so far in health issues. The life sciences curriculum is one of numerous places in the report where *knowledge* appears to be a thin veneer over adult control of youths' behavior.[24]

In the section on teaching for critical thinking, the authors state:

A primary goal in choosing curricula and teaching methods . . . should be the disciplining of young adolescents' minds, that is, their capacity for active, engaged thinking. A student with a disciplined mind can assimilate knowledge . . . challenge the reliability of evidence . . . recognize the viewpoint behind the words . . . see relationships.[25]

These examples of cognitive competencies seem reasonable and desirable, but if we look more closely, the verbs tell a different story. For example, in the section, "enroute to a lifetime of meaningful work," young adolescents will *understand, be aware, not feel bound,* and have *learned to learn.* In the section on being a good citizen, young adolescents will *accept responsibility, understand,* and *possess a feeling of responsibility.* Under goals for becoming caring and ethical people, our youth will *recognize, embrace,* and *understand.* The goals regarding becoming a healthy person are described as possessions: *will be physically and mentally fit and will have a self-image of competence and strength.*[26]

The tone and language in these curricular sections fit most easily with the image of attributes that are poured into passive objects or qualities purchased whole and possessed. The ideal teenager to be created by the report's efforts is a 15-year-old "thinking, productive, caring, and healthy person who takes seriously the responsibility of good citizenship." Although this description pays homage to mind, feelings, work, and physical/psychological well-being, as well as social relationships, these ideal people generally only *understand* or *accept responsibility*. Again and again the report presents youth as vessels to be filled with predetermined feelings, understandings, and competencies. This language of indoctrination strongly undercuts the rhetoric of developing critical thinking, except as prepackaged, isolatable "skills." In the 106-page document a student's voice appears once: in a poem about confusions and the lack of answers by an eighth grade boy from Columbia, Missouri. Students are only spoken *about:* as problems to be solved, as future workers, and as massed bodies on which moral panics are played out. In this way, the model middle school harkens back to the dominant turn-of-the-century construction of youth as problems and as competent only in the future.

Development of the "success for all students" revolves around the institution of cooperative learning and peer tutoring. Both of these strategies are widely endorsed. However, the political dimensions of redistributing school resources so that all students succeed is omitted from the report. It is as if cooperative learning and peer tutoring can be added to existing school practices without disturbing any other expectations.[27]

When youths present so many risks, adult reason and authority in the schooling of young adolescents are unquestionable. Youth, meanwhile, have no power or authority. Even though the *Turning Points* report includes many valuable, important ideas regarding changes in pedagogy, I read them as framed by a primary interest in controlling and indoctrinating youth for economic stability and social unity. Thus the *Turning Points* report fails to question the prevailing discourse of adolescence. The emphasis on control of youths' thoughts and behavior is central to many current teenagers' disenchantment and alienation from school, since teenagers are carefully attuned to adults' overt and covert messages.

Conceptions of Young Adolescents

Repeatedly the *Turning Points* report says that young adolescents need guidance and attention to become "healthy, thoughtful, and productive adults." The future adults are in control of their lives and their worlds, not at the mercy of their environments or their passions. The report lists the five characteristics associated with being an effective human being:

1. Intellectually reflective;
2. Enroute to a lifetime of meaningful work;
3. A good citizen;
4. A caring and ethical person; and
5. Healthy.[28]

The emphasis on health would appear to be only a contemporary interest. However, turn-of-the-century preoccupation with potency also had health at its core. Historian Peter Gay's analysis of the panic in the late 1800s around sex education to eradicate masturbation emphasized the relationship between proper heterosexuality and mastery of the world.

> [Masturbation] . . . seemed a pointless and prodigal waste of limited and valuable resources leading figuratively . . . to impotence. It constituted a loss of mastery over the world and oneself. The campaign to eradicate self-abuse was . . . a way of conserving strength and maintaining control, both highly cherished and maddeningly elusive goals in the nineteenth century.

Gay argues that sex education responded to fears of weakness that had political, military, and biological dimensions.[29]

The interweaving of education and health in *Turning Points* seems similarly grounded in fears of losing dominance, of losing potency—economic, political, and international. Unhealthy behaviors are irresponsible and pernicious, self-abusive, and corrosive of the health of the body politic. Health can mean many things; here it refers to commonsense associations of young adolescents with alcohol, drugs, and sexuality. In using imagery, language, and pedagogical strategies with roots in the late nineteenth and early twentieth centuries, the *Turning Points* report reiterates concerns for dominance, albeit coupled with humanistic psychology and student-centered pedagogy. It is through the report's twin emphases on rationality and health that dominance into the twenty-first century is to be maintained.

Seamlessness and Harmony in Turning Points

An air of unreality engulfs the reader of this report, due to the way it flattens contradictions and particularities of youths and their lives in school.

Part of this flattening and sanitizing is the result of the conception of adolescents' education based upon a one-way view of socialization and development. Adults and organizations socialize youth; through affectional ties and cooperation, youth will internalize the values and practices of productivity and responsibility.[30]

The consequences of this one-way view of socialization are that youth are absent from the report as active participants in education. They are present as the passive objects of teachers, administrators, and parents, but they do not actively contribute to life in schools nor to the production of the goals and aims of middle-grades education. Thus even though critical thinking, peer tutoring, and team learning are present in the recommendations, there is still an overriding passiveness accorded youth. An especially telling sentence about inactiveness occurs in the section on teacher empowerment: "Students who *witness teachers making decisions and discussing important ideas can envision what it is like to participate in decisionmaking.*[31]

This one-directional, passive conception of education is critiqued by numerous scholars who advocate for a radical, active, multicultural democracy in schools.[32] The diminished, flattened young adolescents in this report are not to be educated into the conflicts and contradictions of American history and society, into the difficult public policy issues around civil rights, social welfare, jobs, and environmental concerns, to name a few issues, but are to be safely harbored from disputes, conflicts, and contestations. The report offers an image of schooling as a safe harbor; but this metaphor harbors its own threats. The *Turning Points* report *sentimentalizes* middle school education by covering its coercive qualities and promoting its caring for youth and for our nation's future.

GREAT TRANSITIONS: PREPARING ADOLESCENTS FOR A NEW CENTURY

The 1995 Carnegie Council report is less overtly behavioristic and economistic than *Turning Points*. The report begins by challenging reigning stereotypes of adolescence, such as, "[s]ocial, environmental, and hormonal factors are all important in shaping development" (that is, it's not just raging hormones) and youth culture is "not necessarily in opposition to adult values" (we must look beyond surface appearances).[33] Despite significant advances, the report's problems stem from its exclusive emphasis on prevention, its heavy accent on health issues, and its overall positivist representation of youth. In these three aspects, *Great Transitions* offers a particular politics of advocacy for youth.

First, the emphasis on prevention can be seen as the least controversial approach to youth problems. In an examination of U.S. federal policy toward teenage pregracy in the 1960s, I found that prevention programs became the sole focus of government efforts when alternative responses were found to be politically unworkable.[34] Senators with Catholic constituents, for example, could not support programs that helped a young mother after the baby was born because that was seen as condoning teenage pregnancy. By emphasizing prevention only, legislators and bureaucrats could represent themselves as responsive to the public problem; however, the prevention emphasis provided support only up to the delivery, which many specialists argued was the time before many problems developed. Thus prevention-centered efforts are likely to be the shortest in duration and the least controversial because public funds are not being used actively to support school-aged mothers drug rehabilitation. In this way, prevention indicates a minimal effort.

Second, *Great Transitions* strongly emphasizes health. With its quite direct echoes of G. Stanley Hall, health is regularly related to nationalism and a sense of youth as human capital for the nation's latest efforts. Health is directly linked in the report with becoming productive workers, reliable family members, and active community members. The life-sciences curriculum from *Turning Points* is revisited as offering relevant and useful knowledge that will help young adolescents to say no to drugs, smoking, sex, and other risky behaviors. Thus health is an arena that continues to be morally laden with proper, good actions into which middle school students are to be socialized. I found no sense that health is a socially constructed arena that is heavily freighted with guidelines derived from particular class, race, and gender experiences and assumptions.

Third, although overall less behavioristic in language then *Turning Points*, *Great Transitions* often espouses a positivist, technical view of youth. This is especially evident in the discussions of the need that young adolescents have of "life skills development." Young teenagers need to "learn to make informed, deliberate, and constructive decisions." Interpretative judgments are notoriously complex, yet the report gives a sense that rational decision-making can be directly taught, learned, and regularly implemented, similar to a skill such as riding a bicycle or sawing wood. The regular use of the term "skills" connotes a fragmented view of knowledge and identity, one that aims primarily to control youth. For example, the report offers these aims:

One such life skill that adolescents often lack and that can be taught is the is the ability to pursue constructive relations with others. Adolescents who are vulnerable because they have been isolated and lonely . . . can be helped through life skills training to form solid friendships, learn from experience, and participate in cooperative groups. Another useful skill is assertiveness. An aspect of assertiveness is knowing how to resist pressure or intimidation to use drugs or weapons or have sex—without disrupting valued relationships or isolating oneself.[35]

This kind of writing utilizes a technical view of human beings and human learning—in which learning discrete "skills" is equated with building friendships and establishing autonomy. Youth are again flattened into trainable beings who will be assertive and friendly and will achieve, all on command. Young adolescents are empty vessels to be filled with the most current and productive skills. Youths' possible responses to such activities are absent. In these ways, a portrait of youth as needing to be controlled *and* protected emerges.

CONCLUSION

The *Turning Points* and *Great Transitions* reports are documents of particular times and places, grounded in 1980s and 1990s concerns for economic productivity and social unity. The themes of wayward youth to be controlled through a life-sciences curriculum and skill development prompted this comparison with the ideas and practices of youth reformers in the late 1800s and early 1900s who also faced economic and social change. Like their counterparts a century ago, the authors of *Turning Points* and *Great Transitions* offer a vision of safety and strength in the order and values of face-to-face communities and shared core knowledge, ethics, and health practices. And like numerous past theorists and practitioners with a model of socialization and education as one-way and passive, these two reports represent contemporary youth as worrisome yet passive recipients of knowledge and values, albeit on topics such as decision-making and reflective thought. Despite the incorporation of numerous, compelling contemporary practices and ideas, the reports remain unsatisfactory trips back to the future.

In offering this critique, I do not dismiss the need to educate young adolescents about rules, ethics, and social relations. My emphasis here has been on the debilitating and dehumanizing ways that young adolescents are talked about. Although each of these reports offers glimpses of the potentials and strengths of young people, the two Carnegie Council documents dwell on the deficiencies. I will argue in a later chapter that the romancing of youth by the Progressive Era reformers, although not without drawbacks, offered a positive valence and potential of youth in society. That romantic vision of possibilities seems less present in the two Carnegie documents, which incite us to act by offering pages of charts of lower ages of sexual activity and higher rates of drug use and suicide. Although the figures for poverty rates, forced intercourse, and use of handguns are alarming, the singular focus on youth and prevention limits the political impact of the reports. The council does not address the gutting of social welfare programs that has plunged families into poverty, fails to mention the refusal of Congress to go against the National Rifle Association and pass gun control legislation, and omits the movement of capital out of rust belt cities to more profitable locations, all of which benefit certain social groups but hurt children and their prospects. In omitting such broader national developments, which translate into greater profits for particular businesses and social classes, young adolescents appear as limited "social problems" disconnected from economic and social policies. For this reason these two reports are politically conservative—focusing on youths' problems but keeping invisible the broader policies and social events that created, at least in part, these youth conditions.

Time Matters in Adolescence   4

There is a general confidence that people between the ages of 10 and 15 or 12 and 18 are unique, in a particular stage of their lives that has particular demands, problems, meanings, and crises. This uniqueness resides in their chronological age and the related physiological, emotional, social, and cognitive changes. When I began talking with undergraduate education students about teenagers, age was always significant and provided a template to judge appropriateness of actions. If a 16-year-old acted in a particular way, it was understood differently from a 14- or 18-year-old doing the same thing. I became intrigued with how adolescence is defined in and through age, and thus, in and through time.

Adolescence and the modern temporal order were creations of the same historical period. In this chapter I explore the rise of uniform world clock time at the turn of the twentieth century as the dominant definer of human lives and the measure of success and failure. A certain temporal order simultaneously grounded new sciences as well as new institutions such as schools. People began to think about the past and the future, about learning, and about criminals, to name only three areas, through a one-directional, linear, cumulative lens of "development in time." I introduce the term *panoptical time* to indicate how adolescence was understood as a chunk of time that could be displayed and manipulated in various contexts. Panoptical time emphasizes the endings toward which youth are to progress and places individual adolescents into a temporal narrative that demands a moratorium of responsibility yet expects them at the same time to act as if each moment of the present is consequential. Like Bentham's panopticon prison, adolescent development has been a way in which adolescents watch and correct themselves. In the latter part of the chapter, I examine how modern linear time influenced ideas about adolescence as well as the experiences of being adolescent. Utilizing Bakhtin's idea of literary chronotopes, I analyze the modern story of adolescent development as a peculiar narrative with identifiable uses of time that have implications for how adolescence is easily trivialized and stereotyped.

MAKING MODERN TIME VISIBLE

In April 1999 Mexicans rebelled against the impending initiation of daylight saving time in their country, stating that such a change of time (to be in temporal accord with their NAFTA partners) was a blow against their human body clocks and their cultural time. Similarly, in the 1980s when Tallahassee, Florida, proposed an adoption of daylight saving time to be in accord with the rest of the state, a fundamentalist religious group opposed the measure with the slogan: "Preserve God's Natural Time." In Joseph Conrad's novel, *The Secret Agent*, an anarchist plots to blow up the Greenwich Conservatory, the base for standardized world time. These real and fictional events seem very strange—why would anyone oppose daylight saving time or a homogeneous world time? The first part of this chapter answers this question by discussing the *making* of modern, standardized time and some of its effects; once one begins to understand the making of time, "time wars" take on greater meaning.[1]

Although the steam engine appears in U.S. history textbooks as the marker of modernism:

> *The clock*, not the steam engine, *is the key-machine of the modern industrial age* . . . in its relationship to determinable quantities of energy, to standardization, to automatic action, and . . . to accurate timing. . . . The clock is not merely a means of keeping track of the hours, but of synchronizing the actions of men [*sic*].[2]

Reinhart Koselleck argues that the *temporalization of experience* (the view that all change occurs in and through time) "*is the defining quality of the modern world*." The temporalization of experience utilized clock time, standardized world time, active measurement, and counting of time. Time was tracked in order *to use it*. "The mechanical clock made possible . . . a civilization attentive to the passage of time, hence to productivity and performance." And productive use of time became a central measure of better, more valuable individuals and groups. E. P. Thompson describes how the new time discipline was imposed across a range of social devices and practices: bells and clocks, the division of labor, the supervision of labor, money incentives, preachings and schoolings, and the suppression of fairs and sports. He summarizes, "In mature capitalist society all time must be consumed, marketed, put to *use*; it is offensive for the labour force merely to 'pass the time.'" Clock time and productivity fell into step with an existing American emphasis on progress.[3]

This temporalization of human life and growth occurred with and through numerous social processes and events. The railroads, for example, were central to the adoption of world standard time, because their profits were intertwined with schedules, with being on time. The Prime Meridian Conference in 1884 hosted representatives of 25 countries who agreed to establish Greenwich, England, as the zero meridian and "determined the exact length of the day, divided the earth into twenty-four time zones one hour apart, and fixed a precise beginning of the universal day." Prior to this coordination, a railroad traveler from Washington, D.C., to San Francisco would have set her watch to 200 different local times. Accurate train schedules were in turn dependent upon the telegraph, which made possible the uniform method of determining and maintaining accurate time signals and transmitting them around the world. Even such a brief introduction to the making of standard universal time provides a sense of modern temporalization and standardization, which otherwise appear natural and inevitable.[4]

Sciences and Time

The sciences were active in modern temporalization, as well. Foucault locates the cutting edge of scientific temporalization in the development of natural history, with its central task of classifying according to structure and taxonomic character.[5] While medieval scientists and citizens had conceptualized the cosmos as comprised of static laws and regularities, natural historians began to describe change and growth over time. The French biologist Lamarck, along with competitors Cuvier and Smith, pieced together fossil remains of extinct organisms and placed them in a chronological order. This was the beginning of a theory of evolution, an altogether original conception of development in and through time. In 1809 Lamarck published the first evolutionary family tree, "showing the branched series by which the complex organisms of the present day were related back to earlier, simpler forms of life, and so to the hypothetical point of the 'first beginnings of organization.'" Toulmin and Goodfield argue that it was in this scientific quest for the "origin" that time consciousness was produced: "*The new epistemic order was development-in-time*" and underlay such new conceptualizations as "the evolution of species, the ages of human life, and the development of society."[6]

Johannes Fabian augments this history of science by examining how the discipline of anthropology spatialized time through concepts of "development" and "civilization." Fabian argues that a defining practice of anthropological research is the locating of primitive others in another time (and space) and that this temporal distance, termed "developmental" or "cultural," rests upon more advanced and less advanced positions on the evolutionary scale. Accordingly, to designate a people as occupying "a different time" was to label them as wholly other, inferior, and occupying a less evolved position. Fabian argues that ideas of "otherness" do not begin with evolutionary frameworks but "they are already built into our very presentations of identity/sameness as an *exclusive* 'here and now,' which we accept without much questioning."[7]

Stories of cultural evolution and of individual adolescent development prioritize the ending; they are primarily *narratives of fulfillment*: "the important thing in tales of evolution remains their ending." This fact links these narratives with Christian millennialist ones. Much of the import of cultural evolutionism, claims Fabian, is that it allows us to read events as *omens* of things to come. *The theory of cultural evolution makes otherness ominous by construing it as "past future."* For example, moral panics around youth regularly call up a sense of "past future"—that the future will be diminished, dragged down by teenagers' failures to act in civilized or responsible ways. The discourse on teenage pregnancy portrays young mothers as signifying decline into an immoral and economically backward society, another "past future."[8]

Adolescence and Development-in-Time

At the turn of the century, daily experiences with inventions such as the telephone, the high-speed rotary press, and the cinema sparked debate about time and more precisely about the past, the present, and the future. Adolescence entered into this dialogue about time, humanity, and productivity, because adolescence was defined as "always becoming." In one scholar's view adolescence was reformulated in psychological and sociological terms as "the promise of individual or collective regeneration." During the decade 1895 to 1905 the new adolescent was invented as turbulent, as the "seed of new wealth for the future," and as the source of progress for the race. The conceptions of adolescence went hand in hand with new social sites and practices: longer stays in school, organized leisure in scouting and in urban playgrounds, juvenile justice policies aimed at prevention, and the outlawing of child labor. Overall, such practices helped define an adolescence that demanded a slow, steady movement toward maturity; reformers were especially wary of peaks of emotional intensity, which were linked with precocity. Precocity, especially masturbation, was a direct path to degeneracy. Protected adolescence needed to become bland, sanitized of even religious conversion experiences, which could be too tumultuous. Youth were defined as always "becoming," a situation that provoked endless watching, monitoring, and evaluating. As time was made and marked in public, standardized ways, the modern, scientific adolescent became a multifaceted social site for talk about the productive use of time, the glorious future, and sometimes the inglorious past. Slow, careful development-in-time was identified as the safest path.[9]

PANOPTICAL TIME

In *Discipline and Punish*, Michel Foucault explains how the design for a new prison signified a radical break in the model of social organization and control. The panoptical prison placed one guard in the center who surveilled all the prisoners day and night; one effect of constantly being watched was that prisoners began to watch themselves. The external guard's gaze began to be internalized in each prisoner, who took on the responsibility to supervise himself. The panoptical gaze is the self-surveillance of those who have been conditioned to being watched, evaluated, and measured. The panoptical gaze produces control through normalization in both guards and prisoners. Just as Foucault's reading of the panopticon promoted an understanding of its totalized mode of surveillance, with both prisoners' and guards' subjectivities affected, so too can linear, historical time moving toward "progress" be examined for how it disciplines subjectivities and objective knowledge.

The idea of panoptical time draws from the new regime of prison discipline as well as from preoccupation with terms such as "civilization" and "development" that spatialized time and represented the least civilized peoples as most remote in time from the present.[10] *Panoptical time*, an understanding of development through time that incorporated the assumed superiority of Western civilizations, could also be utilized by individuals in governing others and themselves:

> By panoptical time, I mean the image of global history consumed—at a glance—in a single spectacle from a point of privileged invisibility. . . . To meet the "scientific" standards set by the natural historians and empiricists of the eighteenth century, a visual paradigm was needed to display evolutionary progress as a measurable spectacle. The exemplary figure that emerged was the evolutionary family Tree of Man.

The tree offered a simple classificatory scheme that easily switched between evolutionary hierarchies within nature and evolutionary progress across human cultures. The Tree of Man portrayed a "natural genealogy of power," a unified world history according to the colonizers. Thus panoptical time is colonial time, although it was as useful at home as in

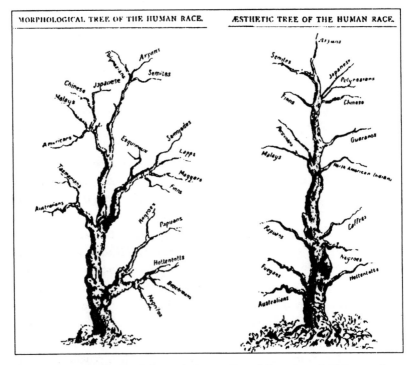

Figure 4.1 Two examples of the evolutionary Tree of Man. Copyright © 1995. From *Imperial Leather* by Anne McClintock. Reproduced by permission of Taylor & Francis, Inc./Routledge, Inc., http://www.routledge-ny.com.

imperial efforts. Diagrams of evolutionary family trees (see Figure 4.1) mapped "natural" social difference through time. The most developed men were white, middle-class, European males in the present: "Aryans" are located at the tips of both trees. The viewer of the Tree of Man has a privileged invisibility and an appetite, an incitement, to understand and classify others in this spatialized time. The Tree of Man provides classification "at a glance" and with equal efficiency a panoptical view of human groups through time.[11]

Psychologists who constructed the stages of individual human development followed the evolutionary tree model and utilized colonial time. Younger children and arrested youth were analogous to older and more primitive peoples (lower branches), and each individual child had to climb her own evolutionary tree. Adolescence actively participated in this reenactment of global history through the theory of recapitulation—the belief that each individual human's growth recapitulates the stages of evolution of the race—and through the weighting of adolescence as a racial swing point, a time when an evolutionary leap forward was accomplished or missed. According to G. Stanley Hall, adolescence marked the boundary between civilized and savage, a time when an individual and his race remained "arrested" or moved toward a higher-ranked position termed civilized. Since adolescence was identified as the cusp, the turning point, the teenager regularly called forth the underbelly of the colonizers' evolutionary narrative: worries over degeneration and contamination and the anxious scrutiny of physical characteristics, behavior, and morals for signs of decay.[12]

I suggest that a dominant aspect of the discourse on adolescence is its location within panoptical time, within a time framework that compels us—scholars, educators, parents, and teenagers—to attend to progress, precocity, arrest, or decline. Adolescence both makes and marks time. The developmental framework is simultaneously colonial (with privileged, invisible viewers and hypervisible, temporalized, and embodied others) and administrative (ranking, judging, making efficient and productive). I develop this idea of the panoptical time of adolescence by examining three images that regularly represent teenagers: physical "stigmata" and delinquency at the turn of the century, pubertal processes and "budding" bodies in adolescent medicine, and psychosocial growth in Erikson's eight stages. Adolescence is not mapped via a tree but by tables and charts of physical regularities, rates of pubertal change, and psychosocial steps. These all function to *rank* individuals according to their placement in time,[13] a process that will facilitate their placement and processing by institutions. In other words, I explore the development-in-time episteme of adolescence by focusing on three schemas that lay out growth, arrest, and decay. Within each image the privileged, knowledgeable reader (who resides in the adult "here and now") may discern problems of atavism, developmental delays, or precocity.

Reading Adolescent Bodies for Progress and Degeneration

In 1896 an article on degenerate youth in *The Pedagogical Seminary*, one of the journals founded by G. Stanley Hall, interpreted deviations from normal growth or progress as ominous for the future and offered an early panoptical view of adolescence. The physical and psychical traits of 52 "delinquent" youth (26 boys from the Lyman School for Boys at Westboro, Massachusetts, and 26 girls from the State Industrial School for Girls at Lancaster, Massachusetts) were compared to those of "normal" men and women. George Dawson, the author, described delinquent youth according to facial, bodily, and behaviorial peculiarities. In one table, reprinted in Figure 4.2, the delinquent girls and boys were compared to normal women and men in incidence of webfeet, protruding ears, large birthmarks, and other "stigmata." Throughout the text Dawson states that criminals and decadent races have round heads, large lower jaws, and asymmetrical faces. Thus delinquent youth were placed with "past types," that is, degenerate peoples, who were neither growing nor in balance, the other two states for organisms. The categorizing of civilized and savage peoples by deviations in general proportions of the body; in asymmetries of face and skull; in oddly formed jaw, palate, or eyes; in developmental irregularities in speech or walk; and in psychical problems (including sexual activeness, explosive activity, and egotism) were common across evolutionary and racial sciences and known as the "stigmata of degeneration."[14]

Youth with degenerate physical traits were referred to as "atavistic," as *throwbacks* to primitive people, in body and conduct "a reemergence of the historical and evolutionary pasts in the present." The criminal was linked by abnormal anatomy and physiology to the insane person and to the epileptic, as well as to those other "others," including "the ape, the child, woman, prehistoric man, and the contemporary savage." Homosexuals were also understood as primitive throwbacks.[15]

Dawson provides an early version of the development-in-time episteme applied to adolescence, one that focuses more on degenerative traits than on markers of normal growth or progress. Dawson located degenerate youth in an earlier time and simultaneously extrapolated the effects of

TABLE III.

Showing Stigmata according to types of Delinquency; also in comparison with Normal Standards.[2]

	Theft Boys	Theft Girls	Unchastity Boys	Unchastity Girls	Assault Boys	Assault Girls	Incendiarism Boys	Incendiarism Girls	General Incorrigibility Boys	General Incorrigibility Girls	Totals for Boys	Totals for Girls	Per cent. of Delinquent Boys having Stigmata	Per cent. of Normal Men having Stigmata	Per cent. of Delinquent Girls having Stigmata	Per cent. of Normal Women having Stigmata
No. of Observations,	10	4	5	10	2	0	3	0	6	12	26	26				
Plagiocephali,	3	1	1	1	0	0	0	0	2	3	6	5	23.0	20.0	19.2	17.2
Platycephali,	1	0	1	2	0	0	0	0	0	0	2	2	7.7	15.0	7.7	0.1
Scaphocephali,	1	0	0	0	0	0	0	0	0	0	1	0	3.8	6.0	0.0	0.0
Hydrocephali,	1	0	0	0	0	0	0	0	0	0	1	0	3.8		0.0	
Asymmetrical Face,	3	1	1	6	0	0	2	0	2	4	8	11	30.8	6.0	42.3	0.1
Prognathous Jaws,	1	0	1	3	0	0	1	0	0	5	3	8	11.5	34.0	30.8	10.0
Large Lower Jaw,	2	1	2	1	2	0	0	0	1	2	7	4	26.9	29.0	15.4	6.5
Precocious Wrinkles,	1	0	1	0	0	0	0	0	0	0	2	0	7.7		0.0	
Bad Eruptions,	0	0	3	0	1	0	0	0	0	0	4	0	15.4		0.0	
Large Birth-marks,	1	0	0	0	0	0	0	0	0	0	1	0	3.8		0.0	
Asymmetrical Ears,	3	0	0	2	0	0	2	0	2	1	7	3	26.9		11.5	
Protruding Ears,	4	0	3	0	0	0	0	0	2	0	9	0	34.6		0.0	
Deformed Palate,	4	1	0	4	4	1	0	0	2	3	10	9	38.6	19.0	34.6	19.0[3]
Asymmetrical Arms,	4	1	2	5	1	1	1	0	2	4	10	11	38.6		42.3	
Web-feet,	0	0	0	0	0	0	0	0	0	0	0	0	3.8		0.0	
"Pigeon-breast,"	0	–	0	–	0		1		2		3	–	11.5			
Total Stigmata,	29	5	17	24	5	0	6	0	17	24	74	53				
No. per Child,	2.9	1.2	3.4	2.4	2.5	0	2	0	2.8	2	2.9	2				

[1] *Nervous Diseases of Children:* p. 12.
[2] Lombroso: *L'Homme Criminel*, 2d French Ed., p. 170.
[3] Clouston: *Neuroses of Development.*

Figure 4.2 The stigmata of degeneration and their association with delinquent activities in boys and girls. From George Dawson, 1896, "A study in youthful degeneracy," *The Pedagogical Seminary* 4(2), p. 237.

degenerate youth on the future health of society. Dawson's categories evoked and would have been understood within an evolutionary chain of being, one in which development was becoming normative and stasis and degeneration were deviant and threatening. We may imagine readers of Dawson's study operating upon an explicit evolutionary history—as portrayed in Figure 4.3—"progress consumed at a glance." Atavistic youth emerged within a framework of desired historical progress. However, young people with physical and moral "throwback" characteristics jeopardized social progress, a worry that helped to entrench the reasoning about adolescence from a development-in-time perspective. Progress and failure to progress were inextricably linked and consumed at a glance in both charts and drawings.[16] Dawson utilized panoptical time in his analysis of deliquent physical "stigmata" and in his adminstrative incitements to cure and prevent such degeneracy.

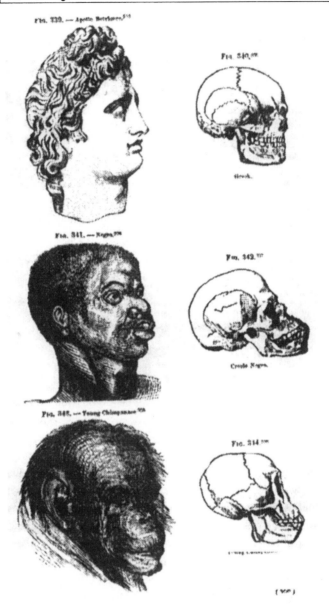

Figure 4.3 Panoptical time: Progress consumed at a glance. Copyright © 1995. From *Imperial Leather* by Anne McClintock. Reproduced by permission of Taylor & Francis, Inc./Routledge, Inc., http://www.routledge-ny.com.

Pubertal Processes

Two effects of the always-imminent *atavism* of youth were especially important for education, social work, juvenile justice, and related fields. First, the potential atavism of youth incited ever finer surveillance of youths and their timely development. Both physical and psychosocial traits had to be carefully mapped, a process that continues in contemporary scholarship, for example, on "young adolescents" or social-emotional learning. Second, schools instituted strict time schedules to minimize tendencies toward degeneracy, with age-grading, daily timetables, and control over clothing and appearance as central techniques.

Panoptical Time Charted on Developing Bodies

In an anthology of state-of-the-art scholarship on adolescence in the early 1990s that was supported by the Carnegie Council on Adolescent Development,[17] drawings of the "pubertal processes" also utilize panoptical time. Figures 4.4 and 4.5 comprise illustrations and a chart that show breast and pubic hair growth stages in girls and penile and pubic hair growth in boys, which were reprinted in the 1990 collection, *At the Threshold*.

These charts emphasize the development-in-time perspective as well as the erotic dimension of looking at adolescent bodies—a scientific scopophilia. Although not as comprehensive as evolutionary trees, these images do call forth a sense of panoptical time as McClintock describes it: privileged, invisible observers (that is, adult researchers) view scientific realities of adolescent development-in-time at a glance. We knowledgeable scientists and educators look and quickly understand the facts of adolescent physical development at a glance. Because *one look* gives us the information that takes years for youth to experience, such immediately consummable facts make adolescents able to be commodified, represented in images and sound bites that can be immediately understood. Such charts incite looking and provide knowledge to be consumed, as well as confirm the reality of adolescent physicality. Adolescent immaturity/development relies upon knowing-by-looking, that is, on an "optics of truth, which has a long history."[18] In the previous section, we saw that Dawson's empirical observations of physical characteristics of delinquent girls and boys also utilized visible body traits as signs of moral and social health.

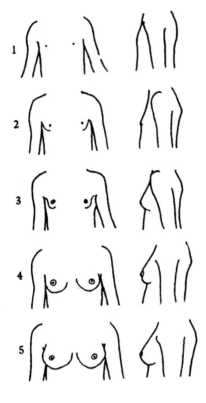

BREASTS

1. No breast development.

2. The first sign of breast development has appeared. This stage is sometimes referred to as the breast budding stage. Some palpable breast tissue under the nipple, the flat area of the nipple (areola) may be somewhat enlarged.

3. The breast is more distinct although there is no separation between contours of the two breasts.

4. The breast is further enlarged and there is greater contour distinction. The nipple including the areola forms a secondary mound on the breast.

5. Mature Stage Size may vary in the mature stage. The breast is fully developed. The contours are distinct and the areola has receded into the general contour of the breast.

PUBIC HAIR

1. No pubic hair.

2. There is a small amount of long pubic hair chiefly along vaginal lips.

3. Hair is darker, coarser, and curlier and spreads sparsely over skin around vaginal lips.

4. Hair is now adult in type, but area covered is smaller than in most adults. There is no pubic hair on the inside of the thighs.

5. Hair is adult in type, distributed as an inverse triangle. There may be hair on the inside of the thighs.

Figure 4.4 Pubertal processes at a glance. The five pubertal stages for breast and pubic hair growth. From W. A. Marshall and J. M. Tanner, 1969, "Variations in the pattern of pubertal changes in girls," *Archives of disease in childhood* 44, 291. Reprinted with permission of the BMJ Publishing Group.

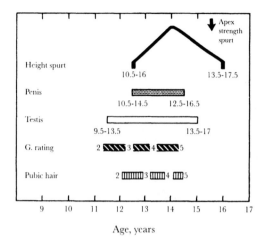

Figure 4.5 Pubertal processes at a glance. The developmental course of four pubertal processes for boys. Reprinted with permission from *Growth at Adolescence*, J. M. Tanner, Oxford: Blackwell Scientific, 1962.

Panoptical Time Charted on Developing Psyches

A vivid illustration of the panoptical time of adolescence is Erik Erikson's influential step diagram. Erikson's theoretical schema, "Eight Ages of Man," was intended to be a "global form of thinking" about childhood, adolescence, and adulthood portrayed as a series of crises, or periods of enhanced vulnerability and potential. Panoptical time is explicitly depicted by Erikson in words and in Figure 4.6:

> An epigenetic diagram thus lists a system of stages dependent on each other; and while individual stages may have been explored more or less thoroughly or named more or less fittingly, *the diagram suggests that their study be pursued always with the total configuration of stages in mind.*[19]

Erikson's diagram, like the Tree of Man, allows the unnamed observer to consume the human life course and adolescence at a glance. This diagram beckons us to locate and evaluate adolescents as well as children and adults by their progress toward the higher stages. Are they in the right box? What evidence of that stage conflict can we discern? Is "resolution" in sight? Erikson's characterization of the adolescent crisis as identity versus role confusion has become synonymous with modern adolescence, as

Eight Ages of Man

	1	2	3	4	5	6	7	8
VIII MATURITY								EGO INTEGRITY VS. DESPAIR
VII ADULTHOOD							GENERA- TIVITY VS. STAGNATION	
VI YOUNG ADULTHOOD						INTIMACY VS. ISOLATION		
V PUBERTY AND ADOLESCENCE					IDENTITY VS. ROLE CONFUSION			
IV LATENCY				INDUSTRY VS. INFERIORITY				
III LOCOMOTOR-GENITAL			INITIATIVE VS. GUILT					
II MUSCULAR-ANAL		AUTONOMY VS. SHAME, DOUBT						
I ORAL SENSORY	BASIC TRUST VS. MISTRUST							

Figure 4.6 "Figure of Erikson's Stages of Personality Development," from *Childhood and Society* by Erik H. Erikson. Copyright 1950, © 1963 by W. W. Norton and Company, Inc., renewed © 1978, 1991 by Erik H. Erikson. Used by permission of W. W. Norton and Company, Inc.

he proposed that it should be: "We may, in fact, speak of the identity crisis as the psychosocial aspect of adolescing." The categorization and placement of the adolescent in psychosocial developmental time defines youth in the United States and, to some degree, around the world.[20]

Erikson's psychosocial stages place adolescence in another time—"there and then"—a lower step, a younger age, a different crisis. The invisible viewer of Erikson's chart understands the full trajectory as well as the imperative to proceed to the top step. We privileged viewers likewise understand our administrative imperatives to aid those others who are progressing normally as well as those who move too slowly or too quickly. Age-graded and morally sensitive educators are especially attuned to timely progress.

NORMALIZING AGE-GRADED SCHOOLS

By the 1870s, age-graded schools were entrenched across the United States. Age-grading was a preeminent structure of schooling and was rationalized as efficient and effective. Joseph Kett traced the beginnings of age-graded curriculum in evangelical Protestant Sunday schools; from there they spread to private and public schools, promoting a systematization of schooling. It had been the norm for one-room schoolhouses, secondary academies, and even colleges to enroll students across a wide age range; it was common for academies (secondary schools) to have male students as young as 12 up through their early twenties. Age heterogeneity had been unremarkable, but the reform efforts of 1830 to 1850 included greater standardization according to age and achievement, working toward a school that was increasingly a controlled environment for children and youth.[21]

Age-graded schools were part of an intensification of age and related norms:

> The establishment of graded schools not only concentrated children of the same age together in a stage-based, factory-like setting but also eliminated incidences and tolerances of precocity.[22]

Four-year-olds were no longer allowed to enter elementary school, nor were ten-year-olds tolerated in high school. This "compressing of age ranges and decreased tolerance of precocity" occurred in American and British secondary schools and also in universities. Textbook writers and publishers accepted and perpetuated age-graded developmental schemes. "Statistical laws" were established primarily upon predictions according to age. Not only could predictions about national population and consumption be based upon age census data, but every aspect of life could be mapped and modeled, including morality, crime, full-time employment, prostitution, divorces, birth of children, and hygiene. "In an era that prized efficiency and 'scientific' data, age statistics were the most convenient criteria for measuring and evaluating social standards."[23]

Leonard Ayres fashioned a high profile educational career by calculating the percentages of overaged students in American schools. His *Laggards in Our Schools* demonstrated that U.S. schools were filled with retarded, that is, *overaged* children. He calculated that 33 percent of students were overaged (that is, not at the proper grade for their age) and argued for greater educational efficiency and a curriculum more in line with average students. Statistics, such as Ayres's 33 percent of overaged students, became "part of the technology of power in a modern state." Proceeding through the grades (not being held back) became normative. Today we automatically anticipate problems if students are held back or if they skip a grade and are out of step with their age peers. Statistical age-based norms became the basis for bureaucratic practices but also became the "classifications within which people must think of themselves and of the actions that are open to them," a topic taken up below.[24]

Schools not only became more age-homogeneous, but they also utilized close supervision of students' time to enforce timely development. Schools for African-American and Native American students, who were perceived as less civilized, demonstrated hypervigilance over time. The "exacting demands of a uniform schedule" were expected to teach the necessity and "the habitual practice of orderly, meek existence," at least for certain youths. The "regulation of time" aimed to create a disciplined habitus in criminal tribespeople, as it did in reformatories in the United States. According to Foucault: "Time penetrates the body and with it all the meticulous controls of power." Then and now adolescents regularly incite moral panics by their failure to embody an "orderly, meek existence." [25]

I have found little evidence of debates over the nature of institutional time in schools and other youth organizations around the turn of the century. Teachers and other youth reformers seemed to accept clock time and its demand for homogeneous, public, irreversible, and fragmented time. Such a view of time supported the belief that youth in public and private schools should be learning and behaving on identical timetables; this view of time helped establish slow children as hopelessly other. Timely development was always interwoven with strict surveillance of the body. Success could be established and displayed convincingly via "normal" dress and deportment and by students moving up at the normal rate, one grade per year. Precocity—in appearance and in age—were signs of deviance, and educators learned vigilance over development on time. [26]

MORATORIUM EXPERIENCES, OR GROWING UP IN "EXPECTANT TIME"

The concept of adolescence as a *moratorium* is part of Erikson's significant impact on popular and scholarly conceptions of youth and adolescence. Although the concept of a youthful moratorium of responsibility may seem quite uncontroversial, when historicized as part of an interrogation of modern temporality, we may consider it differently. The concept of an adolescent moratorium is a specific example of panoptical time, with its invisible observer and contradictory imperatives. In this section I focus on some experiential dimensions of panoptical time. What are some aspects of living within panoptical time? How does the time of a moratorium affect youth? How can we conceptualize teenaged time experiences within such a modernist temporal order?

Stephen Kern explores how modern emphasis on productive time was experienced by persons in different social positions. Kern coins the term "expectant time" to describe how "the assembly line and Taylorism [that is, scientific management of factory production] diminished the factory worker's active control over the immediate future in the productive process and relegated him to an *expectant mode*, waiting for the future to come along the line." Kern argues that this *passive temporal mode, oriented toward the future*, has material effects on people: "Individuals behave in distinctive ways when they feel cut off from the flow of time, excessively attached to the past, isolated in the present, without a future, or rushing toward one." This section explores how the moratorium of adolescence may have material effects on youth.[27]

Children and youth are positioned like Kern's factory workers—waiting passively for the future. According to Allison James and Alan Prout, children and youth are both imprisoned in their time (age) and out of time (abstracted), and they are thereby denied power over decisions or resources. Teenagers cannot go backward to childhood nor forward to adulthood "before their time" without incurring derogatory labels, for example, "immature," "loose," or "precocious." The dominant concepts regarding youth's position in the western societies, "development" and "socialization," make it impossible for youth to exercise power over life events or to represent themselves, since they are not fully developed or socialized. Kern's historical analysis of "expectant time" pushes us to consider the experiences of being caught in age and time.[28]

Despite the passivity of the adolescent moratorium, Erikson's norms for a healthy personality demand an *active mastery* of one's environment, a unified personality, and accurate perceptions of oneself and the world.[29] I want to call attention to the difficulties of actively mastering one's environment and securing "identity" when youth are simultaneously contained within an "expectant mode." In the sections below, I explore the conflicted experiences of "becoming but not being." Because the naturalized discourse of youth is so powerful, it is difficult to conceive of how the normative age-grading, vigilance over precocity, and incitement to activeness might affect youths' experiences of being teenaged, and how these powerful pulls and pushes help produce the knowable and known adolescent. In order to denaturalize adolescent "identity conflicts," I juxtapose postcolonial theory with sociological studies of Norwegian childhood and life-history accounts of American college students. This bricolage portrays some aspects of "expectant time" and suggests the regularized, material production of youth crises.

Knowing Subordinates

> The most formidable ally of economic and political control had long been the business of "knowing" other peoples because this "knowing" underpinned imperial dominance and became the mode by which they were increasingly persuaded to know themselves: that is, as subordinate to Europe.[30]

Postcolonial scholarship offers broad, incisive, and useful critiques of Western knowledge, which help place the facts of adolescence into an unfamiliar perspective. If we take common attributes of adolescence— for example, they are emotional, confused, controlled by hormones, unstable—as a *set of relations* rather than as the natural qualities of people between the ages of 12 and 19, we begin to emphasize the processes of producing and consuming certain knowledge about the inferiority of youth. The system of colonialism kept certain knowledge invisible and trumpeted other ideas constantly; that is, colonialism kept social structural inequalities muted, while the colonized and their psychologized "dependency complex" became hypervisible. As economic and political constraints faded from view, colonized people appeared as the rational source of a colonial order because they "need, crave, demand dependency." In Bhabha's theoretical terms, colonial discourse involves a *splitting*: it obscures the relationships of institutions and apparatuses of power while it emphasizes the inadequacies of the colonized. This process of splitting and the highlighting of the inadequacies of the subordinate people pertains to knowledge about adolescence too.[31]

Family Relations and "Big" 12-Year-Olds

Anne Solberg, a Norwegian sociologist, has documented how different sets of family relationships make children "big" or keep them "little." She contrasted a 12-year-old girl in a family that distributed both household responsibilities (cooking, cleaning, laundry) among two adults and two children and household resources (private time and discretionary spending), with a 12-year-old boy in a family that expected little from him (occasionally he was asked to help out with a particular task) and also accorded him few rights (no regular discretionary income, for example). Solberg found that in the first family both the adults and the girl considered the

12-year-old as *big*, responsible, and capable. The second family tended to view the son as little and childlike. Solberg's point is to suggest that chronological age must be supplemented by a concept of *social age*, that is, of age as socially produced through material practices. Of course, Solberg's study is on a small scale, but it suggests the usefulness of questioning "knowledge" about chronological age and sets of material practices.[32]

The variability documented by Solberg in "big" and "little" 12-year-olds is vigilantly absent in schooling, which enforces rigid age-graded expectations:

> By the early 1900s, passage from elementary school to junior high school and from junior high school to senior high school marked important transitions for youths and nurtured precise expectations and norms for each age-bounded grade and type of school. A fourteen-year-old who was still in the sixth grade was keenly aware of being out of step with peers, as were boys who did not switch from knickers to long pants at thirteen. Equally important, these peer groups and accompanying age expectations were bolstered by new scientific standards for physical and intellectual attainment.[33]

"Feeling Your Age"

My interviews with U.S. college undergraduates preparing to become teachers provide sharp images and feelings of being teenaged that suggested an unsettledness from dimly perceived power relations and from heightened competition with one's age-mates. Renee, a white Midwestern daughter of a veterinarian, described adolescence as a growing consciousness of herself as a social being:

> You begin to actually become conscious of who you are. When your body goes through . . . puberty. . . . You really become concerned about what you look like or how you present yourself. I think that's when you start becoming aware of your effect on the world and your place in it. In adolescence you realize that this is the place you're going to have to live in. *You start feeling your age.*[34]

But what is *feeling your age*? Renee discusses a consciousness of her pubertal body and becoming concerned with how she looked and how others perceived her. So she began to *manage herself* in line with how others responded to her. In Foucault's terms, the disciplinary gaze, or biopower, began to operate in more explicit ways on and through her body and social relationships.

Renee provided clues to other aspects of feeling her age. Her middle-class background, niceness, and Christian values seemed to prevent her from directly critiquing her parents, but over the seven months of the study, she talked more openly about their conflicts. At the beginning of the study in the autumn of 1991, Renee described the conflict as *awkwardness*.

> If I'm looking at my middle school years . . . you wanted to be somebody so big yet you were still this kid that was under your parents' control. You didn't know what to do. I mean, if you tried to act big, you could get in trouble, and yet if you acted like a baby then people would make fun of you. . . . I just felt it was a very awkward in-between time, to make those decisions for yourself, yet your parents are still in control of you. So *are those decisions really yours?*[35]

Here Renee questioned one premise of the discourse of adolescence—she had been informed that middle school youth should act big and make decisions, yet she also knew that the decisions weren't really hers; that is, if they chose wrongly, it would be held against them. Here was a shaky *performance of autonomy* in which the audience, her parents, were like puppeteers controlling her actions via encouragement and enthusiasm.

Renee provided a specific example to illustrate her "awkwardness" around decision-making:

> I have an older sister who plays soccer and she was actually an All-American, and I remember when I was little I just started playing soccer because she was. Then as time went on, I don't know if I was actually making a decision to play soccer or it was just, that was what I should be doing according to my parents . . . 'cause I remember at times I wanted to do other things and yet I was afraid to say something. I thought I'd hurt their feelings, yet I wanted to be the big person to say, I want to do other things . . . if I would have had enough courage to say something, I might have. . . [voice trailed off].[36]

Here Renee described power struggles with her parents over who made decisions. Expressing only frustration, not anger, as she recounted it, Renee termed the experience "awkward," a minimizing term for what seemed vivid and troublesome memories.

Two months later in a group interview with three other undergraduates, however, she dramatically rewrote the story, omitting the power struggle and calling it her identity crisis:

> I think you need to have them [identity problems]. I had an identity problem in high school . . . I played soccer because my sister played soccer and . . . [pause] I didn't really like it, but I played it. So I think that was an identity problem. But *looking back on it, I wouldn't have had it any other way because I met so many of my friends through soccer and I wouldn't have been in shape or anything like that. I don't know where I would have been without it, so I think you have to go through the identity crisis to continue to develop.*[37]

In this revision, Renee adopted an instrumentalist position that soccer helped her find friends, get in shape, and find a place in the world. She concluded that this "identity crisis" was necessary in order to develop. *Only when we look at both versions of the story can we see that an "identity crisis" was a conflict with parents over use of leisure time. Conflicts with her parents were rewritten as* her *identity crisis, an example of the splitting off of context and power relations and the psychologizing of youth.* The second version affirmed the necessity of adult control of youth. "I don't know where I would have been," she summarized, if her parents' perspective had not dominated. *In order to develop, she needed dependency.* According to Fanon, in a colonial society that proclaims the superiority of one race, others must "turn white or disappear," that is, become like the dominators or face erasure or censure. Similarly, in a society that proclaims the superiority of adults, children and youth must become like adults or face censure. Renee's acceptance of her parents' perspective on her middle school activities was a process of legitimizing adult power, recoded via the psychological concept of an identity crisis and her need for others to make decisions.[38] To paraphrase Fanon, she had to have an identity crisis or disappear.

I have used Renee's statements to argue that the discourse on adolescence, like colonial discourse, omits material conditions of existence and focuses solely on the psychological state of youth to position the psychological traits as the logical source of the social structural inequities, or the reasons adolescents have to be controlled. In this example, I emphasized Renee's readiness to interpret power struggles in terms of psychological problems of the youth and simultaneously to drop any attention to the structuring conditions that affect the problem. Homi Bhabha argues that the colonial space is agonistic: the relationship between the colonized and colonizer is one of constant, if implicit, contestation and opposition. Most often when conflict between adolescents and adults is described, teenagers are defined as *rebellious*, that is, the source of the conflict is within them, their hormones, emotionality, and inability to see beyond the present moment. The concrete interactions of rebellious youth with adults are seldom make visible, so that the simple, unitary description of teenagers as rebellious stands. In this way, the discourse on adolescents tends to produce a fixed opposition between adults and youth approaching the permanent opposition of the colonizer and the colonized.

For Renee, *feeling her age* involved doubting her decisions, distancing from her own desires, and accepting her parents' decisions as "in her best interest." In this view, feeling one's age was learning to accept a form of manipulation over decisions and to see oneself as others see you, thereby creating a doubled self. In my analysis, the adolescent "identity crisis" has a social origin and is materially produced in the passive and expectant mode of "growing up."

For Melanie, another white undergraduate, feeling one's age meant competition and always coming up second best.

> There is just something about being a teenager that makes you think that you're not very good . . . no matter how hard you try, there is always someone in the classroom that gets better grades than you are. Or no matter how hard you try there's always . . . some other girl gets to go out with the guy you wanted to go out with since the beginning of the school year. No matter how hard you try, the other team always wins or the other girl can always run faster than I can. Or, my best friend wants to talk to her brother instead of talking to me. Or there is always something there . . . or no matter how hard you try, your boyfriend still breaks up with you. But there is always something there, that once you get out, once you get up a step, you get knocked back down one.[39]

Melanie felt her age in enhanced competition for social status and self-worth. Chudacoff confirms that narrow age-groupings force continuous comparisons among age-mates, and meeting those well-defined expectations for life accomplishments confers social status. In my view, the expectant time modality plus the psychosocial emphasis on active mastery of one's environment, staged within the corporate model of U.S. high schools, contribute to an intensified search for self-and-social-status. This effect of power relations, in which adolescents are defined as irresponsible and rightly without much power, is what is often referred to as "peer pressure." As in colonial discourse, the colonized are declared naturally unfit to be in any other situation. Youth, like colonizied peoples, "need, crave, demand dependency."⁴⁰

Thus the position of youth is multiply inferior. They are expected to measure up to finely tuned assessments of productivity, learning, morality, and achievement while remaining in a social position that is dependent and watched over not only by adults but also by their age-peers. Their dependence communicates their inequality, and their "becoming" status appears to legitimate it. Being 14 or 16 is measured by peers and by adults within a system where adolescents' position remains one of lack or absence. Adults are people who *are*, adolescents *will be* in the future.⁴¹ In these ways, adolescents, like the natives portrayed in ethnographic accounts, are imprisoned in their age as absence and suspended outside historical time.

Expectant Time and the Loss of a Sense of Past, Present, and Future

Reinhart Koselleck provides another dimension of living in "expectant time" in his interpretation of dreams from concentration camp inmates as an inversion of temporal experience.

> In the camp, conditions prevailed that made a mockery of all previous experience; conditions that appeared unreal, but were real all the same. The compulsion to de-realize oneself in order to become paralyzed at the final stage of existence led also to an inversion of temporal experience. *Past, present, and future ceased to be a framework for orienting behavior.*⁴²

In "utopian camp dreams" the inmates dreamed along the lines of daytime fantasies, that is, about life beyond the electric fence. The past was transferred into wishes for the future; however, "such dreams were the harbingers of death," since within the camp system, courage and perseverance could lead to destruction. The "salvational dreams" ceased to try to "anchor the person of the dreamer in reality and thus became, apparently paradoxically, the sign of a chance for survival." Koselleck argues that *salvational dreams corresponded to the experience of the camp and were devoid of both images and action*; that is, they were without a modern, temporal order. This destruction of the person's self-constructed world, which usually heralds schizophrenia, is an inversion that had some effectiveness in concentration camp confinement:[43]

> The timelessness to which the inmates were condemned assumed in the salvational dreams a redeeming significance, more precisely, a redeeming power. *Estrangement from the empirical self* became a silent weapon against the system of terror that ran through both inmates and overseers in the concentration camp. The diabolic inversion, that death appeared to be a better life and life a worse death, was what had to be confronted. Only in salvational dreams did the inferno find its fictive termination "outside" of time and at the same time offer the inmate a grasp of reality.[44]

I read Koselleck's analysis to suggest that under extreme conditions of terror, when no self-confirming or self-making action is possible, time—any sense of past or present or future—also ceases. The empirical self separates from the unspeakable horror of the camp internment by splitting from the self via dreams that reject a time consciousness and the possibilities of action related to past, present, or future events. Here the "mastering" of one's environment totally ceases as indicator of the self.

I am using the shock of an analogy between adolescence and concentration camp inmates to highlight the possible disorientation and self-estrangement that could be effects of stringently patrolled confinement in expectant time. In extreme conditions, those dwelling in expectant time lose altogether the connection with temporalness and with a purposive sense of past, present, and future. Confinement in the seemingly interminable present, the waiting for something to happen, the sense that others know your past and future while you remain in the dark—all of these characteristics of youths' times do not add up to the Holocaust. However, I draw on Koselleck's work to dramatize the sense of *confinement in temporality* and *its possible connections to disorientation and self-estrangement* that are possible in adolescence.

I am suggesting that we consider the powerful effects of teenagers being condemned to an "expectant time"—a moratorium of responsibility and of power. Expectant time is supported by theories that tell us that youth need dependency because they are confused about their identities. Solberg's work points out that 12-year-olds can be big or little in relation to the facts of variable material practices. My interviews with Renee and

Melanie suggest that in adolescence they felt both a youthfu power and strong pressures to "master their environments." Kosu analysis of Holocaust dreams suggests that within a confinement of passivity, the suspension of temporal identity and ability to act and mast one's environment can be "salvational." This means that youths' refusal to consider the consequences of their actions (a familiar refrain in secondary schools) could be considered as salvational rather than as evidence of immaturity.

For me, these pieces suggest that youths' passive temporal position, always "becoming," waiting for the future to arrive, may *effect* the identity crises that, in turn, *prove* adolescents' need to be kept with little power and few decisions. This section has examined the seemingly insurmountable "tasks" and the sometimes surreal experiences of "expectant time" in order to cast a different light upon commonsense meanings of "peer pressure," "conformity," and "rebellion." Extreme experiences of expectant time may produce a withdrawal from modern temporality, from a sense of past, present, and future; and teenagers may hang on to atemporality as a psychic salvational dream, while many of their teachers offer the timeless axiom that the high school years are the "best years" of their lives.

CHRONOTOPES OF ADOLESCENCE

This section offers a Bakhtinian perspective on the construction of adolescence with and through time. Bakhtin's ideas about distinctive chronotopes within novel genres may help distill some conclusions about time and the discourse of adolescence. He analyzed different novel genres on the basis of how they create identifiable relations between time and event. He follows Einstein in defining a chronotope as a particular relation between time and event. There is no such thing as time-in-itself. And Bakhtin believed that "time in real life is no less organized by convention that it is in a literary text." The chronotope of adolescence suggested in this chapter has several characteristics. First, like many novels, adolescent discourse is set in *abstract adventure time;* that is, time appears to have a chronology, but the characters do not age and remain unaffected by time and events. Television series such as *Dawson's Creek* and *My So Called Life* occur in abstract adventure time, where changes do not register on the characters; for example, their minds do not develop. "It is as if the hands on the clock in Einstein's exemplary railroad station moved, but the trains all remained stationary on their tracks." This abstract adventure time produces narratives that are ahistorical and decontextualized and makes it notoriously hard to paste on context.[45]

Second, because of the panoptical gaze, the institutional frame around the discourse on adolescence, nothing much is supposed to happen. Avoiding precocity through slow development means that the present is emptied of meaningful events; the past may have significance, but really *only the future matters*. Holding onto the turn-of-the-century millennial and evolutionary narratives' *focus upon fulfillment*, the end of the adolescence story is primary. Adolescence is usually understood to end when a person finishes school, gets a full time job, marries, and has children.[46]

Third, since the end of the story matters, and adults know what the correct and happy ending is (increasing maturity and responsibility, school achievement, full-time employment, marriage and children, property ownership, in that order), only deviations or pitfalls along the prescribed plot merit attention. The panoptical gaze makes youth into cartoonlike or clownish figures. Although youth themselves are expected to take each moment seriously, we, the adult audience, know that these things are relatively trivial. Since we know the panoptical sequencing, we may watch and comment on adolescence with detachment and humor. Thus the characters in the narrative of adolescence may easily loose their humanity and become stereotypes.

Finally, to put adolescence into this narrative framework is to consider the "readers" of the stories, as well. We consumers of adolescent narratives are bound emotionally to the story. We are happy, satisfied, and comforted by narratives of fulfillment (conventional adolescent development); we are disturbed and alarmed by precocity and risk. We may blame families, bad schools, uncaring governments, lack of economic opportunities, and crazy kids, all of which may be in part accurate. But what is generally absent from view is the narrative structure and conventions of the discourse on adolescence, in which we are emotionally and professionally invested (in both the problems and the solutions).

My analysis calls into question conventional "findings" from sociologists, psychologists, and educators that youth and the social niches they occupy are temporally out of sync, that is, that there is a *mismatch* between developmental needs and youth circumstances. For example, Csikszentmihalyi and Schmidt utilize a sociobiological view to argue that the evolutionary traits of youth, for instance to challenge boundaries, are mismatched to the school and social environment, which is either too constraining or too dangerous. Coté and Allahar utilize an Eriksonian perspective to ask how youth can "formulate a viable and stable identity under uncertain and even hostile circumstances." With relatively few rights and economic resources, youth are denied possibilities to act, which means they cannot develop a "sense of temporal and spatial continuity." Because they cannot take up meaningful roles that connect them to a future, argue Coté and Allahar, they suffer identity confusion, which "incapacitate[s] them or lead[s] them to high levels of risk-taking and gratuitous violence." These scholars offer a critique of adolescence that utilizes a sense of temporality, but one that accepts the modern development-in-time episteme that I have questioned.[47]

This familiar out-of-sync temporal analysis accepts the expectant temporal mode that is foundational to the modern, scientific discourse on adolescence. I agree that there is a tension between the private times of youth (as well as of adults and children) and public institutional standardized time; but I have also argued that basic ideas of adolescence were formed within that "world standard time," not in conflict with it. What these critiques fail to acknowledge is how adolescence is profoundly *a construction with time*, not just empirical objects that can be placed in one temporal sequencing or another. I have suggested that this is a panoptical time and an expectant time that require youth-as-subjects actively to use time, not just pass time.

SUMMARY

In this chapter I have explored three dimensions of the discourse on adolescence—the teenaged years as panoptical time, as expectant time, and as abstract adventure time. My aim has been to understand how adolescence remains so resistant to critique and revision. By foregrounding the modern development-in-time episteme and then examining the ways adolescence is made with and through time, I suggest how adolescence is naturalized via objective, commodified knowledge-at-a-glance and subjective experiences of expectant time, with their constructed anomie and rebellion. Taking up both the objective and subjective pieces, the narrative chronotope of adolescence located in abstract adventure time, where events occur but nothing really changes, cobbles the pieces together. Adults patch together their subjective experiences through the panoptical concept of identity and the developing pubertal body; but the chronotope of adolescence works to trivialize the intensity of the expectant time while simultaneously reinforcing it by endless retellings (in social science research but also in popular culture, say in television, novels, and documentary films). With these various pushes and pulls, I think adolescence has become a comic figure, serious yet trivialized, institutionally ordained and reduced to stereotypes, commodified and malleable as a sign of futures, pasts, fears, and hopes. So viewed, the adolescent is endearing, frightening, unavoidable, and exploitable.

"Before Their Time"

Teenage Mothers Violate

the Order of Proper Development

5

The crisis of teenage pregnancy claimed headlines and sound bites across the latter half of the 1980s in the United States. For example, the New Right portrayed young mothers as immoral social problems who cause family deterioration, a portrait that draws heavily on familial and reproductive ideologies. More critical interpretations presented teenage pregnancy as a moral panic and as a keyword of the U.S. welfare state. Feminist analyses emphasized the gender, race, and social class dimensions of sexual activeness, birth control, abortion, and keeping a baby. Indeed, teenage pregnancy approached an "epidemic of signification."[1]

Though highly visible in the last decade in American society and politics, school-aged mothers have remained marginal to educational discourses of curriculum, school reform, and pedagogy.[2] The empirical research on school-aged mothers has sprung up primarily in fields such as medicine, social work, psychology, and history. In this chapter, I examine the marginalized presence of teenage mothers in educational discussions by scrutinizing normative age chronologies in both theories and institutionalized practices. I examine normative coming-of-age scripts utilizing Homi Bhabha's concept of the disjunctive present—a time that emphasizes contingency and the possibilities of the indeterminate.

The concept of a disjunctive present prompts us to examine the staging and timing of social order, and here that means investigating the life scripts of youth. The concepts of the disjunctive present and normative age chronologies allow us to reflect on how our theories and school practices promote and maintain "socially young" adolescents. When we maintain "socially young" teenagers, their sexuality is thereby staged as a "shock" and pregnancy as a terrible, inconceivable blow to our views of them. Using the vantage point of the disjunctive present and feminist political theory around reproductive rights as central to democracy, I argue that our marginalization of school-aged mothers is emblematic of our denial of sexuality among youth and our ambivalence about sex education in schools. In order to see teenage mothers in different ways, we need to add a sense of contingency to coming-of-age narratives, perhaps via a concept of social age. The concepts of social age and reproductive rights for sex education make school-aged mothers visible to us as figures of both necessary change and hope.

MODERNITY, FUTURE-DRIVE, AND THE DISJUNCTIVE PRESENT

Homi Bhabha interrogates the temporal ordering of modernity, and his work situates the future-directed order of schools within a larger critique of modernity. When the view of modernity as progress (with its negative ontologies of "lack" or "excess") is halted, as it is in the problem of teenage pregnancy—a problem that "rends the social fabric" and creates familial deterioration—the production of modernity as forward movement is visible. Bhabha theorizes that in such situations, binaries of past/present are decoupled: "The linear, progressive time of modernity" reveals its construction, its necessary terms, and its structures. When the past/present dialectic of modernity (that is, the dynamic that we in the present are more advanced and advancing than those in the past) is brought to a standstill, the "temporal action of modernity, its progressive future drive" is temporarily halted. Bhabha identifies this temporal lag—the unmasking of the constant drive toward the future and the interpretations of past and present tied to that future-drive—as a "disjunctive present" when the past, rather than being speedily surpassed, is "sutured to the present." Thus the disjunctive present is produced through an accidental bumping up and overlapping of past and present, terms usually set as binary opposites, kept separate and hierarchically ranked. "This lagged temporality . . . is a mode of breaking the complicity of past and present to open up a space of revision and initiation." Conceptualizing life as uncertain, as contingent, rather than through the veil of progress in which the future is deemed to be brighter and we are working our way "forward" opens possibilities. Bhabha marks this contingency as positive:

Indeterminism is the mark of the conflictual yet productive space in which the arbitrariness of the sign of cultural signification emerges within the regulated boundaries of social discourse.[3]

Adolescent as an Emblem of Modernity

I am utilizing Bhabha's theorizing to emphasize the problem of school-aged mothers as a disjunctive moment, a moment when conceptions of adolescents and youth are revealed as "staged" or produced. Adolescence is a thoroughly modern concept imbued with the dynamics of past/present, as youth point unflaggingly to the future. Youth are invariably talked about as *our* future. *Adolescence is an emblem of modernity, and time is its defining mode.*

In my view, adolescence enacts modernity in its central characterization as *developing* or becoming—youth cannot live in the present; they live in the future, that is, they exist only in the discourse of "growing up." Adolescence reenacts the evolutionary supremacy of the West over primitive others in its psychologized (internalized) progress from (primitive) concrete operational stages to (advanced) abstract ones. Adolescence continuously enacts Western progress carried in the oppositional positions of past and present and ever points toward even greater futures.[4]

Central to successive psychological prescriptions for adolescents to lead to proper human development and the progress of the race was the postponement of sex, for unrestrained sexuality was the hallmark of "savages."[5] Teenage pregnancy and motherhood call into question the future-drive and the present-is-better ideology. When New Right critics label school-aged mothers as the source of family and social deterioration, it clearly communicates a sense of backwardness for them as individuals and for society. The future of sleek, technological progress on the information superhighway and in the global economy is disrupted by images of young pregnant women. The progress through education to work to stable family life is disturbed. This disturbance allows us to examine the staging of the progress and upon what bodies the progress works. Thus teenage mothers exist in a disjunctive moment that focuses us on the present and offers us the possibility to think differently about the future.

THE TIME OF ADOLESCENCE

Age and normative life chronology are central in the linguistic and visual representations of school-aged mothers: Teenage mothers are "children having children"[6] and mothers "before their time."[7] Thus integral to depictions of teenage mothers as social problems is their violation of normative chronology. Annette Lawson explains:

> the overwhelming hegemonic ideal orders events much as follows: childhood and education, work and sexual experimentation, marriage and children. . . . The very young mother is deviant by virtue of her obvious rebellion against the proper chronology of events as she flaunts her out-of-time acts.[8]

The moral panic over teenaged mothers is aroused, in part, by the disorderly, out-of-time acts.[9] Lawson's analysis supports the importance of temporal (dis)ordering in the problem of teenage pregnancy and motherhood, which is in keeping with Bhabha's concept of disjunctive time.

However, another aspect of the disjuncture of teenage pregnancy is the sexuality of girls and young women. Children have been defined as pure and nonsexual, and part of the force of the term "children having children" is the juxtaposition of children with childbearing.[10] The time of childhood and young adults is meant to be asexual. The pregnancy of a 15- or 16-year-old flies in the face of such deeply entrenched beliefs, and news magazines have regularly featured photos of young-faced girls with swollen bellies to emphasize the out-of-time acts.

Bakhtin and Time/Space Mediation

Bakhtin's study of the relation between chronology and plot in different narrative genres is useful to point out how time and event are related. Holquist explains that "there is no purely chronological sequence inside or outside the text." Holquist links Bakhtin's work with Einsteinian ideas about the inseparability of time and event.

> An event . . . is always a dialogic unit in so far as it is a *co*-relation: something happens only when something else with which it can be compared reveals a change in time and space. . . . *[E]verything will depend on how the relations between what happens and its situation in time/space is mediated.*[11]

From this perspective, the meaning of an event resides in the process of comparison with another event and its time/space location. Thus teenage pregnancy or children having children is implicitly compared with orderly childbearing once schooling is finished, employment secured, and a marriage consummated.

Discursive Constructions of Youth in and through Time

Historian Harvey Graff finds that children and youth only exist within the "discourse and experience of growing up," although numerous paths to adulthood exist in different historical periods and among children of different social, racial, and gender groups. Sociologists Allison James and Alan Prout similarly identify time as central to the construction of childhood and youth and urge the systematic study of the "temporal underpinnings of different representations of childhood." James and Prout write: "It is during childhood (and old age) that time and perceptions of time have the greatest social significance."[12]

Drawing upon the work of Graff and James and Prout in order to examine childhood and youth critically, we need to extricate them from the discourses of growing up, to *represent* children and youth; that is, to consider empirically and theoretically the temporal dimension of childhood. We need to be able to consider children and youth separate from the narratives of growing up and biologically based developmental schemas. In order to make youth differently visible, we need to disrupt the normative narrative of youth with its dominant time/event relation. To begin this task, James and Prout recommend scholarly focus upon age-prohibited activities of youth, for example, sex, and transition times. School-aged mothers provide a focus upon both the prohibited sexual activity of youth and upon the transition time of teenaged motherhood, and thereby respond to James's and Prout's proposed sociological agenda.

In the next sections I examine the changes in contemporary life scripts, life chronologies of some teenaged mothers, and how they exemplify the concept of "social age."

CONTEMPORARY LIFE SCRIPTS OF YOUTH

In his recent historical work on youths' narratives of growing up, Graff claims that there is a compacting of the growing up narrative in the contemporary era, at least for some youth. That is, a series of transition events were once ordained to occur over a number of years to allow a slow ("developmental") process of maturation. Graff finds that for some contemporary youth, growing up occurs in one event and that fact produces tremors among adults and youth. Concluding from his own work and that of other historians, Graff finds: "an absence of uniformity across a cohort or age grade, and a lack of a lengthy period of postponement or moratorium in youth or adolescence, regardless of theories and expectations to the contrary, which nonetheless retain their force."[13]

The work of sociologist Marlis Buchmann confirms Graff's view of the greater variety across life scripts. Her research compares the life events of 1960 and 1980 U.S. high school graduates. According to Buchmann, three transitions have historically marked the move into adulthood: the end of formal schooling (and entrance into the workforce), marriage, and having children,[14] and these occurred in that order. In the contemporary U.S., adults and youths may be in extended formal schooling together (due to economic uncertainty and job instability), marriage has been replaced with cohabitation and a substantial increase in single adult households, and having children has been decoupled from marriage. Buchmann concludes that her research "suggest[s] a greater complexity and diversity in transition patterns to adulthood." While socioeconomic position still exerts a strong impact on life chances, Buchmann writes that "the 1980 cohort's orientations and actions show more individually stratified patterns." Traditions and customs constrain her 1980 cohort less, while increased standardization (through rationalization and bureaucratic credentialing processes) of public identities works against individualization:

> More flexible and discontinuous, and increasingly diversified and individualized, life course patterns have been discussed as effects of the mutually reinforcing processes of rationalization at the level of social organization and the elaboration of the ideology of individualism.[15]

The transition to adulthood, in Buchmann's macrosociological and actor-centered perspective, is transformed into a "more extended, diversified, and increasingly individualized period." She thinks that the differentiation between adult status and youth status is increasingly blurred. Buchmann writes that "structural and cultural changes over the last two decades have made youth as a life stage increasingly obsolete, while they have simultaneously extended it indefinitely." Here is another illustration of the disjunctive present—the disordering of a well-established time/event relation. If the contemporary coming-of-age patterns vary more, other social institutions, such as the media, may work harder to reinfantilize youth.[16]

In the next sections, I examine teenage motherhood from the perspective of increasingly individualized scripts of life, which may involve all-at-once growing up accompanied by structural maintenance of a young status.

TEENAGE MOTHERHOOD AS ALL-AT-ONCE GROWING UP

Teenage motherhood appears to be a narrative of swift and all-at-once growing up. Thus the problem of teenage motherhood is a violation of proper age chronology and what is believed about biological age; it is also a compacted or condensed narrative of growing up that violates the leisurely, extended adolescence thought proper and necessary by psychologists from Hall to Erikson and institutionalized in compulsory school attendance laws and child labor prohibitions. Teenage motherhood perplexes secondary school educators and their assumptions of schooling's role in "preparation" for adulthood. If school-aged mothers are already adults, at least in one domain, what can school do for them? And how should it treat them?

In the next section, I use interviews with school-aged mothers to explore the all-at-once growing up scripts and some of their time/event relations.

Students at Bright Prospects Alternative School

Debbie, a 16-year-old mother attending Bright Prospects Alternative High School[17] for school-aged mothers, noted: "*It seems when you get pregnant, you mature just like that.* We're not old," she added quickly to uniform laughter from her peers, "You just mature." Debbie portrayed an all-at-once growing up experience, in which responsibilities appear to demand that youth become serious about their actions and consequences. The group of six young mothers whom I interviewed agreed with Debbie's perspective and supported it with other examples. Suzanne claimed that she had decided to give up drinking and smoking pot in order to set an example for her son. Esther recounted her maturity in her relationship with school: "Before [I got pregnant] I didn't go to school; I partied all the time. . . . Now I respect myself more. I don't do things to embarass myself."

Evelyn, a 13-year-old eighth-grader at the time of the research,[18] was eight months pregnant when I interviewed her. Like many girls, when Evelyn discovered her pregnancy she thought her "life had ended":

> At first when I found I was pregnant, I didn't want to go anywhere. I thought my life was ruined. But here [Bright Prospects School] they help and say, "Your life isn't ruined." You just go on.

Evelyn's middle-class background supported her in clinging to her plans to become a lawyer. She planned to enroll in a private high school while her mother cared for the baby.

For some of the young mothers, the all-at-once growing up occurred in strict, religious family settings that utilized ignorance as an approach to morality.[19] Theresa, a 16-year-old junior at the time of the research, explained the role of Catholicism in her young "social age":

> It's not that I didn't know about birth control, it's just something we [Theresa and her steady boyfriend] never really thought about—till I got pregnant. . . . I was brought up in a strict Catholic family, so even the thought of having sex before you were married was not allowed. That kind of shied me away from talking to my mom about it [birth control].

When they found she was pregnant, Theresa and her boyfriend made some hard decisions. First, they decided not to get married. Second, they decided to release the baby for adoption. Together they went through the open adoption procedures, and they reviewed applicants' files, interviewed them, and chose the adoptive parents:

> [Open adoption] makes me feel better about what I did, knowing that he's [her son, Nicholas] in a good home. I got to choose the parents, so he didn't just get placed in a home. And I get pictures and a letter three times a year, so you don't feel so isolated.

Theresa found being at Bright Prospects during her pregnancy was important in that she was among girls in the same situation, one in which understanding and nonjudgmentalism were promoted. Her comments on learning about the labor-intensive work of caring for a child shed further light on "social age" and pregnancy, for both boys and girls. She believed that few of the teenaged fathers, like the mothers, knew anything about caring for a child. Even one day in the Bright Prospects nursery would temper certain attitudes:

A friend of mine—the father of her baby won't let her give it up for adoption. *He* wants to keep the baby. Well, he's sixteen years old and I don't think he has any idea of what it's like to take care of a baby. And if he came over here and worked for one day [in a nursery], he'd lay off and leave her alone.

Two alumni of Bright Prospects also presented their pregnancies as all-at-once adulthood scripts. Betty, 24 at the time of the interview, described the state she was in when she got pregnant at 16: "I was headed for dropping out; I was headed down. I hadn't been doing well in classes. Getting pregnant really made me grow up. . . . It sort of saved me."

Gina was 21 when I interviewed her, having graduated from Bright Prospects two years earlier. Before her pregnancy and enrollment at Bright Prospects, she had been suspended from several schools in two states. Gina reminisced: "In a way I wanted to get pregnant. She [my mom] was so strict: no phone calls, no dates, no makeup. At sixteen I could only wear mascara."

Social Age

I am using these recollections and perspectives of teenaged mothers to demonstrate all-at-once growing up and to illustrate the concept of social age. In various contexts and dynamics, these young women were kept "young," both in their own behaviors and in what was expected of them by others, especially parents. Part of the precipitating events in young pregnancies, in these narratives and elsewhere, was the failure to take one's life and especially one's sexuality seriously. Prudence Rains maintained that the failure of young women to use contraception was interwoven with their inability to see themselves as *rightfully* sexual. To have sexual feelings was difficult to accept, and the girls she interviewed "resolved" this difficulty by denying the issue of conception and seeing themselves as being swept away by particular situations. Thus they could continue to view themselves as virginal and childlike. Their negotiated "young social age" maintained their innocence concerning contraception—and helped create unplanned pregnancies.[20]

The concept of "social age" denaturalizes biological age and allows us to see the negotiated, thus, *produced* character of age, a topic I began to address in Chapter Four. As noted in the previous chapter, Anne Solberg researched 12-year-olds in Norwegian families, and her study revealed a range of practices around the household obligations and rights of children that either made them "grow" (i.e., have an older social age) or stay small (maintain a younger social age). In this intriguing work, Solberg shows the constructedness of age through obligations and rights of children in households and develops the concept of a mutually negotiated social age that is variable while biological age is constant.[21]

Although I have no comparable empirical studies of negotiated social age in U.S. schools and families to draw upon, the concept of social age can be employed to read the above-quoted statements by school-aged mothers. Strict attitudes toward sex and contraception or toward dating, or few expectations for school achievement, seemed to be part of a negotiated "young social age." Schooling, with its emphasis on preparation and slow development, may help construct the problems of teenage mothers in the maintenance of the "young social age." The maintenance of a young social age in the area of sexuality is common across the United States. Comparative studies of the United States and other industrialized countries demonstrate that the United States has less of an open attitude toward sexuality, and reproductive information and services are harder to find and travel to.[22] An illustrative anecdote from Indiana portrays one way schools perpetuate young social ages around sexuality.

On a fall 1996 visit to a high school in Indianapolis with my undergraduate multicultural education class, a counselor referred to the "epidemic proportions of teenage pregnancy" in the school. Of course, the counselor added, the Indianapolis school board policy prohibited discussion of birth control and permitted only abstinence to be taught. My students and I had numerous encounters with teenaged mothers that day. The student I shadowed had a nine-month-old son; she was an honor student in a highly visible program for college-bound youth (in a strongly working-class school). There were many other honor students and average students who attended school while they were pregnant and as young mothers.

This school system refused to acknowledge the sexuality and sexual activeness of teenagers. In its prohibition of useful and meaningful sex education, these students were defined as sexually immature and, by virtue of lack of knowledge and ability to discuss themselves as sexual beings, were kept at "young social ages." I argue that this young sexual age is part of the production of the problem of school-aged pregnancies.

In this interpretation, school practices and theoretical perspectives on adolescence and human growth and development perpetuate a "young social age" that is particularly significant in effecting a childlike approach to sexuality. These practices help produce unplanned pregnancies, which disproportionately impact young women. These immaturity-maintaining practices are both within the domain of sex education and contraception and more generally in secondary schools that normalize slow development toward adulthood. Finally, when all-at-once maturity occurs, with pregnancy its most potent symbol, schools generally cannot adapt or connect with these "too quickly mature" youths. Once again, schools fail them in lack of child care faciles, lack of sex education, and minimal coursework regarding childrearing and parenting. My argument is that the assumption by schools of a normative and proper slow development of youth is effective in keeping many youths "socially young," a fact which clearly contributes to being "sexually young"; being sexually young, in turn, contributes to an inability to consider responsible sexual practices, including use of contraception (but not limited to that).[23]

Young mothers at Bright Prospects School spoke about their maturity regarding contraception. Numerous students emphasized their regular use of birth control. Dolores spoke for many others: "I have my son on my lap. There is *no way* I will forget to take my birth control pill, with him there as a constant reminder."

Most of the girls with whom I spoke wanted more children but not until they were ready. "Maybe when I'm out of college and I don't have to depend on anyone, when I can take care of myself," Esther summarized. "I know not to do it again until I'm ready."

FEMINIST POLITICS, REPRODUCTIVE RIGHTS, AND SOCIAL AGE

Feminist politics can aid us in reconsidering school-aged mothers and sexuality from the perspective of age domination.[24] Zillah Eisenstein's argument that reproductive rights must include health care, sex education, AIDS prevention, and so on will shift the present immoral status of teenage mothers. Eisenstein argues that focusing on *reproductive rights* as a central facet of a feminist, antiracist, and progressive politics is different from abortion politics:

> *Reproductive rights enlarges the issue of abortion to related concerns*: affordable and good health care; a decrease in infant mortality and teenage pregnancy; reproductive health; health services for infertility; and access to appropriate contraceptives.

Eisenstein writes that "contraceptive services, sex education, and AIDS prevention outreach are as important to any woman needing them as abortion is for others." Reproductive choice is an essential part of this right. The Supreme Court has upheld restrictions on teenage access to abortion, via a required parental consent or a court approval; these restrictions mean that teenagers do not have reproductive choice. Eisenstein argues that we must reinvent democracy from the starting point of the pregnant bodies of women of color, building connections across women of color and white women around reproductive health, broadly conceptualized. These ideas regarding feminist support of reproductive rights, the centrality of pregnant women's bodies in a reinvention of democracy, and the roles of schools in those processes focus our attention on the necessity of reproductive rights education in schools.[25]

CONCLUSION: VISIBILITY, REPRODUCTIVE RIGHTS, AND SOCIAL AGE

The analysis presented here argues that the dominant life script of adolescence is a slow, over-a-long-time development from young person to adult. This coming-of-age narrative is assumed to be universal. However, by looking at school-aged mothers we see that this chronotype ignores reproductive bodies, that is, women's bodies.[26] It assumes and maintains a youth sheltered by affluence, white privilege, and a male body who can grow up slowly, planning and reflecting on his future adulthood. In these ways the dominant theory of adolescence, with its narrative of a developmental moratorium, makes sexually active and reproductive young women impossible to consider. They can remain only marginal and deviant. *Furthermore, this normative view makes sex education marginal to education, rather than a reproductive necessity.*

A second major emphasis in this chapter is the rethinking of teenage mothers, from social problem to an emblem of the disjunctive present—a time in which the staged emphasis on the present surpassing the past is stalled by school-age mothers, who are said to deteriorate the social fabric of family life. Views of slowly developing youth and views of children as nonsexual are belied by scores of school-aged mothers.[27] Sociologist Buchmann articulates the disjunctive present through her vision of the obsolence of youth yet its perpetuation for more and more years. This disjunctive present allows us to see how we produce youth as "socially young" and keep them that way. It allows us as educators to consider the social age of youth and schools' roles in treating them as "young." Thus the concept of the disjunctive present points to how schools help produce "forever young teenagers"—as part of their structural relations to other social institutions (families and workplaces); furthermore, this structural relation is supported by theoretical narratives which make it seem natural and proper to maintain teenagers as youngsters, especially in the arena of sexuality. From this perspective we see how the social age roots of teenaged mothers must remain invisible and how seemingly universal theories of adolescence privilege white affluent males.

In these ways, school-aged mothers bring our narratives of adolescence and imbedded scripts of growing up into relief. Shall we continue to make school-aged mothers visible only as disordered chronologies and sexual deviants? To do otherwise involves educators' active renegotiation of social age and political support for the feminist agenda of reproductive rights.

Our Guys/Good Guys 6

Playing with High School Athletic

Privilege and Power

Whatever mythologies we had at the end of the nineteenth century, they've become sports mythologies today.[1]

The faces of the [football] players were young, but the perfection of their equipment, the gleaming shoes and helmets and the immaculate pants and jerseys, the solemn ritual that was attached to almost everything, made them seem like boys going off to fight a war for the benefit of someone else, unwitting sacrifices to a strange and powerful god.[2]

[T]he athletic complex is a great machine for generating communal Selfhood. The teams are great hearts pumping Self-substance into the anemic Self of the community—students and school included. . . . [W]hen the team wins, the communal Self is replenished.[3]

The Super Bowl has become *the* cultural event of American life, one of many indications that sports, especially the more violent ones like football, have become like a religion or a nationalist ideology to which everyone bows. Sports seem to unite the races, social classes, and the political left and right as well. Although women may watch the Super Bowl in growing numbers, football idolizes that other thing that women can never have—muscle mass. Sports events like the Super Bowl are filled with military language at the same time that football imagery has become the "root metaphor of American political discourse." George Bush dubbed the 1992 Gulf War his "Super Bowl." The potent mix of football, political order, war, and scripted emotion, which was starkly and regularly paraded during the Persian Gulf action against Saddam Hussein, grounds this examination of athletics in secondary schools.[4]

The most popular and highest status boys are in the "athletic clique" of high schools. Athletic programs demand huge slices of school budgets, and coaches can be gods with a capability of making or ruining a school and its community. Despite these undisputed facts, little attention has been given to the significance and effects of competitive athletics and their brand of masculinity within contemporary discussions of teaching, schooling, and school reform. That is, sports in schools, especially in high schools, have generally been treated as a separate sphere—extracurricular, court- or field-based. This chapter seeks to understand male-dominated athletics as a systemic "logic of practice" and to map their influences on school culture, teaching, curricula, and our ideas of successful teenagers.

I utilize the personal narratives of one coach-in-training who was a football star in high school to help map the circulation of football-politics-war perspectives and how they impact the social relations of youth and teachers from the gridiron to the classroom. I examine the competitive relationships of playing football and the implications of schools becoming "level playing fields"; the privilege and power conferred on male athletes; and the implications of these masculinized, stratified, gridiron social relations for high school curriculam and teaching. Thus I am in pursuit of the rewards that await successful school team members; the ways that the logic of competitive athletics affects school discipline, management, and curricula; and how team loyalties and values sustain an intolerance of "outcasts," those who do not meet the criteria of successful athletes, the "winners."

Since studies of teenagers are usually stocked with stories of problems, risks, and crises, I devote this chapter to the "good guys"—the idealized stars of secondary schools, those young men who garner positive media attention and enhance school histories and local real estate values. These boys often conform to the successful kid image: "attractive, well groomed, articulate, and doing well in school or in some enterprise, like sports."[5] In examining the successes and problems of school athletics, I keep my eye on those outside the athletic circle as well, those kids who do not meet the standards for appearance, success, and social presence. I want to consider the athletes in relation to the less prestigious students. This chapter looks at the *winners*, and Chapter Seven examines the multiple effects of the dominance of competitive athletics on the culture of schools and on the *losers*.

This analysis begins with the understanding that competitive athletics *masculinize* schools, by which I mean that schools support and highlight the processes and persons who represent particular masculine interests, traits, and attitudes. British scholars have described a new wave of male dominance amid school change, which they term a *remasculinizing* of schools and school management. A particular version of masculinity— "competitive, point-scoring, overconfident, sporting, career and status conscious"—has come to dominate school management, writes Lynn Davies. In a detailed study of one British secondary school, Mac an Ghaill recorded a resurgence of English nationalism among male teachers, which he linked to various school practices, such as a renewed demand for boys learning their place through coercive discipline, a yearning for the old days of all-male schooling, and an emphasis on traditional "masculine" subject areas, for example, natural sciences, mathematics, and competitive team sports. The continuing popularity of caning, considered to be part of a "proper British upbringing," further supports this analysis of a yearning for more orderly and disciplined times.[6]

In the United States, the remasculinizing of schools includes a number of features: the spread of competitive sports; higher standards through increased testing; a more rigorous curriculum; zero-tolerance policies; and redoubled efforts in math, science, and technology.[7] This chapter pursues themes that might be imagined as circulating among these high stakes testing and other changes—a logic of competition and an absence of compassion for people with different abilities and/or critical perspectives. This analysis also examines variations in schools' promotion of all students' learning. I am trying to understand an attitude that seems based in schools but is also more broadly operative in domestic and international political realms.

POSITIONING FOOTBALL, MASCULINITY, AND THE GULF WAR

My interviews with Woody Rockne,[8] the subject of this chapter, were part of a larger study of a secondary teacher education program.[9] They began in August of 1993, slightly more than a year after the Persian Gulf War ended. The emotional tenor of his narratives, coupled with the alleged efficiency and rationality of his life, sounded familiar. For me, Woody's stories echoed the mix of irrationality and reason surrounding the U.S. invasion of Iraq during the Gulf War. I felt a similarity between the plot and emotional pitch of this preservice teacher's life stories and the popular response to the attack on Saddam Hussein by George Bush. My mental, emotional, and visceral responses to Woody's stories focused on the mix of rationality and boosterism in his tales of his school years, his sports involvements, his coaching practices, and his beliefs about teaching and coaching. Ann Laura Stoler has termed this intersection the link between nationalism and desire, or the "harnessing of affect to political life," and this chapter examines school athletics as a powerful site where a particular set of emotions and desires gets harnessed to a political order. Connell suggests that life history narratives afford an invaluable and unique perspective on schools as masculinizing institutions, which is elided in other approaches.[10]

This re-presentation of Woody's stories of playing football, coaching, and preparing to teach within the context of the Gulf War's nationalistic aggression begins with the need to view the following topics as linked: (1) sports and war, (2) sports and nationalism, (3) football as nationalist spectacle, and (4) the militarization of civilian life through "permanent war." The latter part of the chapter examines the individual and classroom dimensions of these sports-war-masculinity connections that are so powerfully fueled in secondary school sports. My broader concern is the impact of these sports and masculinity connections on expectations for all adolescents.

Sports, War, and Nationalism, or the Epistemology of the Bunker

The language of football draws heavily on military argot: attack, blitz, bombs, ground and air assaults, offense, defense, penetrations, flanks, conflicts, and battles for territory are standard terms in sportscasters' vocabularies. Both coaches and generals speak of victories, defeats, and casualties. In addition, sport/war metaphors have had currency in U.S. politics since the Civil War. The government often uses sports language as code words; for example, Richard Nixon's pseudonym for himself was "Quarterback." American political discourse would be straining for words and metaphors without its staple football imagery.[11]

Connections between sports and the Gulf War were everywhere: "[F]rom the beginning sports and the actual [Persian Gulf] conflict were linked in the media." Nadelhaft points to sports-inflected language in the Gulf War coverage; references to the war appeared on the sports pages and the *Chicago Tribune*'s full-page, brightly colored "Young Reader's Guide to the Gulf War" was at the back of the sports section. Columnist

Mike Royko established similarities between football coaches and Gulf War generals in strategies, establishing the air game and the ground game, and loathing the press. Sports imagery both rallied support for the war[12] and justified it:

> Sports, used as a metaphor for the Persian Gulf war, provided a sense of parity between the combatants and a sense that the war was governed by a neutral structure. . . . Sports metaphors, wrestling included, helped to legitimate the war and show merit and Justice to lie with the United States. . . . They imparted a structure to the war and made it into a contest, not a slaughter.[13]

The intimacy of sports and war simultaneously offers strong connections between *sports and nationalism*. Sports provide an ideal of physical fitness and its related moral health which are regularly linked to national strength. The physical body—often portrayed as a strong, white, muscular, male body—represented the German nation and its moral health at the beginning of the twentieth century.[14] Sports are seen as the proving ground for soldiers before going into battle for their country; when U.S. airmen survived being shot down in enemy territory, news accounts often linked their bravery and strategies to having been stellar athletes. Team loyalty was highly rated as preparation for war by the boyologists, and these connections remain strong today.

Although I have emphasized the multiple, concrete connections between football and the Gulf War, a specific war context may be superfluous, for the United States can be considered in a state of permanent war, a state in which a militarization of nationalism and civilian life occurs. This militarization takes place on the terrain of ignorance and knowledge and through the psychologies of good citizens and threatening others. Persistent ideas of dangerous others who might brainwash upright citizens and images of subversion of the American way of life are aspects of Lutz's "epistemology of the bunker." The "permanent war" mentality can be mobilized through complex, portraits of evil Others, who threaten invasion or the diminishment of American institutions or interests. It seems possible that school sports, with their valuing of aggressive triumphs over "others," might partake of and support an epistemology of the bunker. This is a place where the feelings of attachment to "our guys" and animosity toward their challengers can be seen as a training ground for national political conflicts with "others."[15]

Feeling Sport Spectacles

The mobilization of emotions is a crucial component of wartime dichotomies of us and them and is essential to the appearance of a noncoercive political order. To conceive of sports events as nationalistic spectacles that include visual, collective, emotional, and symbolic dimensions is to consider how football mobilizes emotion. According to Guy DeBord, we must think of public spectacles as "*a social relation among people, mediated by images*. . . . The spectacle is the present model of socially dominant life." DeBord elaborates on the modern spectacle, which demands a passive acceptance via a commonsense attitude: "that which appears is good, that which is good appears." Since football spectacles are seldom critiqued, they have a "monopoly of appearance."[16]

The monopolizing visual spectacle asserts the dominant social relations as an accepted fact and charges these images with emotion. Sporting events are highly emotional occasions, although thoroughly scripted and "hostile to all spontaneous feeling." "Apathy and boredom are considered bad form; if the game is that bad, you're expected to get mad and boo. Fans are expected to be *enthusiastic* in the literal sense of the word." The intense emotions that surround sport spectacles "*can be directed only into approved and conventional channels*: like competition or school or national spirit."[17]

As Friedenberg advises us, spectacles are central to the formation and maintenance of nations and nationalistic feelings.[18] Nationalism is brought to life through the visible, ritual organization of familiar objects, for example, flags, uniforms, and anthems, and through collective spectacles such as provided by team sports, military displays, or mass rallies. Media reports of international sports events have greatly expanded and often use the language of the "national interest" when "our" competitors are analyzed and ranked. Questions that underlie such reportage—such as how are "we" going to do? and how have "we" done?—promote an identity with the nation through sport. Writing about British national identity and sports, Hargreaves concludes that the sports ceremonies with national symbols, for instance, flags, parades, uniforms, and anthems, "signal preferred conceptions of national unity which powerfully invoke feelings of identity."[19]

Spectacles such as athletic contests invent nations and at the local level imagine communities. Since all the members of a nation or even a metropolitan area cannot know each other, national and local identities must be *imagined.*[20] Sports spectacles with uniforms, flags, and music are central to imagining the unities of school teams, local communities, regions, or nations. Bissinger's portrait of high school football in Odessa, Texas, overflows with evidence of ritual organization, from the watermelon feed in August to the motorcades of cars and vans trekking to away games; football was the site of Odessa community-making, a "compulsive self-gorging" on ritualized community.[21]

Sports spectacles also take up the "imaginative" role of nationalist spectacle; spectacles can both transform past social relations and reflect authentic cultural values from a common past. Nationalistic spectacles *invent* images of the past to identify what is "new" about current efforts. The Permian Panthers of Permian High School in Odessa, Texas, exhult in the tradition of the enormously successful football team situated within the grim realities of a town consistently named among the ten worst places to live in the United States. "The legends of Odessa football had a deep and abiding sense of place and history, so unlike the town, where not even the origin of the name itself could be vouched for with any confidence."[22] The start of each football season gave townspeople something to live for, which the economically depressed realities of their lives did not.

The townspeople were "desperately devoted" to the football team and considered all the players like their own children, until players were injured. African-American players who were benched reverted especially quickly from beloved sons to no-good blacks. Football in Odessa, Texas, provided an imagined community out of economic boom-and-bust cycles and dust storms, an imagined community with a glorious past (in football victories) and a record-breaking future. In providing emotional spectacles, a sense of history, and a sense of communal identity in relation to outsiders, football mimics nationalism. Emotion is produced through spectacles and stories of success and failure against "outsiders"; this emotion is attached to what the team/community are in the present, thus establishing an emotional connection to a given political order. The desire for success, for power, is yoked to the community's team, or "our guys."

In this section I have argued that sports are intimately linked with war and nationalistic political discourse. The concept of "permanent war" necessitates sports/war/nationalism as a continual process of the militarizing of civil society. Sports events such as the Super Bowl provide the material spectacles, which are a preeminent form of contemporary nation-building. *Spectacles invent group ties, by creating both pasts and futures*; as illustrated in Bissinger's study of one Texas high school team, football calls forth community and scripted emotions and enacts, legitimates, and revivifies a dominant form of social relations. Thus I am postulating a permanent discourse of sports/war/nationalism as the context in which school athletics operate and within which they must be viewed.

The football spectacle as the model of "socially dominant life"[23] will be explored on the individual level with Woody's stories of his football career, his disciplined body, and the social relations of playing and coaching football. I will investigate Woody's narratives of football as parables for a successful teenage career and as policy statements for how young people should act and how society should be organized—as on a playing field. If we are encouraged to imagine schools as "level playing fields" and teachers as "coaches," we need to look more closely at the assumptions about adolescent social relations carried in those images. Woody's life history will help us specify the social relations of football and coaching before examining their implications for teaching.

WOODY'S DISCIPLINED BODY

Woody was a white, middle-class, 20-year-old junior in college, dividing his coursework among physical education, history, and secondary education, when he narrated his own adolescence. Unlike the adolescents he characterized as "trying to become as adult as possible as quickly as possible" or those he described as reactors to stimuli without self-determination, Woody presented himself as always fully rational and purposeful:

> I knew, probably from day three in the womb, I was going to play football. . . . My parents swear on my baby book that the first two words I ever put together were my high school, Holy Cross. They swear that ever since day one, it was just football and that was it. That's all I wanted.[24]

Although he described many of his teenaged friends as confused and acting on whims, Woody portrayed himself as masterful, reasoning, and autonomous.

> I never did anything because I had to do it. . . . I did what I thought was right . . . 99 percent of the time. It wasn't like, Well, I'm in high school now and if I want to be a big, big star, I'm going to play football and get As and Bs. Na, I just lived my life how I was going to do it. . . . Did I

succumb to peer pressure? No, I never did . . . other than like styles or clothes . . . I was just, you know, I think I should do this. It would be right if I did this.[25]

Woody's story portrayed a boy-man[26] who knew exactly what he wanted; he wanted, like other adolescent males, to be an athlete, for boys are judged according to their ability in competitive sports.[27] He pursued his goal single-mindedly except for his eight-month "James Dean" period, which he described with relish:

> I guess my teen years did not start until I was 16, when I got a car. . . . [A]ctually like 14 I bought an old Mustang, '68 Mustang. Me and Dad restored it. . . . When I turned 16, everyone thought I became this big James Dean kid, . . . and I kind of started trying to live up to that attitude. I was driving fast and getting into all kinds of trouble. . . . I was running around with some guys that were a little older than me and they were a lot crazier than I was. . . . [28] After they graduated, [and entered the Marines] I went back and refound myself. . . . The only thing that mattered to me, after the rebel period, was playing football and getting grades, because I had been recruited to play ball by Notre Dame, so I was just kind of straight and narrow. . . . I just kind of wanted to be a football player, go to work, come home, and coach my little brother is all I really wanted.[29]

Except for the lapse of eight months, strategically positioned between the end of one football season and the beginning of the next, Woody never was an adolescent, if an adolescent is rebellious, confused, and prone to be influenced by others. He was purposive and focused, and his life was an orderly progression toward football stardom and academic achievement. He did not *learn* rationality; his orderly development was naturally occurring. Woody's narratives indicated that he had strength of will—"one of the distinguishing marks of the proper male ideal as opposed to so-called weak and womanly men,"[30] a popular male attribute with turn-of-the-twentieth-century boyologists, too.

In describing his younger brother (about to turn 13 at the time of the interviews) and his brother's best friend, Woody elaborated on several dimensions of strength of will: self-directedness, purposive living, decisiveness, and competition:

> Those two kids are more mature than any other kid I've every
> coached. . . . They're not totally independent, but they're in control of
> what's going on. They tell their parents what they want to do instead of
> just sitting back. . . . [T]hey pick out what they want and they take it.
> They are more determining kids.[31]

Being mature is being "in control" and "determining."

When Woody talked about his coaching experiences, he admitted that
he found it difficult to work with kids who were not like himself. The
"lackadaisical athlete" reminded him of his middle brother, an irritant,
who barely made it to practice on time. As a coach, he ran lackadaisical
team members to death, which did not accomplish much but rid him "of
the problems of having to deal with them."[32]

In these excerpts, Woody portrayed several aspects of ideal masculinity
that begins in adolescence: rational, purposive, disciplined, and focused.
Woody and his younger brother remained self-determining, except for
Woody's short "rebel" period. As we track these rational, disciplined, self-
determining men into competitive sports, additional aspects of the social
world governed by football are clarified. Woody's rational, purposive,
focused "citizen" believes he has earned his privilege, believes that his is
the standard for all other team members (and citizens), and rebukes suggestions of pluralistic diversity.

PRODUCING WOODY'S PRIVILEGED POSITION

In this section, I trace some connections between sports and the establishment of a sense of privilege, the belief that one is superior and deserves
special treatment. The limitations of regular people drop away for superior athletes as they receive adulation from fans, families, and the media;
the "pain principle" mandates that they give until it hurts (and beyond),
conferring a sense of superior will and courage. The ability to take pain is
part of the embodiment of masculine privilege that distinguishes strong
men from weak others.

Privilege

In both Woody's narratives and other sociological studies, success in
sports creates a sense of privilege that involves specific material rewards,
status, and an exemption from ordinary routines. In Odessa, Texas, the
football coach began each new season by telling his players, "You guys are

a very special breed."[33] Sociologist Don Sabo recalled the pull toward high school football in very specific terms: "Winning at sports meant winning friends and carving a place for myself within the male pecking order."[34] Girls were part of the bounty won by athletes, as Woody explicitly described: "Our football coach used to always say: 'If you guys win this sectional or if you win this big game, there's going to be girls waiting for you when you get back.' "[35]

Having been deemed special, athletes come to believe that they are "supposed to win—every game" and they count on other entitlements as well.[36] Both Bissinger's report on West Texas and Lefkowitz's account of athletes in New Jersey demonstrate how successful athletes assumed they were above the law. Woody's sense of superiority was also produced through a private school education:

> I competed in Catholic leagues, but then I played football and baseball in the city leagues and . . . the kids I played with, I always thought they had no manners, I was more adult acting than they were. . . . *I just always had an idea in my head that they were lollygagging around all the time while I had to sit and study and learn. Our grade scale was higher, so we definitely thought we were smarter when we graduated.*[37]

Woody's sense of superiority is a phenomenon widely chronicled in scholarship on masculinity and sports, but I am emphasizing its impacts on all young men and young women, when sports stars rule.

Don Sabo connects the privileges of competitive athletics with domination of women and other men. It is a hierarchical system in which men dominate women and a minority of men dominate other men: "The inter-male dominance hierarchy exploits the majority of those it beckons to climb its heights. Patriarchy's mythos of heroism and its morality of power-worship implant visions of masculine excellence and ecstasy in the minds of the boys who ultimately will defend its inequities and ridicule its victims."[38] The social relations of sports create a small group of privileged young men who dominate women and lower-status men, which they learn in their teens.

The Pain Principle

High status athletes must embrace pain; facing pain with courage distinguishes strong men from weak others. Football, of course, is especially brutal. In a recent survey of retired football players, 78 percent reported that they suffer physical disabilities related directly to football, and 66 percent believed that having played football will negatively affect their life spans.[39] "Boys are taught that to endure pain is courageous, to survive pain is manly." Reflecting on his own football career, Sabo writes:

> I learned to be an animal. Coaches took notice of animals. Animals made first team. Being an animal meant being fanatically aggressive and ruthlessly competitive. If I saw an arm in front of me, I trampled it. Whenever blood was spilled, I nodded approval. The coaches taught me to "punish the other man," and to secretly see my opponents' broken bones as little victories within the bigger struggle.[40]

The path to privilege and domination was via becoming an animal. Masculinity draws vigor from animality, a theme that connects contemporary sports with G. Stanley Hall and Theodore Roosevelt.[41] If men are to dominate they must draw upon the primitive, animal energy that competitive sports offers.

Male athletes learn to view their bodies as instruments and thus, while dependent upon their bodies, athletes may also be alienated from them. Bodies may become merely tools or a machine to be utilized. Physical and emotional pain are nuisances to be ignored or minimized, often through the use of alcohol or other drugs. Coming to see the body as an instrument often accompanies violence expressed toward others and ultimately toward oneself.[42]

Athletes who reject the pain principle become pariahs among their teammates, coaches, and fans. Michael Messner tells the story of Bill S., who injured his knee before the state football championship game:

> I was hurt. I couldn't play, and I got a lot of flack from everybody. The coach said, Are you faking it? And I was in the whirlpool and a teammate said "You fucking pussy." That hurt more than the injury. Later, people told me it was my fault that we lost . . . not just other players and coaches, but people in the whole town. It hurt, it just really hurt.[43]

Players with suspicious injuries receive the silent treatment, which often makes them frantic to play: "They will plead with the team physician to shoot them up so they can play. The player will totally disregard the risk of permanent injury."[44]

Painkillers are an illegal but necessary part of the brutal culture of professional football. As National Football League (NFL) medical staffs try to contain the use of prescribed painkillers, players trade tickets or locker room passes to pharmaceutical sales representatives for drugs. Playing in pain is typical in the NFL, since the sport consists of 300-pound guys smashing into one another. Painkillers are a necessity, according to New York Giants quarterback Dave Brown, because: "No one cares about how hurt you are. The coach doesn't care, the fans don't care and the media doesn't care. They just want you to play."[45]

The pain principle causes young men and boys to place efficiency and the goals of the team as priorities and to ignore personal hurts and injuries. In language that often appears in media stories about domestic violence and murder, men become adept at channeling the feelings that boil up inside them into a "rage which is directed at opponents and enemies."[46]

Woody's stories of playing high school football exemplified these themes: the stifling of personal pain; the prioritizing of the team, efficiency, and doing one's best; the trivializing of others' hurts and pains; and the channeling of feelings toward opponents and those who did not subscribe to the same principles that he did. Woody enumerated his injuries as a separated shoulder, a fracture in his left hand, a torn-up ankle, and, of course, his major knee injury:

> When I was a freshman, I got hit by a kid who is the middle linebacker for the University of Illinois now. I actually went unconscious, the only time I've ever been blacked out, and my knee cap was laying on the inside of my leg when they woke me up.

Woody elaborated on playing through the pain, a story that resembled innumerable ones reported by sports sociologists and journalists:[47]

> I played sometimes in so much pain I didn't know if I could make it through the game. I mean my knee would act up in the middle of the game, and I'd come off the sidelines and tell the coach, "I don't know if I can go anymore." He'd say, "You've got to go. You have to do it." It's just that . . . I mean, I never really had, I always had like not bad knees but kind of weak knees, even when I was younger, you know, I would twist it or something. I wore a knee brace from when I was 11 on and . . . I

anticipated it because I always watched ball players get hurt all the time. I mean, I remember when I was little, my dad always wanted me to play regardless. . . . [N]one of us are quitters. They [his parents] never wanted to see anybody quit if you started something. . . . I've always lived by that and always tried to do that as much as I could, play as hard as I could for however long.

Woody restated his perspective on the pain principle:

I just learned I'm not going to live forever and that's how I've always lived, is that I'm going to try as much as I can do. . . . I'll probably get real crippled at some point with arthritis, but I don't care as of now.[48]

The pain principle has an additional implication for social relations off the field. Violent sports support male dominance, not only through exclusion of women but also through the association of males and maleness with sanctioned use of aggression, force, and violence. Thus modern sports help to naturalize the equation of maleness with physical power[49] and to place those values at the center of secondary school life.

In this section, we saw how sports is a means for producing and reinforcing social hierarchy of a small group of men over women and other men and channeling emotions against structurally ordained enemies. But in "permanent war," the enemy can take many forms; and sporting spectacles likewise signify deficiencies and superiorities of class and race.[50]

WEAK OTHERS

My interviews with Woody occasionally moved to educational and public policy and he invariably emphasized hard work within an assumed meritocracy.

I always had to work for whatever I got, so I think everyone should have to do that. . . . No one's going to get anything for free. I don't believe in the free stuff, and I don't care how much you have to work for everything, I won't give grades. I won't give playing time. . . . I've had parents come up to me and holler that my kid's not playing enough. Well, he's not good enough, you know. I'm sorry, he's not, and maybe if he practiced or whatever. I mean, I'm not going to just give anybody anything.[51]

Woody's backing for "the level playing field" image of schooling and social policy became emotionally charged when I queried him on youth rights issues. Woody advocated the prohibition of rights, such as voting, marriage, and so on for persons under 21 years of age: "These kids are so immature, they have no clue of what's going on. . . . You just end up with too many problems."[52] If parents are abusive or neglectful, should a young person be able to instigate a termination of their parents' rights, I asked. Without knowing much about the high profile 1992 case in which "Gregory K." wanted to legally replace his biological parents with more responsible parents of his choosing, Woody wondered whether Gregory K. was just a *whiner*:

> How was his father abusive? What did his dad do? Holler at him? Well, you're a little girl, kid—not little girl, but you know what I mean—little baby. I'm sorry you're a little baby, but things happen. You're going to get yelled at in your life.[53]

Woody adeptly retreated from his gendered denigration of the whining, and made his derogation age-based instead, calling Gregory K. a baby. Woody proceeded to portray teenagers as apt to make up stories about things that happened to them. On a rhetorical roll, he asserted that "35 to 40 percent of date rape is a farce."[54] He was convinced that it was a combination of teenagers lying about what had happened or whining over trivial occurrences. In this way he trivialized both child abuse and date rape, saying that many of these kids were either wimps or liars. Thus Woody demeaned those who failed to endure pain courageously and silently, and identified all "outsiders" as lacking control of their passions.[55] Being tough and macho, the core of competitive, sporting masculinity, became a central criterion for good citizens beyond the playing field—people who complained were seen as wimps and their protests were not taken seriously.

In this section I have highlighted the intertwined construction of privilege through success in high status school sports and the value placed on the attendant discipline and pain. In the deadening of athletes' attention to their own bodies and emotions and in the conscious fostering of an animality to beat the opponent, a complex and volatile brew of reason and emotion results. Woody portrayed himself and other good teenaged athletes as self-directed, autonomous, and rationally moving toward a goal.

He spoke almost lovingly of his disciplined body and mind. Weak or emotional people, notably girls, people of color, and other whiners, were chastised for not being able to take a little of what life offered.[56] Woody's ideas were in line with a broader recasting of national patriotism as "proper public expression, loyal self-censorship, and personal self-discipline."[57] What becomes of this emotionality/rationality construct when Woody moves from coach to classroom teacher?

Traditional, Teacher-Centered Pedagogy Meets the Terminator

Although Woody had coached for years, he had not been a classroom teacher. When we talked about his expectations and fears of teaching, Woody aligned himself *against* images of student-centered teachers who might try to make history and math relevant and try to understand students' lives outside school.[58] Woody's concerns were not for his students but for his coaching career: "I want to teach at the biggest school I can possibly go to. . . . I don't want to be a teacher. I just want to coach football, and you've got to go to a big place to get a good square where you can move on."[59]

Without irony or embarrassment, Woody eagerly fleshed out his version of the highly caricatured, familiar, and strategically upwardly mobile teacher: "I'll be the kind of teacher that . . . puts a movie in two days a week and the other three days gives notes for 35 of the 50 minutes and then says, 'Read your books and I'm going to be up here.'"[60] Woody's description of a perfunctory teacher is focused on what really counts—coaching. On top of the stereotyped social studies teacher, who is also a coach, another image emerged, a fantastic Woody-as-terminator:

> I guess I want to be the . . . one that everybody wants to take as a teacher, but the players are just scared to death of him, you know. They respect him, but they're just scared to death that at any moment he could just blow up and just smash them.[61]

I quote at length here to provide a stronger feel for Woody's authoritative yet playful, boy-man pedagogy, a pedagogy sure to connect with athletic boys:

> I base my teaching, or how I want to teach, on three teachers I had in high school. One was the social studies, one was science, and one was the economics/psychology/sociology type area. The history teacher . . .

was the most popular teacher. He was my football coach. He was the wrestling coach, but he was just laid back. The tests were hard, but as long as you came to class, you knew the material. As long as you took notes and read your notes, you knew the material, nothing more than that. You watched movies a lot, and you watched stuff that interested you and you talked about stuff that interested you. I didn't care if Betsy Ross made the flag. I mean, I could care less if she made it or not, so you didn't talk about that. You talked about Vietnam, something that mattered to you.

And then like my chemistry teacher, he was always in control of the class, but it was always just like right on the verge of just going out of control. You made comments to him and he'd holler back at you . . . but when he wanted control, you [the students] totally were in control. He was in control.

The same with the psychology teacher. You know, discussion is mostly what should occur in psychology and sociology classes, I think, and he'd allow discussions, but when he wanted control, he'd say be quiet and everyone was quiet. I mean those guys were popular because they allowed you to learn basically what you wanted to learn or what they needed you to learn, but they also allowed you to enjoy your classroom.[62]

In these portraits of his own favorite teachers, Woody described a gendered pedagogy that caters to verbal, athletic boys' interests. The teacher ignores the conventional curriculum when it is not interesting [to boys], and the most important things are being in control and having a good time.

When I asked: "What kinds of teaching situations or students will be hard for you?" Woody replied in his hyperbolic mode: "I can't handle idiots." He explained that he had difficulty with "below-level" students: "That's what, I guess, I'm most worried about is not being able to handle the below-level kid."[63]

Woody also railed against what he termed favoritism on the field and in the classroom and he vowed to never give playing time or good grades because of parental pressures, because "everybody's equal. No one's better than anyone else."[64] As noted above, the level-playing-field rhetoric projects an image of fairness and justice on situations where that is far from the case.[65] So, although Woody clearly favored students like himself, he argued that this was giving everyone an equal chance.

In humorous and vivid images, Woody presented his aspirations to be a worshipped teacher who could hammer any male student into obedience in or out of the classroom. He pulled from classroom experiences with three male teachers who promoted discussion of topics that interested him (e.g., the Vietnam War), allowed banter (at which Woody excelled), and drew the disciplinary line in the sand when necessary. The social relations he described were based on male-to-male relationships, with laughter, competitive talking, and put-downs, but always within the teacher's ultimate control. Woody acknowledged that patience, necessary for teaching of diverse students and historically linked with women and nurturing, was not in his repertoire.

Against Multiculturalism

The rage of a white male just beyond adolescence deprived of his privilege surfaced when Woody discussed his experience with the required course on multicultural education.[66] Woody had filed a formal complaint for reverse discrimination against the African-American woman instructor:

> I seriously think that she is the worst teacher that I ever had because everything that she did was to degrade white males. White males were the downfall of everything. White males cause abortion. White males cause black kids not to get educations. White males cause Chinese kids to be, you know, come over here on boats from Bangkok and be sick. You know, the last time I checked, I never chartered a group of aliens over here and I never caused a black kid to not get an education.[67]

The focus of the course on racism in schools and society was intolerable for Woody, who reached his limit one day and recalled giving a "I'm mad as hell" speech:

> I said, "Look, I'm sorry if I have offended anyone for being a White male, but you know this is ridiculous. I'm really pissed, so I'm just going to leave now" and [I] walked out of class. This was in fact during one of our panel discussions. . . . I just got up and left for lieu of later, you know, causing myself to be an ass. . . . In all honesty I was really disappointed with this university at that time.[68]

In these statements, Woody took the position of the beleaguered white male who was held responsible for all the nation's shortcomings. He deflected the criticism by saying that he personally never did any of those things. Woody concluded that he had never been prejudiced and rejected ideas that emphasized past patterns of race relations: "Everything that occurred in that class was prejudged on past racial tendencies, and . . . I don't want that [racial, ethnic, or class discrimination] to occur in anything I've ever done or will do."[69]

I can only describe Woody's response to the multicultural education class as *rage*; and his rage led to contesting his grade and the instructor's approach to the course. That is, he challenged her authority to grade him and her legitimacy in teaching about racism. Given Woody's descriptions of good teachers and his expertise in exerting control over classroom dynamics, pacing, and topics, it is small wonder that he reacted so strongly to the multicultural course. Not only were the social dynamics, topics, and perspectives beyond his control, but his usual privileged position (as clown, as articulate student, as high status student) was diminished. Indeed, his usual position of dominance in classroom dynamics was a topic of the multicultural course, for such patterns perpetuated certain students' achievement.

Although Woody occasionally critiqued high school history courses for presenting a sanitized version of the past, we can expect that his curriculum will remain Eurocentric and dominated by the study of the accomplishments of white men and that his classroom will similarly be dominated by young men who are skilled at athletics and verbal repartee and demand a disproportionate amount of the teacher's time and attention. His appropriation of the traditional image of social studies coach/teacher combined with the ultimate control of a science fiction Terminator offered a contemporary remasculinized coach and teacher, who alternated between entertaining, giving lecture notes, playing the dozens, and putting students in their places.

RE-MASCULINIZING SECONDARY SCHOOLS

> WOODY: Let's put it this way. I'm not going into education because I want to teach children.[70]

Gendered school change—coded as upward mobility; academic rigor; the importance of math, science, and technology; and moral standards—can be viewed as part of a broad remasculinizing of schools, into which Woody fits nicely. When this competitive, point-scoring sense of privilege is established in schools, it will combine with the epistemology of the bunker to hunt down spoilers: critics of athletics, of the academic canon, and of male-centered school practices.[71] When coaches become school administrators, it is nearly impossible for them to see the combination of privilege and violence to others that schools typically enact.

The problems of hypermasculinity in athletics and in gendered violence have begun to receive some national attention as a social problem, no longer completely dismissed as "boys being boys." Nevertheless, given the mounting scholarship on gendered violence and athletics,[72] schools have a long way to go in seeing, understanding, and changing the hypermasculinity that is often synonymous with being a successful teenage boy. This chapter has traced Woody's youthful enchantment with football and how this enmeshment of a teenage boy and sports grounds his orientation toward teaching and coaching the next generation. He remains the athlete-boy as he plans to become the coach-man. His evocative story of boyhood to manhood enacts the early twentieth-century reformers' vision and beliefs on raising courageous, strong-willed leaders. Woody's life accords perfectly with the boyologists' scientific character-building program.

Utilizing critiques of competitive athletics and explorations of the hegemonic masculinity of sports, I have emphasized the social relations produced in football spectacles, with their scripted emotions and linkages with nationalism and war. The hierarchy through unity of competitive athletics, its violence, loyalty, and emphasis on winning are principles that would seem quite distant from classroom life. However, using one preservice teacher's life-history narratives, I began to track the circulation of disciplined bodies, the pain principle, and privilege across fields and classrooms. Woody's ideas about teaching were in part rooted in its unimportance, while coaching counted. Through flashbacks and imaginary forwards, Woody figured himself as a domineering teacher, a boy-man who moved between jokes and serious history, between being the most popular and the most feared teacher. These teaching fantasies gave preeminence in the classroom to those with Woody's characteristics: athletic, joking, articulate, competitive, and masculine. Woody eschewed all student-centered teaching and acknowledged an impatience with all but the best and the brightest.

Education conceptualized as a game open to all players repudiates multicultural education, at least any version that contains a serious examination of structural racism and sexism in schools. Woody's view of the classroom as a level playing field glossed the educational process as an athletic event, with the imputation of fairness and justice; everyone was equal to compete. This perspective, combined with his violent rejection of the existence of racism or sexism (those people just need to stop whining) and the failure to see his own privilege, kept Woody-as-teacher/coach within practices that will connect with the male athletes. The social relations of the gridiron are smoothly embraced within a teacher-centered, level-playing-field approach that is staunchly against affirmative action and antiracist policies and practices. In these social relations, persons who do not hold the same values and physical prowess will be labeled weak or whining and will be dismissed. The hierarchy within the alleged unity of the "team" perspective will prevail in classrooms and curriculum. The emphases on team loyalty, playing by the rules, energetic participation, and self-determination contain strong links to the boyologists' ideas and practices. These values and the practices in which they are imbedded are difficult to question; they are so familiar that few question what and how they teach. The familiarity must be created over and over, of course, but the long tradition begun by turn-of-the-century boy reformers around the inherent value of team sports for the individual, the team, the school, and the nation remains strong.

Competitiveness, aggressive masculinity, dominance, and privilege are key players on and off the football field. If educators and taxpayers accept the inevitability of high status athletics in secondary schools, it is questionable whether the problems of hegemonic masculinity, school management, and hierarchical social relations in the classroom can be raised, much less changed. Woody's narratives raise disturbing questions about "athletic discourse" and its logic of practice in schools.

Furthermore, Woody's ideas are in line with a broader recasting of national patriotism as "proper public expression, loyal self-censorship, and personal self-discipline."[73] Community spirit via athletic spectacles can be seen as a powerful training ground for these new "civic values." In Woody we see the harnessing of affect to a political order via football. The political order he espoused was a peculiar blend of the New Right, team spirit, and can-do masculine football fervor, companioned with a sense of privilege masquerading as merit. The Persian Gulf war was one occasion in which this football-and-nationalistic discourse was clear and wildly popular. That event stands as a reminder of the power of desire linked to nation and mobilized against others. The Persian Gulf war is also a marker of the connections between nation, war, and football, and a glaring instance of the necessity to critique spirit-building events and the related body images, affect, and discipline. Educators must pay heed to the masculinized and racialized spirit embodied and advocated by Woody, for it offered no hope for progressive school change. Woody's version of coaching was not a model for future teachers who will teach an ever more diverse student body. Although the pleasures of playing well and winning football games must be acknowledged, it is imperative to evaluate Woody's perspectives in relation to what we believe the future of public schooling ought to be. Woody's image of himself as Terminator Teacher does not carry the public school toward a more responsible position in society. Nevertheless, the seeming "naturalness" of football and the logic of discipline and pain (present in high stakes testing and zero-tolerance policies, too) make the interrogation of aggressive adolescent boys imperative and still immensely difficult.

When the Romance Is Gone ... Youth Development in New Times 7

A nation's politics becomes a child's everyday psychology.[1]

In Chapter Two I described the boyologists' approach to adolescence as a *romancing* of youth. By this I meant a tendency both to see youth in the best light with rose colored glasses and to emphasize the expansive human potential of youth as a route toward progress or improvement of the human condition. Although this romancing was of white boys and was accompanied by programs and administrative arrangements that fettered the romanticized youth, there was something important and valuable in the boyologists' *devotion* to adolescent development and education, understood broadly. The romantic aspect carried a fair amount of idealism, belief in unlimited potential, and a willingness to invest time and energy in youths' lives. In saying this, I remain aware of the place of both desire and fear in this romantic devotion to youth and to the future they came to represent.

I believe that the romance with adolescence is now over. The almost century-long belief in "child-saving" ended in the United States with the Welfare Reform Bill of 1996, which plunged 60,000 children into poverty.[2] What remains are the bureaucratic arrangements, programs that promote loyalty and team spirit, rhetoric of adolescent stages and raging hormones, and the commodified images of youth in the media. But the love and desire that in part animated the original ideas about adolescent development seem to be turned toward younger children or simply dissipated. Fear and outrage against youth can still be mobilized, as evidenced by the short-lived attention to school shootings, such as in Pearl, Mississippi, and Littleton, Colorado, and Proposition 21 in California, which sought to criminalize youthful legal offenses.[3]

In this chapter I return to a more panoramic view of adolescence, race, gender, and nation and argue that the slow adolescent development prescribed by turn-of-the-century reformers has hit the wall of social welfare downsizing and global economic pressures. The conditions of many youth in both developed and developing countries are rapidly deteriorating. Global economic pressures intensify time and space, making the slow development of middle-class white youth untenable.[4] These changes further support my view of the inadequacy of the ideas and concepts from the child-savers, which this book has articulated. The idea of the developing adolescent utilized raced, classed, and gendered concepts of civilization to frame the path of development. The reasoning around the "developing adolescent" was also firmly grounded on a nearly complete opposition with adult maturity (again, with race, class, and gender characteristics). These concepts have undergirded programs and practices that have had the effect of making gender and race hierarchies more difficult to see and to change. Characterizations of adolescents have repeatedly demonstrated that they wanted and needed dependency.

As I argued in Chapter Four, the temporal ordering of adolescent development is central to narratives and experiences of being teenaged. The panoptical time of youth spurs us constantly to consume this condensed image of adolescence-as-developing and simultaneously to trivialize it. The panoptical time of adolescence is a kind of temporal protectorate in which nothing much can happen, we believe, and we can be lulled into apathy because we know in advance what is supposed to occur. While the developmental framework is supposed to accentuate attention to youth, it also works to mute their conditions largely by way of the temporal narratives, as I detailed in Chapter Four. The global economic pressures and social welfare downsizing make the panoptical time of adolescence especially difficult, because the moratorium/mastery works for an ever smaller group of teenagers. Time and space compressions suggest that youths' lives will continue to be affected by the speedup of global expectations, and that these changing conditions will likely go unrecognized.

INTENSIFYING COMPETITION IN SECONDARY SCHOOLS

Why are secondary schools such unpleasant, hostile, and humiliating places for so many students? Columbine and the other school shootings raise the issue of school cultures and politics. Despite the high-profile nature of the school shootings, most violence by youth is not committed in schools, and overall crime by youth in the United States is down, although the most violent youth crime increased slightly during the 1990s.[5] In this chapter I pursue an etiology of episodes like the Columbine massacre and examine their sources in school culture and the power that some students hold over others. How could some students become murderous toward hundreds of others in their school? The local sheriff concluded that the motive for the Columbine High School killings lay in the two boys' desires to become famous. He looked for sources only in the psychology of two teenagers, but in this chapter I argue that, adapting the (above) quote from Coles, *a school's politics becomes a teenager's everyday psychology*. I imagine that such violence directed against others, as well as the self-directed violence of girls who cut themselves or binge and purge, is in part generated by the politics of the social and academic institution that dominates teenagers' lives.

We have almost come to accept, even expect, that secondary schools will inevitably be hostile places for most students. What are the sources of peer groups and their conflicts, which seem to be central to the successes and failures of secondary schools? Do peer groups and hierarchies become naturalized in the same ways that adolescence is naturalized? When violence (toward others or toward oneself) is threatened or occurs, how do adults respond? Does the discourse of adolescence, which I have laid out in earlier chapters, contribute to the *chains of reasoning* around secondary school practices related to students' peer hierarchies and conflicts? And do school practices in turn confirm deficient views of youth?

This chapter answers these questions with a focus upon the competitive, masculinized nature of secondary schools and the acceptance by secondary school administrators, teachers, and policy-makers of the problems of cliques, competition, and dominance as natural and inevitable. I link the dynamics of secondary schools to the colonial image of adolescence as emotional, becoming, naturally dependent, and confused; the "natives"/ students are, as a mass, semihuman. Those students who speak the teachers' language and share their values share the institutional power. Because adolescent development, like child development, purports to be color-blind and gender-blind, the gender and race of secondary school successes and failures is largely downplayed, invisible to those in power at least. As the last chapter demonstrated, the successes are "our guys," who can make educators and the supporters of schools feel that our policies and practices

are good and working correctly. As global competition and the disman-
tling of the welfare state proceed, amounting to a hyperstratification of
social life, the competitive dynamics in secondary schools are likely to
become more conflict-ridden and less accepting.

Schools Unify and Differentiate

Basil Bernstein's work has been helpful in understanding that school practices, especially those occurring again and again in a ritualized way, have
contradictory effects. Rituals such as school assemblies, sports events, academic competitions, musical performances, and so on, both unify students under the banner of "our school" or "our team" and differentiate
students as athletes and nonathletes, cheerleaders and fans, brains and
nonbrains. A more explicitly politicized interpretation of sports events
suggests that assemblies and games are relatively open spaces which may
contribute to the status quo of schools and communities and/or provide
opportunities for new meanings, politicizations, and resistances.[6]

Historians of American education have also portrayed the comprehensive high school as divided in its aims and methods. As the social-efficiency
approach to curriculum became dominant during the 1900–1920 period
and secondary schools increasingly differentiated students according to
their likely futures in different tracks, extracurriculars such as athletics and
student government were proposed as the unifying and democratic anti-
dotes to curricular differentiations and separations. While the belief that
schools should prepare students for different jobs and lives after high
school prevailed, and as many as 13 different coursework tracks were created to separate and differentiate students, extracurricular activities in student government, athletics, the arts, and service organizations were supposed to unify students. And in British studies of secondary schools,
athletics did sometimes bridge class differences. American schools place
the greatest emphasis on athletics, as evidenced by regular in-school assemblies and the size of athletic programs' budgets, and the emphasis is not on
playing the game well or building character, but on *winning*. Athletics may
unify the school and the community and they may build character, "*provided those teams are successful*." The unifying power of sports needs the
resources to triumph if school spirit is really to be developed.[7]

However, such "balanced" analyses mislead if they lull us into imagining that an *equilibrium* between differentiating and unifying prevails. If
there is some resistance to the stratifying and conservative football
processes, then high school life is not as bad as we might think. The bal-

ance approach also downplays the fierce competition among adolescents for control over the definition, norms, and values of their social and political peer group lives. In U.S. high schools, the competition for recognition and rewards from the school is dominated by a small group of students, and *the social tracking of different peer groups dominates both academic and nonacademic aspects of high schools.* Thus a small group of students, usually identified as Jocks, garners most high status school rewards.

I follow Eckert's definition of Jocks: in a general way, Jocks are the "leading crowd" who are enthusiastic in their participation in school activities and who are in some ways sponsored by the teachers and the school. "The term Jock originated in sports," but it signifies people whose "lifestyle embraces a broader ideal associated in American culture with sports":

> The high school Jock embodies an attitude—an acceptance of the school and its institutions as an all-encompassing social context, and an unflagging enthusiasm and energy for working within those institutions. An individual who never plays sports, but who participates enthusiastically in activities associated with student government, unquestioningly may be referred to . . . as a Jock.[8]

Understanding the norms and organization of secondary schools is necessary to appreciate what this means. Penelope Eckert argues that secondary schools partake of a *corporate organization and culture* in several common features; in other words, high schools expect and produce the following characteristics in students' relationships:

1. Isolation from outside communities
2. Internal hierarchical structures
3. Emphasis on role-oriented individual identity
4. Task-oriented determination of interpersonal associations

This corporate organization matches the Jocks' own social organization: "Hierarchy and competition within a closed corporate community characterize Jock social structure." Because of this close match in norms and values, there is a "domination of productive roles in the school by those who fit the Jock stereotype." Thus as students move from elementary and middle school to high school, students whose lives are in sync with the institution are now "in a position to enjoy ascendancy over their peers in the control of many aspects of the social life of the institution." Jocks have access to information of what is happening and about to happen; some mobility in an age-graded institution; recognition and political contacts from a wide friendship network; the ability to negotiate with and "handle" adults; and certain freedoms (such as freedom from suspicion of wrongdoing) that stem from being trusted by adults.[9]

Given the central position of secondary schools in teenagers' lives, demanding 32 percent of their time, the rewards that the corporate school has to offer go to a few students. Despite public school ideology that they promote democracy and want all students to succeed, secondary schools seem to want all students to be like Jocks. However, the norms of the Jocks are not those of all students. The individualized success, the acceptance of hierarchy, the tacit acceptance of adult authority and oversight, and the tendency to play a role rather than to be oneself—all of these approaches to life are anathema to the Burnouts. The "Burnouts" in Eckert's study saw themselves as more adult, more adventurous, and more egalitarian. They scrupulously resisted adult control at home and at school, and this was one strong turnoff from the corporate culture of the school. They worked against giving adults any control over their lives. They wanted school to apply to their future lives with working-class jobs, and only vocational education courses came close to doing that. Even from a reason-centered analysis, the Burnouts were not positioned to get much that they needed or wanted from high school.

As Jocks ascended to control of school power, the Burnouts rejected school, its values, norms, and activities. They were, of course, rejecting the corporate system, which had already rejected them unless they changed to adopt Jock attitudes and behavior. Their identities and biographies connected them with other schools, neighborhoods, and age groups. The hierarchy and adult authority of secondary schools were repugnant to Burnouts, who demanded an egalitarianism in their relationships. Their social relationships were neither individualized nor narrowly role-determined, such as only having friends from your team sport or your academic track. Their friendships were more heterogeneous, especially across different ages. And "narcing" (that is, informing on others) is the Burnouts' ultimate transgression.

Eckert's portrait of the dynamics of high school peer categories helps us imagine how marginalized boys like Harris and Klebold, despite strong academic abilities and parents' affluence, might have experienced life in school. In schools with high-profile and successful sports teams, and

Columbine High School's teams are always champions, *Jocks rule*. Burnouts and "in between" students might as well disappear, for they were "in the wrong" in their values, style, relationships with teachers, and ability to compete for school rewards. Insults toward lower-status peers are regularly couched in terms of sexuality, gender, and race, with *faggot* and *wimp* vying with racial- and class-based denigrations.

In-between students, those who may have some of the values, interests, and norms of both Burnouts and Jocks, end up having to adjust to a social landscape that is divided into two camps. Although additional settlements of peers may exist, such as visual and performing arts students, the corporate culture may likely push such students toward inclusion on its terms or toward marginal cooperation and thereby a social linking with Burnouts. It is not clear that a corporate model can tolerate more than one set of norms, values, and preferred roles.

Philip Wexler's study of three high schools drops the academic ideology of schools and claims that "becoming somebody" in the school society is the central labor and meaning of schools. His analysis offers further elaboration of the symbolic labor of achieving identity in differently classed schools, although his analysis provides school-specific identity politics in three high schools whose students came from different social class and racial backgrounds.[10]

Eckert emphasizes that adults often "choose to ignore their own role in the development and sponsorship of this society" in which Jocks rule. Since Jocks are skilled at winning teachers' trust, they may all too frequently be "assumed innocent." Rather than examine their own school's corporate culture and their investments in certain kinds of students, teachers are likely to blame bad families, psychologically disturbed youth, and raging hormones for Burnouts' and In-betweens' failures or slipping between the cracks. Furthermore, since high school is the "normalized" social institutional setting for teenagers (prisons and residential treatment centers are the two other "total institutions" that youth may be mandated to attend; malls, video arcades, and part-time jobs are the other places where youth spend time outside their homes), it is increasingly regulatory and increasingly problematic.[11] Because of schools' corporate culture, Jocks are in sync with the values and expectations. They can use the school for their purposes and over time control more and more of the resources. Their association with high status athletics only consolidates their rule. Writing in the late 1980s, Eckert claimed that high schools were getting larger and serving fewer and fewer students in that the few rewards that secondary schools had went disproportionately to a fraction of the students. Eckert explained this in primarily social-class terms, but I want to explore the effects from gender and race perspectives as well.

Schools Are Masculinizing Institutions

The feminist interrogation of gender in schools has led to recent claims that schools are fundamentally masculinizing institutions. Although this argument has been only recently established, primarily through scholarship from Australia and England, even standard histories of U.S. schooling provide ample evidence for the marked flat-out pandering to boys and male teachers almost from the beginnings of mass education in the late 1890s. However, the expansion of schooling during the Progressive Era and its aims for greater efficiency and effectiveness included a thoroughgoing masculinization of secondary schools in both formal curricula and extracurriculars. Graves's history of high schools in St. Louis demonstrates how the move from one common academic-focused curriculum to multiple curriculum tracks diminished the position of girls who had distinguished themselves in the classical course of study. As commercial studies grew in popularity, boys dominated the most visible courses of study and their interests became normalized as central.

Thus the vocationalization of secondary schooling, at least in the North, was simultaneously a masculinization. The decline of academic-focused studies was coincident with the value placed upon keeping boys in secondary schools. Bissell-Brown documents the replacement of Los Angeles high school girls' athletics, despite their state basketball championships, with boys' sports and the demotion of girls to cheerleaders as central features of attracting and keeping more boys in school. School leaders and, I assume, taxpayers also worried about girls' school success over that of boys. Secondary schools hired more male teachers with higher pay than their female colleagues; enhanced extracurricular programs; especially athletics; and offered increasingly practical courses of study, because "[b]oys . . . were more perceptive than girls of the sham of the academic studies." As noted in Chapter Two on the boyologists, there was widespread fear of the feminization of boys in female-dominated schools and homes. Thus schools were masculinized in curriculum, in extracurriculars, in preferred teachers, and in value placed upon boys' over girls' retention.[12]

Vocational education was also racialized, most visibly in the South. Classical academic programs of study were deemed irrelevant for black students, and most of them were denied secondary education until the

1940s because school philanthropists and local whites wanted them to have only the minimal vocational education, an education for life. In urban areas like New York City, students could often choose from a wealth of different school programs, some of which were theoretically racially integrated and coeducational. Nevertheless, black students were often treated worse in integrated schools or outright rejected.[13]

One accompaniment of this early white masculinization of secondary schooling is a blindness to its presence and effects, especially those related to the status and privilege of high status males, most often male athletes. Athletics' effects on school retention remains a truism of secondary education today, often repeated by male teachers and teachers-to-be: "If it hadn't been for football (or basketball or baseball), I wouldn't have stayed in school." It suggests that, consciously or unconsciously, athletics are believed to keep boys in school. But a focus on athletics does much more, as I have suggested above. Athletics and a masculinizing school firmly legitimate the reign of white hegemonic masculinity, with its dominance of girls, students of color, and less-masculine boys. I turn to this topic in the next section.

Global Competition and the Remasculinizing of Schools

Many commentators on schools have promoted smaller schools and the creation of school communities as the response to issues of violence as well as school dropout, truancy, and achievement issues. I agree with this assessment, and I conducted studies of schools in this vein several years ago. However, I want to emphasize the contemporary pushes and pulls in secondary schools that remain quite traditional in size, ethos (e.g., the shopping-mall high school), and fragmentation. In other words, I want to address schools that will remain the norm, although small changes—for example, advisory groups or therapeutic services—may make them seem more humane. Rather than just focus upon individual youth who shoot others, or their families, I wish to focus upon the relationships between schools as masculinizing institutions and the escalation in global competition and conflict, which are also masculinizing forces.

I am arguing that violence in schools, which takes various forms, must be understood as a remasculinizing, or a hypermasculinization, that echoes and responds to global competition. I refer back to the last chapter on "our guys," the football team, the teenagers who are doing it right, whom we hold up as successes. In this chapter, I lay out an analysis of the contexts in which Woody's (see Chapter Six) views are reasonable and popular. In other words, *I examine the chains of reasoning in which competition, sports, standards, and hypermasculinity are intertwined and valued, and within a school logic of dominance and absence of compassion for "losers," student-to-student harassments are simultaneously created and tolerated.* When the system erupts in public (school shootings, fights, and harassment) or private (eating disorders or self-cutting) violence, the system can only blame isolated individuals, promise to be more watchful for "early warning signs," or hire anger management experts. The system appears unwilling to examine itself.[14]

Global Economic Competition

Although it is beginning to sound clichéd, the swell of global economic competition increases the overall emphasis on becoming and staying competitive that we witness in businesses, as the rationale behind educational vouchers, and in school standards. This is not a phenomenon just in the United States but worldwide, although unevenly disbursed. According to David Harvey, flexible accumulation of capital produces a postmodern condition of fragmentation, ephemerality, discontinuity, and chaotic change. He makes much of time space compression which would likely intensify pressures on people as "modern developing time" is cracked by technological and capital flows across space. I believe that the heightened speed and flexibility of capital accumulation demands a competitive quickness that promotes increased competition in all domains of life.[15]

The Welfare Wars

The global economic developments would not likely have been sufficient unto themselves, but the concomitant rise of the New Right and the erosion of welfare state policies is a second substantive movement toward competition and a new social Darwinism, a second-millenial struggle for survival of the fittest. The welfare wars in the United States have meant the legitimation of rhetoric and policies that are selfish and mean spirited and that move toward more blatant punishment strategies toward the have-nots (as opposed to intact welfare policies which discriminated in more subtle ways). The political elites and conservatives have revolted and refuse to support social groups through welfare programs such as Assistance for Families with Dependent Children (AFDC).[16]

I am most interested in the chains of reasoning that surface successfully in these welfare wars. Other people's children are no longer to be protected by society at large; decent living conditions and good schools are no longer considered a "general welfare" issue in which wealthy and poor citizens alike have some broad *interest*. If Michael Katz is correct, the sound bite of turn-of-the-century reformers who established the progressive foundation of the modern welfare state was "child-saving." The sound bite of the New Right reformers is "self-sufficiency," which means something quite different for the haves who receive welfare subsidies through government contracts to local governments and corporations. Welfare for corporations remains invisible from the self-sufficiency criticism.

The rhetoric of self-sufficiency, despite the obvious political economy of networks and patronage, resonates with many who have felt outside the welfare state's (seeming) largesse, beyond the East Coast corridor of power, who believe they have "worked for what they have" and others should do it, too. No matter that white skin color or educational background or affirmative action policies provided the first few (unmarked) steps up the ladder of success.

Taking the global economic pressures for fast, flexible capital and absence of responsibilities to workers, environments, or human living places such as cities and towns, along with the cries for "self-sufficiency," we have the portrait of a society that is becoming more focused on the creation of e-millionaires and television game shows with high stakes than on educating "other people's children." Only one's own children count, but even they must measure up, in school and in the "leisure curriculum."[17]

SOURCES OF "RIGOR" IN CHILDHOOD AND ADOLESCENCE

I argue that the enhanced competition of fast-track capital and the replacement of welfare supports with demands for self-sufficiency have begun to effect changes in students' relations, in the politics of secondary schools, and in the enhanced rigor of schools being promoted through high-stakes testing. The effects are diffuse and yet marked, as the following snapshots suggest.

- There has been a movement away from appreciation of and support for the "slow and demanding process of becoming literate" synonymous with childhood and youth, accompanied by the technologically quickening of success or failure.[18] In Chapter Six, for example, Woody displayed sharp criticism for those who were not aggressively self-determining and tough, and, in Chapter Five, Melanie described that for her, being a teenager was synonymous with always being judged "less than" someone else as a valued friend, as a student, or as a romantic interest. If Jocks' values resonate with school norms, we witness the schools' practices in Woody's perspectives.

- Pressures for increased "rigor" in secondary schools take various forms. One marker was the 1983 report by the National Commission on Excellence, appointed by President Ronald Reagan, entitled *A Nation at Risk*. It bemoaned the tide of mediocrity in U.S. schools, indicated by so few students enrolling in advanced math and science courses, as analogous to military disarmament, and linked America's ability to compete economically with students' academic courses of study and their achievements in rigorous, advanced subjects. That report seems to have been the battle cry to raise standards in schools, with the twin policies of high-stakes testing (adopted by over 30 U.S. states' legislatures) and educational vouchers. While the standards-and-testing approach aims to raise all students' achievements, vouchers foster competition between schools. Thus competition is intensified both between students and between schools.

- The global spread of youthful competitive sports is another domain in which fast-paced accomplishments are given very high-profiles. The increasing net of competitive sports (girls and women are new markets) educates all of us about what a valued person is like: "[A] person is competitive, a person dominates (his) body, a person dominates nature and technology, a person dominates time (measured in increasingly small fractions)."[19] The valued person is usually male but can be female. Certainly participation in sports offers many advantages, such as increased self-esteem, sense of accomplishment, and greater physical strength and endurance, among others.[20] Especially for girls, sports may teach competition that balances out the supposed collaboration that is often preferred. Nevertheless, the hypervisibility and status of competitive athletics supports my analysis of increasing competitive pressures.

- Sports and competition are also a familiar route to nationalism. Other spectacles also support flags, uniforms, and marching bands, but global sports spectacles such as the Olympics provide a perfect spectacular package tied into nationalism.[21] As I demonstrated for turn-of-the-century England and the United States, the demands of empire brought boys' physical and moral health into the spotlight. Similarly now, the feverish competition, team loyalty, and incitement to win are experiences that can lead to successful entrepreneurship as well as be funneled into nationalistic aggression.

- Schools respond to potential student violence by becoming more like prisons, which, as we know, are anything but safe. Zero tolerance policies are appealing because they suggest a return to learning-centered and orderly schools, but they impose a punitive and arbitrary juvenile justice system mentality and cannot take into consideration students' understandings of safe and unsafe zones, both in school and between home and school.[22] Zero tolerance means that the moratorium of adolescence has been greatly shortened for some, while others still have time to accumulate credits in the leisure curriculum.

- White, suburban, young men who feel left behind in the escalating global competition and see women and people of color taking away their jobs and benefits are responding by taking up white supremacist ideology. A recent report by the Southern Poverty Law Center, which tracks hate groups' activities, states that "a larger—and, apparently, growing—crop of white supremacist youth has sprung from the soil of socioeconomic discontent."[23] Thus the negative effects of the speeded up global competition also reach beyond school territories into community life, extending hate and intolerance.

These various dimensions raise the visibility of success, making it more important to be valued by others but still inaccessible to many young people. The media trumpets the need to compete, now and always, and provides innumerable scenarios in "news," entertainment, and sports programming that endlessly show us those who "have it." The have-nots may be pitied but are usually ignored. Celebrities from politics, Hollywood, and sports and captains of e-industries shower us constantly with their success stories. Teenagers are famously attuned to those around them, watching and listening closely. Teenagers are thus primed to accept the escalation in competition and dominance that everywhere besieges us.

Reasserting Racialized and Gendered Institutional Power

Stuart Hall argues that the 1990s witnessed a return of recharged nationalism in England and elsewhere which was an effort to restore national culture as the primordial source of national identity. Studies of U.S. film and literature after the Vietnam War evidence a broad social remasculinization that emphasized women's and people of color's subordination. Some studies of secondary schools also document the resurrection of nationalism and attendant masculinities. Lynn Davies finds that a particular version of masculinity—"competitive, point-scoring, overconfident, sporting, career and status conscious" has come to dominate school management. Roger Rees concludes that "'win oriented' or 'achievement' sport is becoming a worldwide phenomenon and that economic factors are playing a major role in its spread."[24]

Mac an Ghaill's description of the masculinities of teachers in one secondary school supports these "winning" conclusions: Mac an Ghaill found a resurgence of English nationalism, which was linked to boys learning their place through coercive discipline and to a professionalism yearning for the old days of all-male schooling and enacting some of that past by emphasizing traditional "masculine" subject areas, such as natural sciences, mathematics, and competitive team sports. Mac an Ghaill's detailed ethnography of Parnell School evidenced multiple masculinities, some associated with nationalism and others with the global technopoly.[25]

Sports is one particular passion of this regendering of schools. But "rigor" is another approach to making school more competitive, efficient, and productive. Increased rigor in school programs points toward traditional kinds of methods and materials, for the language of "rigor" does not make sense, for example, in the performing or visual arts. Rigor typically means more pages of reading and more writing assignments. Rigor also reinscribes conventional forms of evaluation which push toward objective and positivist understandings. We also have a good idea of which students are likely to respond to calls for greater rigor—those who are certain that schooling will pay off well. High-stakes testing is another component of this remasculinizing movement in which students must prepare and perform, prepare and perform, in a constant evaluation mode. At the policy level, vouchers have won support in many states as the best way to promote competition and school excellence.[26]

What kinds of emotional tenors are associated with this interpretation of changes in schooling? Certainly, with an increase in expectations for self-sufficiency, there is a lot less tolerance for "disorder," "whining," and exceptions. Despite well-publicized curricular reforms around multiculturalism and anti-sexual harassment efforts, secondary schools are likely to promote informally a narrower normed idea of what a good student is and does. Certainly, more of a focus on physical dominance through pumping iron, competitive athletics, and, unfortunately, harassment of perceived weaker students is occurring. In short, hegemonic masculinity is reinforced, ever more vitally performed, and strictly enforced. Fewer gender border crossers may be tolerated. For girls there may be a stronger pressure for clearly emphasized femininity. Gender-bending and outright homosexuality will continue to be punished among students. I expect an enhanced emphasis on emotional choreography of noncontroversial perspectives, such as in school spirit, patriotism, community service, and academic achievement.[27]

EFFECTS ON STUDENTS AND PEER RELATIONS

The possible effects on students of increased normative discipline—to be school-spirited and sports-obsessed, to accept that the domination of the athletes and other privileged groups is right and meritocratic, and so on—are both multiple and large and small. If fitting in and being accepted necessitate ever finer proscriptions, students may be humiliated and resistant in various ways. Gendered differences suggest that girls are more likely to turn their hurt inward, and eating disorders and self-cutting are two widespread expressions of lack of control over one's environment. The calls for increased rigor suggest a tightening of discipline and control over youth's movements. This may produce ever greater senses of frustration and lack of control over their lives.

If Columbine High School illustrates this new school order, the complaints of Klebold and Harris offer ideas about the effects on nonathletic students. They were called fags, made fun of, and humiliated for being emotional and lacking self-control. They had feelings and showed them, which is proscribed except for scripted emotions of team loyalty, ritualistic put-downs, and righteous anger. It is a complete trap—school controls the majority of a teenager's life and most of that is outside personal choice and control. If one is constantly hounded and disrespected during those unending hours spent in school, it is easy to imagine the situation as intolerable. The Secret Service has been conducting research on people who attempt assassinations of U.S. presidents and has described the assailants as having uniformly experienced repeated and prolonged humiliations. Writing of Australian schools, Kenway and Fitzclarence similarly document the horrific and lasting impacts of taunting, bullying, and other harassments and humiliations.[28] And there is no escape; regardless of a young person's response to tauntings, he or she can be additionally degraded as emotional, a wimp, as well as the other epithets already strung together. This is by no means a justification for killing, but it is an attempt to understand the impact of the hypercompetitive, corporatized social order on both marginalized and dominant kids.

As I have argued in Chapter Three, a political response that targets individual crazy kids or violent youth is a limited, conservative approach to the problem. Youth must be seen within a broader context, which means understanding the relationships among the powerful and the less-powerful in adolescent society and in adult-controlled institutions.

SUMMARY

I began this chapter with questions of how to understand not only school shootings like the incident at Columbine but also the increasing evidence that life in secondary schools is hostile, violent, and often intolerable. I understand the normative order of secondary schools, and the ability to maintain "business as usual" despite high-profile, international media attention to problems, to be in part connected to the discourse of adolescence. My tentative anlaysis of why secondary schools are increasingly awful places is because of a process of restratification through increased rigor and pressures to compete. Students are to compete in athletics and on high-stakes tests; teachers have begun to be evaluated and ranked on the basis of their students' test scores; and vouchers force schools to compete against other schools. These pressures to achieve in highly visible ways are accompanied by youth's weakening position *vis-à-vis* senior citizens and young children. These changes may be further exacerbated by a narrowing of acceptable social roles within schools (or less tolerance for a broad range of social roles). These bureaucratic arrangements are contextualized within and influenced by a nationalistic exhortation to compete harder and better. Be tougher and more rigorous and have zero tolerance, proclaim our state legislatures, school boards, and educational policy-makers! The broader U.S. society and our schools boastfully advertise these traits and their benefits, yet we expect our teenagers to follow another generation's path of sexual abstinence, belief in authority, and living for the future.

Schools are based upon adult authority over youth, with teenagers usually understood as passive recipients of adult rules, knowledge, and resources. Some students accept and thrive in this adult-centered system, but secondary schools succeed with a diminishing proportion of adolescents. As described in this chapter, adults perpetuate a particular kind of violence through neglect of marginalized students and through failure to understand their own investments in the success of one group, typically the Jocks. As socioeconomic pressures accelerate competition, adolescents in school are bombarded with prerequisites for them to be valued by others and by themselves. Unfortunately, schools are largely conducting business as usual, distracted by high-stakes testing, and with little attention or resources devoted to peer group dynamics, intolerance, harassment, and other forms of "poisonous pedagogies."

Cutting Free from the Great Chain of Being

8

Toward Untimely Teenagers

> An untimely attitude to our present [is] one that is capable of "acting counter to our time and thereby on our time, and, let us hope, for the benefit of a time to come."[1]

This book is the result of my efforts to think in "untimely" ways about youth. My interest in doing so arose from many interactions with "real" teenagers, social science research on youth, and theories of adolescence and from my own dissatisfaction with how youth were represented in scientific and popular cultural texts. Youth were usually presumed to be deficient, a little crazy, controlled by hormones, and educators and parents were warned that their actions and effectiveness were always broadly circumscribed by teenagers' immaturity, by their being in transition. Thus it seemed that a circular reasoning was in place, and I went from hormones to peers to self-esteem to age and back again in attempting to get out of the loop of common sense. The common characterizations of youth, I slowly realized, comprised a sealed system of reasoning, and the inability to talk and think about youth outside the discourse of "adolescent development" limits educators and parents in considering how different interactions and schooling practices might in effect make adolescence different. Thus a belief in the social constructedness of youth and age was one starting assumption of this work.

Static ideas about youth have helped to keep in place a range of assumptions and actions in and out of secondary schools. For example, since adolescents have raging hormones, they can not be expected to do sustained and critical thinking, reason many educators. Since adolescents are immature, they cannot be given substantive responsibilites in school,

at work, or at home. And since there has never been a shortage of anec-
dotes and images about this "separate tribe,"[2] teachers, parents, social
workers, and psychologists, among others, have always been able to
muster evidence to demonstrate their deficiencies. Another set of images
and feelings shadow these immature and irresponsible characterizations.
When teenagers take on forbidden adult behaviors, from having sex to
breaking laws, they become monstrous. The boys who killed people in
American schools in the late 1990s, for example, could only be understood
as inhuman and outside of society and human relations, as criminals who
were banished and punished. This is the effect of seeing adolescents as natural beings who exist outside of social life and relations; when kids go
bad, society is helpless and our only recourse is punishment.

This circular reasoning is a problem, I believe, especially for educators.
In the process of conducting research in numerous public, private, and
alternative schools, I came to understand how conceptions of adolescence
play a "conserving" role; that is, unexamined assumptions about youth are
a foundational element of secondary schooling that helps make traditional
ideas of teaching and curriculum reasonable and necessary. How can
teachers be expected to have in-depth discussions of, say science and the
environment, with all those raging hormones in a classroom? Commonsense ideas of adolescence are a grounding element in the edifice of
teacher-centered and authoritarian schooling practices. By interrogating
the assumptions and chains of reasoning around adolescence, I aim to
contribute to a broader rethinking of educational aims and practices.

Given this set of overarching hypotheses and interests, this project has
both theoretical and practical aims. Theoretically, I wanted to explore how
the idea of adolescent development was created in specific historical circumstances primarily through the new sciences of psychology, anthropology, and pedagogy and through "child-saving" reformers working in
juvenile justice and in organizations such as the YMCA and scouting.
Moreover, I questioned how youth were conceptions "in and through
time," that is, how age and ideas about history (in other words, ideas
about past, present, and future) were and are central to how we think
about adolescence. Because of these theoretical or conceptual aims, I
entered into interdisciplinary conversations about how specific areas of
study and their related theories are connected to broader social debates,
such as what we mean by a rational adult, a productive citizen, femininity
and masculinity, "race," maturity and immaturity, and proper sexuality,
among others.

In tracing "adolescent development," I have taken its contemporary stage, or step, structure as central and I have thus emphasized how developmental stages of adolescence mimic or reenact a particular view of evolutionary theory, as it was understood in the late 1800s and early 1900s, primarily in the United States. The mimicking of evolutionary theory means several things for conceptions of adolescent development. First, it means that adolescent theory has been about developing people according to raced, classed, and gendered experiences and criteria formulated in the West. As I have noted, this means that "adolescent development" has been about creating and endlessly re-creating whiteness and developing masculinity, which were seamlessly fused and unmarked in "civilization" at the turn of the twentieth century. These dimensions within adolescent development have gone largely unrecognized.

Second, adolescent development has been driven by an imperative for individual improvement and "higher" achievements in cognitive, emotional, and psychological understandings. Because this developmental demand seems to come from nowhere, we are barely aware of its pull toward a certain set of characteristics that define maturity, rationality, and responsibility, and the simultaneous demotion of other possible definitions of adulthood. The hierarchy and selectivity are muted. Third, the evolutionary roots of adolescence impose a strong interest in *the future* over the present or the past; one eye is always on the ending, which spurs the documentation of movement or lack of it toward the desired characteristics. The temporal movement into the future is understood as linear, uni-directional, and able to be separated from the present and the past. Finally, evolutionary theory was part of broader histories with particular problems and concerns. When adolescent theory of development echoes evolutionary theory certain problems are prioritized, for example, How do we help young adults to become more responsible or How do we keep teenagers from "gateway drugs?" A continued emphasis on evolutionary-like development means that certain problems and questions will remain priorities and alternative questions and needs will be elided.

Some scholars who have recognized the partiality and selectivity of developmental stages have proposed alternative sets of stages, say for women or for youth of color. Although this approach has been important, I see it as ultimately limited. To argue that Asian-American children have a different developmental trajectory or that girls may develop moral reasoning in distinctive terms is to challenge the universalizing discourse of developmental stages with a minoritizing one, which states that particular minority groups have different needs or patterns of growth.[3] Under this critical stance various "minority" differences flourish, but the universal stance remains untouched. I think that the minoritizing discourse is a mirror image of the universal perspective, and we flip-flop between them. Furthermore, making minority claims "stick" to an abstracted, universalized adolescent is hard and the universal adolescent remains as the grounding idea.[4] My approach has been to challenge the underpinnings of all developmental schema, universal and minority, in order to consider ideas of teenagers that do not rely on evolutionary trajectories and linear temporality. Thus, a more useful target remains the development-in-time epistemology that has dominated modern adolescence.

We can think of "adolescent development" as being, like former U.S. president Ronald Reagan, Teflon-coated; critical assessments and specific historical and sociological questions slide off it. Attempts to point to specific youth are easily wiped away. The power of this one set of ideas to define and redefine youth in generalized and abstract ways is not inevitable, and it was produced by human beings. Our inability to think differently about youth with and through "adolescent development" has been the central problem and project of this book. In order to reenvision adolescence and their growth and change, I had to go after the Teflon coating.

Linking adolescent development with the Great Chain of Being, with Western imperialism, and with the imperative—*Become civilized!*—has been the key to chipping away at the Teflon coating. My title, *Act Your Age!*, with its exclamation (i.e., the directive to do it now!) carries within it an older imperative: Become civilized! I have drawn from other historians' and theorists' work to demonstrate how adolescence and its status as always "becoming" are interwoven with the cultural and historical emphases on progress defined in limited ways. The value and preoccupation with becoming civilized occurred as the U.S. was establishing an international empire as well as keeping a particular "civilized" social order at home, which involved keeping white middle-class men dominant. In addition to imbedding hierarchies based on race and gender, adolescent development also spoke to the context of building a nation with an international reach, the third theme of my analysis. Building a nation and an empire put a positive valence on developing human capital and producing useful citizens. In Baden-Powell's efforts in Great Britain in and around the Boy Scouts I see this citizen/worker theme of adolescent development most clearly articulated.

I have consciously interspersed chapters of historical analysis with contemporary interpretations to highlight the continuing significance of the turn-of-the-century ideas and to illustrate that "past," "present," and "future" are more interwoven and enfolded than discretely marked segments along a unidirectional chronology of progress. Alternating past and present echoes a view of history as recursive. In the problem of teenage pregnancy, for example, I see another iteration of the command to "become civilized." The route to and the definition of that "civilization" bear the stamp of particular values, social positions, and interests. Teenage pregnancy is a problem that should be avoided because it interferes with a smooth transition into being a member of a good family, a good worker, and a good citizen. Teenage pregnancy is avoided by abstaining from active sexuality and becoming deeply immersed in the communities and houses of middle schools, for example. This kind of rhetoric and reasoning was as familiar and comfortable in the early 1900s as it is today.

In addition to questioning the epistemological foundation of "adolescent development," I have also examined how sets of concrete practices, such as team sports, help support particular reasoning around youth. I believe that the ideas and theories are created at the same time as concrete programs and practices that help make the theories believable and reasonable. For example, I traced how our current belief that youth are "peer-oriented" may be an effect of strategies of the early twentieth-century reformers. As a tactic to exert control over youths' behavior even when the adults were not present, reformers emphasized team games and other ritualized practices, in which teenagers would "supervise" other teenagers. It appears that the practices of youth-watching-youth were invented, or at minimum enhanced by reformers' emphasis on group activities to structure leisure time. Today peer pressure has taken on a life of its own—segmented from adult interventions and understood as part of adolescent pscyhology—and become a new social problem to be remedied by yet another group of scientists and reformers. The historical problems and their contexts within which peer dynamics were discovered, utilized, and intensified remain obscured, while the "facts" of adolescents as naturally occurring beings are highlighted. To work against this tendency to see youth as natural beings, I have historicized psychological theory and interpreted the "facts" of adolescence as the effect of a "splitting" off of power and authority; so while the adolescent hugs the spotlight, the political machinations such as who has the ability to make choices, to force others' actions, and so on, remain in the shadows.

In closing, I pull out important dimensions of this recursive discourse of adolescence that I think must be revisioned if we are to have a chance for different youth and different relationships with youth. As I argued in Chapter Seven, inherent inadequacies and social changes make the continued use of progressive-inspired, romantic ideas about young people impossible. I conclude that *we must seek to advocate for young adults and children in new ways*, because neither abandoning them to the global economy nor reiterating the well-worn claims for developmental needs will suffice. In order to advocate for teenagers in different terms, we face three substantial challenges. To reason differently, we need three revisions: in the conception of young people's growth and change; in the relations among past, present, and future; and in our articulation of public problems and their implications for definitions of adolescents' "needs."

ALTERNATIVE CONCEPTIONS OF GROWTH AND CHANGE

"Development" rules in the discourse of adolescence. As I have indicated, this conceptual framework has a legacy that includes racism, sexism, and classism and works to reinstate social hierarchies. Another problem with development is that it generally refers to what occurs at the intraindividual level, and it is hard to paste on context to what is essentially an individualized phenomenon. Thus we want a concept for growth and change that allows us to see and talk about collective social practices as well as individual responses to broader social contexts. These problems with psychological theory have been widely discussed, but they continue to cripple thinking otherwise.[5]

Running a close second to development is the idea of "socialization." It is hard to talk about children or young people without invoking the term socialization, which suffers from some of the same problems as development. Although socialization of girls or of a young man of color can be discussed because processes grounded in group and social structured involvements are significant, the process of becoming socialized remains unidirectional, as with development. There is also an assumption that socialization occurs in a straight line, one thing after another, so a blizzard of socializing factors is unlikely to be considered. Most importantly, socialization implies a profound passivity of young people. We all accept that teenagers are socialized into peer groups' norms, for example, which suggests that they are mindlessly duped and overcome. Conceptions of children and youth portray them as "oversocialized," passive, without critical awareness or active agency.[6]

If we try to move away from "development" and "socialization," what other possibilities exist? A common response to this question is to produce a combination framework—that adolescent growth and change are a result of an interaction between individual characteristics and traits and social influences and opportunities. I do not think this solves our dilemma, because the individual remains without a context and passive when he or she comes into contact with social dynamics. It retains the original two concepts but tries to give them equal weight rather than making us choose between individual development or group socialization.

One part of charting a path toward some new prospects is finding a theoretical framework that heightens our awareness of how individuals are necessarily always active, social beings. I see several theoretical possibilities that might help us reconceptualize adolescence growth and change. Scholars utilizing feminist theories to examine gendered identities have provided us with conceptual frameworks that seem to allow for collective social practices and individual movement within and across those. R. W. Connell and Máritín Mac an Ghaill, for example, discuss how men become masculine through collective social practices. In this work there is attention to the specific agency and meaning-making of individuals, but always within the collectively identified and historically provided contexts and range of possibilities. Poststructural feminists, such as Bronwyn Davies and Valerie Walkerdine, also offer discursive constructions within which individuals must articulate positions. Even though the positions are theoretically unlimited, Wendy Hollway,[7] for one, argues that once a mainstream position has been articulated, if you want to talk back to it, relatively few powerful options exist. This means that individual agency is constrained at any given time.

What I am suggesting here is that ideas of growth and change must be investigated and not presumed in *a priori* frameworks such as development or socialization. Work on the construction of masculinity and femininity provides some useful perspectives on the necessary sociality of identities. A related issue with development and socialization is that they are rationalized concepts, while growth and change are highly contingent, not cumulative but, rather, recursive. I think that if we assumed that growth and change are *contingent*, we would need to specify the contingencies and that would lead us to examine and document multiple microcontexts. I also think that a conception of growth and change as *recursive*, as occurring over and over as we move into new situations, would reorient us. Rather than the assumption of cumulative and one-way development that is now in place in both science and popular culture, a recursive view of growth and change directs us to look at local contexts and specific actions of young people, without the inherent evaluation of steps, stages, and socialization.

CONCEPTIONS OF TIME: PAST, PRESENT, AND FUTURE

The linear, unidirectional, and cumulative conception of growth, development, and change of which adolescence is a part participates in a view of history that is more like war, in which the present always overtakes the past. It seems obvious that as we advance in time, "each successive stage outstrips the preceding one." But Michel Serres replies that such a sense of time is "a trajectory of the race for first place—in school, in the Olympic Games, for the Nobel Prize. This isn't time, but a simple competition— once again, war." Serres replaces the modern belief of time with this conception: "[T]ime alone can make co-possible two contradictory things."[8] So, if we are to radically remake adolescence, we will have to revise our idea of time, and, relatedly, of history.

In thinking about the relations among past, present, and future, we are used to assuming segments of life and segments of time which are cut off from other parts. The concepts of childhood, adolescence, and old age suggest radical changes and differences between those times of life. I want to hold onto Serres's idea that in time we can be two contradictory things, which he illustrates by saying that he is "both old and young." He also maintains that "the temporal rupture is the equivalent of a dogmatic expulsion."[9] This "dogmatic expulsion" is what I have called the opposition between children and teenagers or between youth and adults. Applied to adolescence, Serres's ideas suggest that youth can write off adults as old and obsolete, responding in kind to the system of reasoning that stipulates teenagers as immature and inferior. Somehow a remade adolescence must take up the contradictions of being simultaneously mature and immature, old and young, traditional and innovative. These contradictions are explored in various texts, fictional and sociological. For example, Johanna Wyn, following in the tracks of Buchmann, argues that youth are simultaneously young and old, learning and learned, working and in school.[10] This idea of time (that is, of past, present, and future) as holding seemingly opposing identities *simultaneously* is, I believe, a necessary dimension of a retheorizing of adolescence.

I think that we need to work against both the idea of unilinear, competitive (who will get there fastest) time and our desire and willingness to consume images of youth within panoptical time. In order to do this we must hold on to a sense of the oppositions within time that Serres, Wyn, and Buchmann, among others, note. If we look toward adults' lives to suggest how education might proceed, we must simultaneously consider how youths' lives and ideas can also inform and transform adulthood. Shifting from clock time, the time of development, requires both new language and new images of time. Serres suggests that we think of time as folds or sieves, as passing but also not passing: "Time doesn't flow; it percolates. This means precisely that it passes and doesn't pass." Serres is certain in his disagreement with the classical theory of time as a "line, continuous or interrupted." His view is more chaotic; "Time flows in an extraordinarily complex, unexpected, complicated way."[11] If time percolates through a filter, then some aspects pass through and others do not; if time is imaged as a fold, some aspects of the past are folded right next to the present and other aspects of the past are farther away. Theorizing adolescence as a simultaneity of contradictions may be necessary to allow it to escape the temporal trap of linear, cumulative development. The global economy and mobilities of people, information, and technologies suggest more fluidity and simultaneous experiences in people's growth and change. These reformulations are likely to spur reconsiderations, or at least allow us to speak of possibilities. However, we must also advocate for youth differently and describe their needs differently.

REDEFINING YOUTHS' "NEEDS" THROUGH NEW "PUBLIC PROBLEMS"

Might adolescence have a future that is different from the past that I have sketched above? If *adolescent development* was part of a broad response to making citizens and adults differently in the beginning of the twentieth century, it originated as part of an answer to a set of problems. Thus adolescent development (this includes theories, empirical studies, institutionalization, and therapeutic interventions) was in part a *reply* to certain problems presented by economic, international, and familial change. Specifically, adolescence helped identify and create a vision of the modern citizen who would be equipped for the challenges of the new social, economic, and world arrangements.[12] Of course, these public problems were interpreted and articulated in certain ways.[13] This analysis suggests that we might anticipate new conceptions of adolescence along with the articulation and popularization of different problems.

Just as at the turn of the twentieth century, there are now challenges to modern economic, intellectual, global, and familial arrangements. Citizenship and nation-states are likewise under revision.[14] Adolescence and children are being redefined in the process, as the global economy expands and discards unproductive processes and people.[15] I want to consider how global forces may intensify, modulate, adapt, and disrupt panoptical time, the development in time episteme, expectant time, and the chronotope of adolescence. What opportunities exist for redefining public problems and youth "needs" in these times?

In many ways the situation appears bleak. The era of "child-saving" in the United States ended with welfare "reform" in 1996. The resources once committed to education, health, and social welfare programs of panoptically viewed youth and children are now utilized to build prisons, install metal detectors in schools, and criminalize younger children as adults. As children below ten years of age have become erotic, spectacular, and marketable, the teenager's market share has sunk. Slow development in time may no longer be functional, and quick leaps from childhood to adulthood may be called for by virtual workplaces and education provided on line. Such a view is in keeping with interpretations that emphasize greater flexibility—of organisms, welfare systems, and individual potential.[16] Flexibility may distinguish up-and-coming life course theories as schooling becomes lifelong learning. The clear boundary between adolescence and adulthood is blurred, as everyone needs to keep *becoming*. This lack of clear boundaries can contribute to the process of further reducing attention to children's and youth's needs.

What I suggest is that we utilize our understanding of these in many ways desperate times to consider advocating for youth in new ways. Can we connect and repoliticize youths' needs, for example, by linking issues of poverty with human rights language? Somehow this process of advocating for youth in different terms, no longer as "developing," must include a clear attention to differences among youth currently elided in theories of development and socialization. We must move between the minoritizing and universalizing discourses of children and teenagers. If we want to make gender and race visible and conscious in our reasoning about and aims for youth, we have to come to grips with how hegemonic masculinity dominates schools and our views of valued and mature youth.

Localized school contexts may again be the place for advocacy, although the advocacy is likely to be around and against specific practices, such as sexual harassment, hazing, or disciplinary "profiling." Despite the risks of doing so, I think we have to advocate in a way that undermines the monolithic view of adolescents as supposedly all the same and as fundamentally different from adults. We must move between and against the confident characterizations of youth, which involves including teenagers as *active participants* (not tokens) in educational and other public policy deliberations. I am not just trumpeting one "student voice,"[17] but calling for the imagining of concrete practices in which youth demand and exercise adultlike responsibilities, acknowledging that teenagers are also affected by the commonsense reasoning about their age group.

These suggestions may seem too small and too peripheral in light of massive changes and inequities in the United States and elsewhere. Nevertheless, one "lesson" of this study is that researchers, educators, and reformers together make and respond to "public problems." What counts as a public problem and how "needs" are conceptualized constitute a major part of political life today.[18] If we reason and advocate for youth in "untimely" ways while trying to be as aware of the current political, social, and economic currents as possible, we may be able to act on our time.

notes

Series Editor's Introduction

1. Pat Burdell, "Teen Mothers in High School." In Michael W. Apple, ed., *Review of Research in Education, Volume 21* (Washington, DC: American Educational Research Association, 1995), pp. 163–208.

2. See, for example, Michael W. Apple, *Official Knowledge*, 2nd ed. (New York: Routledge, 2000), and Michael W. Apple, *Cultural Politics and Education* (New York: Teachers College Press, 1996).

Introduction

1. In method and questions, I draw substantially from the work of Michel Foucault, specifically from *Discipline and punish* (1979) and *The history of sexuality, Vol. 1* (1978). The idea that "knowledge cannot situate itself within the same framework as its object of study because the result is nothing more than recapitulation" is from Bender (1992, p. 62). I am grateful to Tom Popkewitz for this reference.

2. Gould (1991) describes the evolutionary dimension; Wood (1984, p. 73) refers to the ideology of emergence in his study of secondary school students and teachers; and Trinh (1989) is the source of the "confident characterizations" as homiletic.

3. Fausto-Sterling's critical analysis of hormones is excellent (1995b).

4. See Russett (1989) on Victorian psychologists' views of women and people of color. See Brown (1990) for critiques of some accepted ideas on adolescence. Gary Schwartz (1987) portrays the dualism attendant in this conformity view: when teenagers (or women or natives) are not oversocialized, they are undersocialized, or rebellious. Neither the conforming nor the rebelling position of youth gathers much positive regard.

5. Macleod (1983, p. 99).

6. The anthology edited by Feldman & Elliot (1990) is a good representation of the naturalized, biological view of adolescence, albeit with some sociohistorical inclusions.

7. There is a lot of work from this theoretical perspective, much of which I utilize in other chapters. Some representative historical work is that of Gillis (1981), Kett (1977), Springhall (1986), Macleod (1983), Hawes & Hiner (1985), and Dyhouse (1981). Recent work that makes the different experiences by race, class, and gender explicit includes Breines (1992), Graebner (1990), and Graff (1995).

8. I follow Popkewitz (1997) in using *postmodern* as an overarching term for this approach, which is informed by different theoretical orientations and offers multiple emphases.

9. Popkewitz (1997, p. 19). A lot of this section is indebted to Popkewitz (1997). The second quote is from Popkewitz & Brennan (1998, p. 6).

10. John Rajchman (1985) examines Foucaultian methods and ethics, see pp. 50–60.

11. My ideas about method and ethics are informed by Rajchman (1985) and Blacker (1998).

12. This paragraph draws on most explicitly on Morrison's, *Playing in the dark: Whiteness and the literary imagination* (1992); Young (1990) is also useful here.

13. Stoler (1995) provides an excellent description of the role of colonial settings in creating theories for raising children; Bederman (1995) demonstrates how racial hierarchies were modified in child raising; Asad (1983) situates anthropology within colonial authority; and Stocking (1982), Fabian (1983), and Stepan (1982) offer analyses and histories of racial sciences. Young (1990) provides an overview of postcolonial perspectives on Western knowledge and theory.

14. Edward Said is the source of the idea of contrapuntal reading (1993, p. 51).

15. On color-blindness, see Nieto (1992) and A. Thompson (1995); the concept of gender-blindness as analogous to colorblindness was introduced to me by Garrahy (1998).

16. For a clear distinction between U.S. public schools and Navaho ideas of adolescence, see Deyhle & LeCompte (1994). For a more general view of contemporary urban youth's hybrid identities, see Heath & McLaughlin (1993).

17. Hall's video lecture, *Race: The floating signifier* (no date) was distributed by Media Education Foundation, Northampton, MA.

18. For studies of students, Nan Stein's (1995) work is helpful, as is the chapter by Mandel & Shakeshaft (2000). Theoretically, Butler (1990) explores how gender is grounded in presumed heterosexuality, and Sedgwick (1990) explains how homophobia is primarily about male-to-male sociality.

19. The quote is from Weedon (1987/1997, p. 105). Her book is good introductory reading on discourse and discourse analysis; also see Luke

(1995/1996). See B. Davies (1989) and MacNaughton (1998) for accessible discussions of feminist discourse work around schools and teaching.

20. The term social administration, or governance, is used by Popkewitz & Bloch (forthcoming). The description of "the conduct of conduct" is from Rose (1999, p. 3).

21. Lyotard (cited in Peters, 1998, p. 3) also claims that postmodernism is a "condition," that is, an ethos, attitude, or style rather than a period.

22. Rajchman (1985, p. 4).

23. Popkewitz and Brennan (1998, pp. 11–12).

24. This interpretation of poststructuralism draws on Whitson's (1991) useful analysis.

25. Rose's (1999, pp. 51–55) discussion of technology, or human technology, is quite good.

Chapter 1: Up and Down the Great Chain of Being

1. Bederman (1995, p. 31).

2. Rydell (1984); Bederman (1995, p. 35).

3. For example, some black organizations refused to support Colored American Day at the Columbian Exposition (Spear, 1967, p. 52). This was part of a broader refusal to accept segregation, which was being established via Jim Crow laws in the South and creeping into the North as well (G. E. Hale, 1998). Race riots, the establishment of the NAACP, the campaign against lynching, and the growth of black communities in Northern cities with a sense of racial agency were additional ways that the racial hierarchy was being challenged (Weiss, 1974).

4. Several colleagues have pointed out competing interpretations of the meaning of the term "race" at the turn of the twentieth century. Tom Popkewitz (personal communication) understands that race was used in the early 1900s to talk about the American race, a cultural and political division; this is not as I have used the term, which is more consistent with contemporary ideas. I draw from scholars such as Bederman (1995) and Hale (1998), among others, who do not make such a distinction between how race signified then and now. In fact, Hale demonstrates how contemporary racial segregation was begun during Reconstruction after the Civil War and supports that the idea that our familiar and contemporary idea of race was also in use in the early 1900s. I am grateful to Ines Dussel (personal communication) and Tom Popkewitz for raising this issue.

5. Gould (1981) and Lovejoy (1936) for metaphors of progress; Gilman (1985, p. 78) on the moral dimensions of the Great Chain of Being; and Eksteins (1985, p. 12) on advance from superstition to reason.

6. The emphasis in Nye's (1985, p. 49) quote is added; Bederman (1995, p. 25).

7. Bederman (1995, p. 25).
8. Bederman (1995, p. 26).
9. T. Lutz (1991); Popkewitz (1998a).
10. The contagion quotation is from McClintock (1995, p. 47); Russett (1989, p. 4), emphasis added.
11. Popkewitz (1997, 1998a).
12. Wiebe (1967); Platt (1977); T. Lutz (1991, p. 9).
13. In addition to Peiss (1986) on women's leisure and social responses, see also Alexander (1995) and Odem (1995); Smith-Rosenberg (1985, pp. 79, 86); practices of self-determination, purity, and unity are discussed in Collins (1979) and Wiebe (1967). Issues of unity also arose in England and Germany at this time; see Gillis (1981), Springhall (1977), and Laqueur (1962).
14. The quote about race riots is from Weiss (1974, p. 6). On challenges to white-dominated society, see also G. E. Hale (1998), Scheiner (1965), and Spear (1967); on Harlem, see Douglas (1995); on the growth of the black middle class, see Frazier (1957).
15. Bederman (1995, p. 15).
16. Lears (1981, pp. 13–14); Frazier (1957, pp. 71–78).
17. Lutz (1991, pp. 3–4) [my emphasis]; see Bederman (1995) for a case study of Theodore Roosevelt's diagnosis as a neurasthenic and his masculinizing cure in the U.S. West.
18. Smith-Rosenberg (1985, p. 88) offers this distinction between how the unknown futures of boys and girls were considered.
19. Ashcroft, Griffiths, & Tiffine (1995, p. 1); Stepan & Gilman (1993, pp. 172–173) offer a helpful portrait of the emerging racial sciences; Lears (1981); Brumberg's (1988, p. 99) study of "fasting girls" provides an additional look at the modernizing tensions of family life at this time.
20. Young (1985, frontispiece and chapter 2).
21. On progressive ideology, see Popkewitz (1998a) and Wexler (1976); Chamberlin & Gilman (1985).
22. McClintock (1995, p. 50).
23. Stoler (1995, p. 150) discusses how colonies helped to create the moral panic and interwoven ideas about "natives" being childlike and vice versa; Siegel (1985); and Haraway (1989) on primates.
24. Russett (1989, p. 51); Gould (1977, pp. 117–118).
25. Gould (1977, p. 126); McClintock (1995, p. 51), emphasis added.
26. Asad (1983).
27. McClintock (1995); Stoler (1995, pp. 151–152), my emphasis.
28. Serres cited in Gould (1977, p. 127).
29. Stocking (1968, p. 35); he also speculated that the significance of race was

linked with a romantic reaction to the eighteenth-century Enlightenment and the egalitarianism of the French Revolution. Russett (1989, p. 7) similarly demonstrates how the discipline of psychology was obsessed with gender. McClintock (1995).

30. Figlio (1976, p. 24); Stepan (1982, p. 14); Stepan cited in McClintock (1995, p. 49).

31. McClintock (1995, p. 50).

32. Le Bon cited in McClintock (1995, p. 54). According to McClintock (1995), the English middle-class male was placed at the pinnacle of the evolutionary hierarchy (this class inversion was due to the fact that aristocrats were generally seen as degenerates), followed by white English middle-class women; Irish or Jewish men were represented as most inherently degenerate "female races," while Irish working-class women were assigned the lower depths of the white race. McClintock argues that domestic workers, female miners, and working-class prostitutes (women who worked publicly and visibly for money) were stationed on the threshold between the white and black races. In Chapter Two, I will argue that white boys were similarly positioned—in the borderlands of white and black races, in the borderlands between progress and decline. The fate of white boys, like that of borderline working-class women, carried great significance for individuals as well as for society.

33. McClintock (1995, p. 56).

34. Smith-Rosenberg (1985, pp. 175–176).

35. Kimmel (1996, pp. 83–87); Bederman (1995, p. 12).

36. Kimmel (1996, p. 90); Mary Ryan (1981) has examined the emphasis on insular domestic spaces among middle-class whites and the creation of the home as the definer of family as a reaction to the urban "jungles"; Kimmel (1996, p. 95); Collins (1979) interprets the rise of the Ku Klux Klan as a manifestation of an Anglo-Protestant counterattack against immigrants and Southern blacks, who threatened their economic and cultural hegemony; Collins does not discuss masculinity.

37. Chauncey (1994); Katz (1995, pp. 83, 72); Nathan Hale (1971) and Linda Nicholson (1998), among others, read Freud as providing a space that facilitated a variety of desires and sexualities, an interpretation at odds with Katz's.

38. Gilman (1985, p. 72); Siegel (1985, p. 213).

39. Smith-Rosenberg (1985, p. 181); Kimmel (1996, p. 93).

40. Young-Bruehl (1996, chs. 1, 5, 9).

41. Kimmel (1996, p. 100); Zinn (1980/1995, p. 308).

42. Anderson (1983); Stoler (1995).

43. These efforts to raise manly boys can be referred to as political socialization; poststructuralists, following Foucault, use the term "governmental-

ity," for the study of how we come to others and govern ourselves (Rose, 1999). I utilize these ideas but not the language here.

44. The first two quotes are from Zinn (1980/1995, pp. 291–293); Lafeber is cited in Zinn (1980/1995, p. 293).

45. Lafeber quoted in Zinn (1980–1995, p. 297); Zinn (1980/1995, p. 299) with my emphasis.

46. Macleod (1983, p. 136).

47. Walkerdine (1990, p. 19); Chudacoff (1989, p. 91); Koven (1992, p. 378) with my emphasis.

48. The first two quotes are from Koven (1992, p. 377); Masterman is cited in Koven (1992, p. 378).

49. McClintock (1995, p. 48) with my emphasis; Koven (1992, pp. 383–384).

50. Koven (1992, p. 366).

51. Sommer cited in Stoler (1995, p. 137); Smith-Rosenberg (1985, p. 88).

52. Lutz (1991, p. 15); Stafseng (1994).

Chapter 2: Making Adolescence at the Turn of the Century

1. G. Stanley Hall utilized the metaphor of ships adrift; the same metaphor appeared on the cover of the 1989 Carnegie Council on Adolescent Development report, *Turning Points: Preparing American Youth for the 21st Century*.

2. Wiebe (1967); T. Lutz (1991); Macleod (1983); Bakan (1972).

3. Haraway (1989).

4. Although the enormous influence of G. Stanley Hall's work on adolescence is broadly acknowledged, the exact nature of that impact is another question (see Grinder & Strickland, 1963, and Curti, 1959 for two competing evaluations of his impact). He succeeded in making adolescence a household word by "democratizing adolescence" from a middle-class phenomenon to a universal life stage (Acland, 1995). Part of his strategy in popularizing the term was to make it a *time of crisis* in which different paths are possible, those leading to prosperity and productivity and morality and those leading to immorality and degeneration. He further weighted the adolescent *crisis* via the insistence that adolescence was not just a crucial transition for the individual but simultaneously a leap (or setback) for *the race*. As described in Chapter One, we know that *the race* stands for white, European, civilized men but also for the morally ordered nations and families that they fashioned and for which they fought.

5. I am grateful to Ola Stafseng (1994) for this analysis of Hall that draws on Basil Bernstein's ideas of a pedagogy that is internally split by both middle- and working-class beliefs. Hall's views were conflicted, or split, on many issues. Although he was clearly allied with bohemians and free-thinkers, his scholarly and policy stances also evinced aspects of a conserv-

ative philosophy that responded to the widespread lack of energy and nerve called "neurasthenia." Neurasthenic perspectives operated upon an "economistic logic" in which efficiency and proper investment of energy were paramount. A second doubleness in Hall's views occurred around racial progress; although he taught at Howard University and supported women students, his science drew from and affirmed racial and gender hierarchies. In reconstructing schools and curriculum according to scientific findings, he utilized both progressive and traditional-authoritarian methods and philosophies. He was genuinely critical of much of modern society, but his ideas participated in a discourse that omitted political and social critique and aimed reforms at individuals and education; see also Hale (1971) and Bederman (1995) on Hall.

6. Steven Schlossman notes that the trans-Atlantic context of nineteenth-century penal and educational reform is generally slighted (1977, p. 36 and p. 220, n. 17). Schlossman's study of juvenile justice showcases the influence of German and French family reform schools on the thinking of U.S. reformers. Macleod (1983) emphasizes the strong impact of British private schools on boyologists in the United States, and on their antiprecocity measures of loyalty and team sports. See also Thistlethwaite (1963) and the recent *Atlantic crossings* by Rodgers (1998). D. Ross (1972); Neubauer (1992) on the European "culture of adolescence."

7. On the origins and aims of the German Youth Movement, see Laqueur (1962, p.p. 4–7). Stafseng's ideas were communicated in our conversations in Oslo in October 1999.

8. Laqueur (1962, p. 35).

9. For example, one former German Youth Movement leader, Gustav Wyneken, founded Wickersdorf, a model of the most progressive schooling. I am grateful to Ola Stafseng for his explanation of the relationship of the German Youth Movement and progressive education in Germany. See Stafseng (1984 and n.d.) for further elaboration. See Mosse (1985) and Parker et al. (1992) for connections between nationalism and the disciplining of sexuality.

10. Hall quotes are from his autobiography (1923/1977, p. 223); Ross (1972, pp. 36–42, and 92); on Hall and Freud, see Hale (1971).

11. Bederman (1995, pp. 25–26).

12. Strickland & Burgess (1965, p. 11).

13. Hall (1904, vol 2, p. 361); Cole (1984, p. 361); Weber (1958, p. 265); on changing social expectations for citizens, see Bederman (1995, p. 14), Lears (1981), and T. Lutz (1991); on the analysis of Hall's search for a biologically based idealism about human society, see Ross (1972); Neubauer (1992) describes the European culture of adolescence.

14. Gould (1977, p. 143).

15. Chudacoff (1989, p. 67); Macleod (1983).
16. Hall (1881, pp. 121); Macleod (1983); Hall (1881, p. 122) with my emphasis; T. Lutz (1991) on the economistic logic of turn-of-the-century health concerns.
17. Macleod (1983, p. 46) on masculine centeredness of Hall and other charac-ter-builders; Hall (1923/1977, p. 203).
18. Hall (1923/1977, p. 217).
19. Kliebard (1995); Guthrie (1976/1998); Curti (1959, p. 411); J. D. Anderson's (1988) study of the education of black teachers at the Hampton-Tuskegee Institute demonstrates Washington's ideas in action: a teacher education that shorted academic study for long hours of fieldwork since teachers needed to learn, and later teach, the dignity of labor. Washington's men-tor, Samuel Armstrong, claimed that blacks were not intellectually inferior, but morally inferior and that the development of morality would take hundreds of years.
20. Hall & Saunders (1900, pp. 590–591); Strickland & Burgess (1965, p. 24).
21. For a feminist critique of Rousseau's preparation of Émile and Sophie, see Martin (1985).
22. Macleod (1983, p. 32); T. Lutz (1991) and Bederman (1995) both discuss urban environments as threats to white men's health; Macleod (1983).
23. Macleod (1983, p. 101).
24. My emphasis in the letter cited in Bederman (1995, p. 98).
25. T. Lutz (1991) on the sources of neurasthenia and for one description of Roosevelt; Beard (1881); on the link between masturbation and neurasthe-nia, and on Roosevelt's cure, see Bederman (1995, p. 85).
26. Hall (1923/1977, pp. 361–362); on definitions of emotions, see Boler (1997); quote on Herbartianism is from McMurry (1925, pp. 297–298). For a discussion of the ideas of Johann Friedrich Herbart, see Pinar, Reynolds, Slattery, & Taubman (1995), chap. 2.
27. Bederman (1995, p. 260, nt. 5) follows Warren Susman in noting that "character" was synonymous with manhood, so here the development of *will* is the development of the *manly* will; Kett (1977) on conversion narra-tives.
28. Macleod (1983); T. Lutz (1991); Bederman (1995).
29. Bederman's (1995) chapter on G. Stanley Hall explains his shift of what feminist poststructuralists call binary oppositions, such as male/female and black/white.
30. Macleod (1983, p. 100); Macleod (1983, p. 37); Kett (1977, p. 135). The physiological changes were most pronounced among middle-class, urban dwellers.
31. All the quotes are from Macleod (1983, pp. 23–24) with my emphases.
32. On dead-end jobs, see Collins (1979) and Kett (1977); the enrollment fig-

ures are from Macleod (1983, p. 24); see Koven (1992) regarding the situation in England.

33. Macleod (1983, p. 27–28) is the primary source for these ideas on age-grading with my emphasis; Bakan (1972) on child labor; Chudacoff (1989) provides additional information on the increasing attention to age.

34. Grinder & Strickland (1963, p. 395); Macleod (1983, p. 99).

35. Van Liew (1895, pp. 99, and 119).

36. Dewey (1896, p. 233) with my emphasis.

37. Anderson's (1983) work on nationalism acknowledges the Janus-faced characters of nationalism, its looking simultaneously to the past and to the future. This same two-faced view appears in Hall and the character-builders and is a link between adolescence and nation-building. In the last chapter of Volume 2 of *Adolescence*, Hall takes up "ethnic psychology and pedagogy, or adolescent races and their treatment" in a primarily paternalistic attitude, stating that savages are "adolescents of adult size" (1904, p. 649), but he also condemns the negative effects of imperialism on many groups.

38. Macleod (1983, p. 55); Kincaid (1992, p. 51).

39. Fanon (1952/1986); Kincaid (1992, pp. 31–32).

40. Kincaid (1992); Kimmel (1996, p. 181) with emphasis added.

41. Stecopoulos (1997).

42. Young (1995, pp. 20–22).

43. Grinder and Strickland (1963, pp. 391–392); Hall cited in Gould (1977, p. 154).

44. Horn (1995, p. 122) with my emphasis.

45. Macleod (1983, p. 136); Nye (1985, p 60); Nye traces the language of degeneration in both France and England at this time. Although the association between individuals' health and national health sounds quaint, we utilize it regularly; for example, when youth crime is discussed, the threat to the nation is so assumed that we need not even articulate it.

46. Nye (1985, p. 65); Springhall (1977, p. 15); Springhall (1986); Springhall (1977, p. 18); overall, Springhall maintains that nationalism and militarism were stronger in Britain than imperialism, that holding the empire and maintaining borders were the primary tasks; in contrast, the United States at this time was actively acquiring colonies and possessions (Zinn, 1980/1995); Popkewitz (1998a).

47. Springhall (1986, p. 45) notes that Dr. J. W. Slaughter, Chairman of the Eugenics Education Society and Secretary of the English Sociology Society, was mentored by Hall, and promoted his ideas in his 1911 book, *The Adolescent* (London), as did Arnold Freeman, author of *Boy Life and Labour: The Manufacture of Inefficiency* (London, 1914); on youth crime, see Springhall (1986, pp. 43–48); Churchill quoted in Springhall (1986, p.

46); Koven (1992, p. 378).

48. The ideas and quotes about changes in reformers' ideas come from Koven (1992, pp. 374–377); Kimmel (1995).

49. Koven (1992, pp. 376–378).

50. Koven (1992, pp. 378–382); Springhall (1986, p. 56).

51. Baden-Powell quoted in Macleod (1983, p. 137); Rosenthal (1984, p. 106); Koven (1992).

52. Rosenthal (1984, p. 65); Macleod (1983, pp. 140, 145).

53. Cavallo (1981, pp. 37–38, 43).

54. Cavallo (1981, p. 37).

55. Cavallo (1981, p. 39).

56. Cavallo (1981, pp. 92–93).

57. Cavallo (1981, p. 94); Gillis (1981, p. 109) on the political utility of sports.

58. On statistics, see Popkewitz (1998b) and Hacking (1991); Trinh (1989) for more on massification.

59. Hall (1903, p. 446); Graves (1998, p. 129).

60. Dyhouse (1981, p. 92, p. 114).

61. Bissell Brown (1990, pp. 506–510).

62. Graves (1998, p. 280).

63. Dyhouse (1981, p. 110).

64. Dyhouse (1981, pp. 136–137).

65. The rhetoric in England over girls sometimes declared them as having too much energy that needed channeling and sometimes not sufficient energy, and these typifications were attached to working-class and middle-class girls, respectively (Dyhouse, 1981). In putting the emphasis on fear of *precocity*, the otherwise contradictory problems can be seen to stem from the same issue.

66. Bakan (1972); Odem (1995, p. 111); Schlossman and Wallach (1978, pp. 70–71).

67. Odem (1995, p. 1).

68. Schlossman and Wallach (1978, p. 72) with my emphasis. The expanded state regulation of adolescent female sexuality was part of a broader trend toward control of sexuality in general. "Expressions of sexuality that did not conform to a marital, reproductive framework were increasingly subjected to government surveillance and control, as evidenced by a range of legal measures enacted during the period. These included legislation prohibiting the dissemination of obscene literature, the criminalization of abortion, stringent measures targeting prostitution, and heightened legal repression of homosexuality" (Odem, 1995, p. 2). Threats to marital reproductive sex were the common denominator in this reading. Such a view is not inconsistent with a Foucauldian reading which sees the governing of

sexual selves occurring in all the talk of sexuality, with homosexuals coming to be regarded as a separate species. So I would add that a populational reasoning is being constructed in the proliferation of sexual
categories as well as an incitement or compulsion to be normatively [het-
ero]sexual.

69. Schlossman and Wallach (1978, p. 73) with my emphasis.

70. Schlossman and Wallach (1978, p. 76) with my emphasis.

71. Mary Odem (1995) describes two stages of the campaign against delinquent daughters. The first stage criminalized sexual intercourse with
teenage girls by raising the age-of-consent laws. This strategy identified
men as the villains in making delinquent girls. In 1885, 36 states' age of
consent was ten years of age, nine states had 12 as the age of consent, with
Delaware at the bottom with seven years of age. By 1920, only Georgia
had an age of consent of 14 and the majority of states had raised theirs to
16 years of age, with 21 states setting the age at 18 years of age. The second
stage of the campaign against delinquent girls focused upon girls themselves and involved the prevention and juvenile justice policies described
in this section.

72. "Tough dancing" was sexually explicit and brought couples into close
physical contact, gazing into each other's eyes, arms around the neck, and
hips touching. Tough dances included the turkey trot, slow rag, and the
bunny hug (Peiss, 1986, pp. 100–104). Alexander (1995, pp. 43–44); see
Odem (1995, ch. 1) for an excellent description of how African-American
reformers' approaches to delinquent girls differed. For example, they
never subscribed to the male-as-villain narrative because they feared black
men would be targeted. They also emphasized sex education and prevention for both young men and young women.

73. Alexander (1995, pp. 45–46); Alexander (1995) and Odem (1995) both
describe how the juvenile courts were used by working-class, immigrant,
and African-American parents as leverage to control their daughters,
pointing out that the juvenile justice system was not just reformers against
girls, but a more complex interplay of parents, reformers, enforcers, and
daughters.

74. Odem (1995, p. 109); on professional opportunities, see Platt (1977) and
Odem (1995).

75. Schlossman (1977).

76. See Schlossman (1977, ch. 3); Schlossman (1977, pp. 38–41, 50, 97).

77. Schlossman and Wallach (1978).

78. Hall discussed female adolescent and sexual development in the following
works: 1904, I: chap 7, II: chap 17, 1911, and 1914 (cited in Odem, p. 209,
n. 15).

79. Popkewitz (1998b).

80. Grumet (1981); see Barthes (1972) on myths, which is a different but related critique.
81. B. Anderson (1983) offers this temporal analysis of nationalism.

Chapter 3: Back to the Future

1. Carnegie Council on Adolescent Development (1989); on intertextuality see Luke (1996); Carnegie Council on Adolescent Development (1989, pp. 12, 9); for alternative critiques of *Turning Points*, see Franklin (1990) and Rosario (1990).
2. Carnegie Council on Adolescent Development (1989 p. 8).
3. Walkerdine (1997); Buckingham (2000).
4. Strickland & Burgess (1965); D. Ross (1972); Carnegie Council on Adolescent Development (1989, p. 8).
5. Carnegie Council on Adolescent Development (1989, p. 14) with my emphasis.
6. Carnegie Council on Adolescent Development (1989, p. 9); for well-developed critiques of the term *at risk*, see Fine (1993); Roman (1996); Holloway & Jefferson (1997).
7. The four principles excluded from discussion here are: "Teachers and principals have the major responsibility and power to transform middle grade schools; Teachers for the middle grades are specifically prepared to teach young adolescents; Families are allied with school staff through mutual respect, trust, and communication; Schools and communities are partners in educating young adolescents" (Carnegie Council on Adolescent Development, 1989, p. 36).
8. Carnegie Council on Adolescent Development (1989, p. 36).
9. On the impersonal quality of large schools see Fine (1993); Wehlage et al. (1989); Powell, Farrar, & Cohen (1985); Carnegie Council on Adolescent Development (1989, pp. 8, 37, 40, 38).
10. A. Ross (1988, p. xi); on a sense of community in alternative programs see Wehlage et al. (1989).
11. This Akers quote is from a series of advertisements in *Fortune* in the late 1980s, quoted in McQuire (1990, p. 110).
12. Cuban (1993a, p. 11).
13. Schlesinger (1992); Hirsch (1987); Rousmaniere (1997).
14. Carnegie Council on Adolescent Development (1989, p. 36); Franklin (1986, p. 6); Rousmaniere (1997, p. 56).
15. Schlossman (1977, p. 53).
16. Grumet (1981); Boler (1999); Foucault (1979).
17. Goleman (1995); Boler (1999).
18. Carnegie Council on Adolescent Development (1989, p. 36).

19. Carnegie Council on Adolescent Development (1989, p. 42).
20. Newmann (1993).
21. This interpretation of the life sciences curriculum as central and illustrative of the goals of the *Turning Points* report stems both from the close reading of the report and from two recent special issues of journals focused upon adolescence, both edited by Ruby Takanishi of the Carnegie Council on Adolescent Development. The issues of *American Psychologist* (Winter, 1992) and *Teachers College Record* (Spring, 1993) both focus heavily on health issues of youth.
22. Carnegie Council on Adolescent Development (1989, p. 46).
23. Rousmaniere (1997, p. 58).
24. Carnegie Council on Adolescent Development (1989, p. 46).
25. Carnegie Council on Adolescent Development (1989, p. 43).
26. Carnegie Council on Adolescent Development (1989, pp. 15–17).
27. Heath & Mangiola (1991); Sapon-Shevin (1989).
28. Carnegie Council on Adolescent Development (1989, p. 13, 15).
29. Gay (1984, p. 317); in Wishy's (1968) history of conceptions of child rearing, he describes the move from the ideal youth as "pious, holy or pure" to "red-blooded" and "manly" as principal words of praise by the 1870s, an analysis that complements Gay's work.
30. Franklin (1986).
31. Carnegie Council on Adolescent Development (1989, p. 54) with my emphasis; see Buckingham (2000) for a good discussion of passive young people in radical and conservative scholarship.
32. For example, see Perry & Fraser (1993); Grumet (1981) discusses how the sentimentalizing of teaching keeps power relations with superiors and children from view.
33. Carnegie Council on Adolescent Development (1995, p. 28).
34. Lesko (1995).
35. Carnegie Council on Adolescent Development (1995, p. 55).

Chapter 4: Time Matters in Adolescence

1. Levine (1997, p. 80); Conrad (1907/1998); Rifkin (1987).
2. Mumford cited in Landes (1983, p. xix) with emphasis added.
3. Koselleck cited in Bender & Wellbery (1991b, p. 1) with my emphasis; Landes (1983, p. 7); E. P. Thompson (1993, pp. 394–395); Popkewitz & Pitman (1986) on American belief in progress.
4. Kern (1983, p. 12).
5. Toulmin and Goodfield (1965) argue that biology was the central science in the discovery of time. Foucault retorts that biology did not yet exist, so he disagrees with the perspective of Toulmin and Goodfield. Foucault

terms the new perspective "natural history" (1973, pp. 127–132).

6. Toulmin & Goodfield (1965, p. 179); Lowe (1982, p. 49) with my emphasis.

7. Fabian (1991, p. 190); also see Fabian (1983).

8. Fabian (1991, p. 193–195) with added emphasis; on Christian millennialist narratives, see Haraway (1997) and Popkewitz & Pitman (1986); on teenage pregnancy see Lesko (1994b, 1997) and Chapter Five of this volume.

9. Passerini (1997, p. 281).

10. Fabian (1983).

11. McClintock (1995, p. 37); space does not allow an extended discussion of the colonial origins of panoptical time and racial family trees, but see Haraway (1989), McClintock (1995), and Lesko (1996b).

12. Gould (1977); Lesko (1996); Stoler (1995).

13. Foucault (1979, p. 146).

14. Dawson (1896); on "stigmata of degeneration," see Fausto-Sterling (1995a); Gilman (1985); Horn (1995); McClintock (1995).

15. Horn (1995, p. 112); Terry (1995).

16. Bederman (1995); Nye (1985).

17. Feldman & Elliott (1990).

18. Terry (1995) on scientific scopophilia; McClintock (1995, p. 50); see also Said (1978).

19. Erikson (1950/1985, pp. 273, 272) with my emphasis.

20. Erikson (1968, p. 91).

21. Kett (1974, 1977).

22. Chudacoff (1989, p. 36).

23. Chudacoff (1989, pp. 37, 91).

24. Ayres (1909); Callahan (1962); on statistics as a technology of power, see Hacking (1991, pp. 181, 194).

25. Anderson (1988) and Lomawaima (1995) on time discipline in African-American and Native American schools; Schlossman (1977, p. 30) on orderly, meek existence in and out of reformatories; Tolen (1995, p. 95) on criminal tribespeople; Foucault (1979, p. 152).

26. Rousmaniere (1997) discusses how teachers and teacher unions opposed the administrative efficiency experts' speeding up of the schoolday and adding to the work load of teachers, but she does not talk about teachers' resistance as based on a different temporal orientation. On public, irreversible time, see Kern (1983); see Alexander (1995) and Schlossman & Wallach (1978) regarding normal dress and deportment.

27. Kern (1983, p. 92) with my emphasis; Kern (1983, p. 3).

28. James & Prout (1990a).

29. Erikson (1968, p. 92).
30. Ashcroft, Griffiths, & Tiffin (1995, p. 1).
31. On the effects of colonialism, see Fanon (1952/1986) and Memmi (1965); Cesaire (1972, p. 40) on the dependency complex; Bhabha (1995a).
32. Solberg (1990).
33. Chudacoff (1989, p. 72).
34. Interview 1, p. 10, with my emphasis; see Lesko (1996b) for further description of this study of undergraduates.
35. Interview 1, pp. 16–17, with my emphasis.
36. Interview 1, pp. 19–20.
37. Focus Group 2, pp. 25–26, with my emphasis.
38. Fanon (1952/1986, p. 100). Waksler (1991) teaches a sociology of childhood class in which she asks college students to write about their most difficult times as children. She found that a "rewriting" of events from the parents' perspective (as in Renee's second account) to be common. When she confronts her students with this pattern of accepting the parents' view as naturally best, most of them drop it. I never confronted Renee in the way Waksler suggests, so I do not know how durable the revised story would have been.
39. Interview 1, pp. 11–12.
40. Chudacoff (1989, pp. 126–132) on narrow age-groupings; Eckert (1989) on competition in high schools; Cesaire (1972, p. 40).
41. Morss (1996).
42. Koselleck (1985, p. 224) with my emphasis.
43. Koselleck (1985, p. 224).
44. Koselleck (1985, p. 224) with my emphasis.
45. Holquist (1990, pp. 115–117).
46. See Buchmann (1989) on changing life scripts. I am arguing that the panoptical time of adolescence affects all youth from diverse backgrounds; however, in the narrative scripts of life I would expect to see a wide divergence in how adulthood is achieved.
47. Csikszentmihalyi & Schmidt (1998); Coté & Allahar (1996, pp. 82–83).

Chapter 5: "Before Their Time"

1. On familiar and reproductive ideologies, see Coontz (1992), Luker (1996), and Murcott (1980); Fraser and Gordon (1994) on keywords; for general social analyses of teenage pregnancy, see Eisenstein (1994b), Kunzel (1993), Lesko (1995), and Solinger (1992); Treichler (1987).
2. Exceptions to this general silence do exist; see for example Burdell (1995/96) and Lesko (1995).
3. *Time* (1985); Bhabha (1995b, pp. 58–59, 48).

4. Graff (1995) for discourse of growing up.

5. Ross (1972, 1984).

6. This phrase is synonymous with the 1980s depiction of the problem of teenage pregnancy and varies from earlier language of unwed mothers. The headline for the December 9, 1985, cover story in *Time* magazine was "Children Having Children." The Children's Defense Fund used this phrase as the title of one of its early booklets, *Preventing Children Having Children* (1985). Leon Dash, a journalist, published *When Children Want Children* in 1989.

7. The phrase "before their time" is not as frequently invoked but does appear often as a shorthand phrase for teenage mothers. For example, see Sander (1991).

8. Lawson (1993, pp. 111–112).

9. The voluminous research on teenage pregnancy and motherhood, much of which begins with an assumption that school-aged mothers are problems, enacts a critique based upon out-of-time perspectives. First, teenage mothers are likely to be bad mothers (thus contributing to the New Right discourse on family deterioration), they are irresponsible (which connects to a failure to have hope for a bright future), and they are likely to become and remain dependent on the state (Lesko, 1995). The "out-of-time" dimension plays in each of these domains: they are too young to be good mothers (still children themselves); they are emotionally disordered in failing to believe ideologies of progress and ability to succeed if they try hard enough; and by not completing their education and entering the workforce before having children (or, failing that, by not marrying), they are plunging themselves into poverty.

    Some analyses have begun to emphasize the problem of young mothers as poverty rather than age (e.g. Weatherley & Cartoof, 1988). Austin (1989) characterizes teenage pregnancy as a failure of the schools, the economy, and the health system to provide education and opportunities for youth.

10. Foucault (1979); Kincaid (1992).

11. Holquist (1990, p. 116) with my emphasis.

12. Graff (1995, p. 10); James and Prout (1990b, p. 217).

13. Graff (1995, p. 333).

14. The compulsory heterosexuality of this account of growing up can only be noted here. Space does not permit a critique of this heteronormativity, but see Sedgwick (1993) for a relevant analysis.

15. Buchmann (1989, pp. 181–184, 186).

16. Buchmann (1989, pp. 187–188); Holland's (1992) study of contemporary print media's portrayal of youth depicts recurrent representations that make the adult/youth border unambiguous and demonstrate clear adult

superiority. Similarly, expert knowledge such as developmental psychology retains its rigid age-based stage demarcations. Thus, despite Buchmann's findings of greater blurring of adult and youth status from the perspective of life scripts, other social arenas continue to promote the view of inferior, undeveloped, and immature youth.

17. All proper nouns are pseudonyms. The perspective of the teachers and counselors and nurses at Bright Prospects High School was that young teenagers can be good mothers. The alternative school was founded in 1980 in a city in the Southwestern United States, a city reputed to have above national averages of pregnancy, drug abuse, and suicide among youth. The city's ethnic diversity was reflected in the school population of 54 percent Hispanic, 30 percent Anglo, 8 percent Native American, and 7.5 percent black. The economic base of the city rests largely upon a military base, tourism, and the main branch of the state university. Salaries remain low.

18. The research at Bright Prospects High School was conducted across 1986 to 1988. More extensive data on Bright Prospects are presented in Fernandez et al. (1987) and Wehlage et al. (1989). Elsewhere I have analyzed the students' perspectives differently; see Lesko (1990, 1991).

19. Research has indicated that higher teenage pregnancy rates occur in countries with the least open attitudes toward sex. In addition to different attitudes toward sex, contraceptive information is differently advertised and made available. See the two volumes of comparative research by Elise F. Jones et al. (1986, 1989).

20. Rains (1971).

21. Solberg (1990).

22. Jones et al. (1986); Jones et al. (1989).

23. Lesko (1995). See Fine's (1988) important critique of sex education from a feminist perspective.

24. Hooks (1981).

25. Eisenstein (1994, p. 220) with my emphasis.

26. Eisenstein (1994).

27. Recent figures report that the rate of births to teenagers is down: from 62.1 births per 1,000 in 1991 to 56.9 births per 1,000 in 1995 (*Education Week*, 1996).

Chapter 6: Our Guys/Good Guys

1. Shelton quoted in Goldstein (2000, p. 42).

2. Bissinger (1990, p. 11).

3. Henry (1963, pp. 190–191).

4. Jansen & Sabo (1994, p. 3); Nadelhaft (1993, p. 27).

5. Lefkowitz (1997, p. 65).

6. Connell (1996) on masculinizing schools; Davies (1992, p. 135); Mac an Ghaill (1994); Lyall (2000) on caning.

7. Rees (1997); Shank (2000); Willinsky (2000).

8. Participants in this study chose their own pseudonyms, and the football influence on Woody's choice is evident. All proper nouns, such as the name of Woody's high school, are also pseudonyms.

9. The research project occurred over the academic year 1993–1994 in a Midwestern university. A research assistant and I interviewed four undergraduate preservice teachers across two semesters while they were enrolled in teacher education courses, specifically educational psychology and multicultural education. We conducted both group and individual interviews to understand the participants' experiences in secondary schools, in their families, and in college, as well as their expectations for teaching.

10. Stoler (1995, p. 136) with my emphasis; Connell (1990).

11. Jansen & Sabo (1994, p. 3).

12. Nadelhaft (1993, pp. 25–27); Jansen & Sabo (1994).

13. Nadelhaft (1993, p. 29).

14. Mosse (1985, 1996).

15. Lutz (1997) on permanent war; on evil portraits of others, see Levidow (1995) and Askoy & Robins (1991).

16. DeBord (1977, pp. 2–3) with my emphasis; Debord (1977, p. 12).

17. Friedenberg (1980, pp. 180–184) with emphasis added.

18. McClintock (1995) on spectacles and nationalism; drawing on Anderson's (1983) work on the imagining of nations, nationalism can take various forms and need not only take the form identified here. See also Parker et al. (1992).

19. Hargreaves (1986, p. 154).

20. Anderson (1983).

21. Bissinger (1990); Berlant & Freeman (1993, p. 195); for other accounts of high school sports, see also Foley (1990a, 1990b), Gruneau & Whitson (1993), Robins & Cohen (1978), and Walker (1988).

22. Bissinger (1990, p. 34).

23. DeBord (1977, pp. 2–3).

24. Interview 2, pp. 29–30.

25. Interview 3, p. 44.

26. In using the descriptor "boy-man," I draw on Jeal's (1990) biography of Baden-Powell, the founder of the worldwide Boy Scout Movement.

27. Messner (1992, p. 24).

28. When asked to describe in more detail what occurred, Woody recounted

getting a flattop haircut (like a Marine), getting an earring, driving fast, partying (but not drinking much), "just popping off to anybody I could" (i.e., "mouthing off" or "talking back" to people) and losing all his manners. Friends of his parents, for example, avoided him because he was obnoxious.

29. Interview 2, p. 45; from Connell's work on the Iron Man (1990), we can see the car-based, masculine rebellion as a collective social practice involving his father, close friends, acquaintances, and various other performers. Also like Connell's Australian Iron Man, Woody leads a life narrowly focused on sports training, studying, and coaching his younger brother.

30. Mosse (1996, p. 100).

31. Interview 3, p. 55, with emphasis added.

32. Interview 2, pp. 17–18.

33. Bissinger (1990, p. 24).

34. Sabo (1994, p. 83).

35. Interview 2, pp. 32–33.

36. Messner (1992, p. 50).

37. Interview 2, pp. 15–16 with emphasis added.

38. Sabo (1994, p. 86).

39. Messner (1992, p. 62).

40. Sabo (1994, pp. 84–86).

41. The direct exploitation of animality (savagery) for Western male domination has a long history in the United States. Gail Bederman (1995) directly links psychologist G. Stanley Hall and Theodore Roosevelt with this turn-of-the-century association between developing masculinity and promoting civilization by using animal or primitive energy. These primitive energies were gathered by being in nature, by hunting, by competitive games, and through righteous wars.

42. Messner (1992, p. 62).

43. Messner (1992, p. 72).

44. Messner (1992, p. 74).

45. Cited in Freeman (1997, p. 22). Freeman (1997) adds that many players face drug withdrawal rigors at the end of each season.

46. Sabo (1994, p. 86).

47. The pain principle and its collective making and remaking are an example of what Connell (1995) calls body-reflexive practices, which are an important dimension of masculinity.

48. Interview 2, pp. 20–23.

49. Messner (1992, p. 15).

50. Jeffords (1989) and Lutz (1997).

51. Interview 3, p. 32.
52. Focus Group 3, p. 11.
53. Focus Group 3, p. 14.
54. Focus Group 3, p. 14.
55. Mosse (1985, p. 134).
56. Woody exhibited a rhetorical "privilege" to make amazingly contradictory statements about youth. One minute he would say teenagers just needed to be left alone and be given responsibility and they would be fine. Then he would state that as a teacher he was not going to pamper kids, but just give them lecture notes and test them on those. He suggested that his own children would be strictly limited in what they did, for instance, no dating before they were 16 years old. What emerged as the most important issue was that Woody remained the ultimate authority in all situations. The substance of his decisions or policies did not matter; what mattered was his authority to make absolute calls, which he labeled as rational, in each of these different domains.
57. Berlant & Freeman (1993, p. 195).
58. Following Cuban (1993b), I utilize the language of student-centered and teacher-centered teaching to denote sets of different practices. In general, Woody's comments place him in the teacher-centered perspective on teaching.
59. Interview 3, p. 50.
60. Focus Group 3, p. 18.
61. Focus Group 3, p. 18.
62. Focus Group 3, pp. 19–20.
63. Focus Group 3, pp. 20–21.
64. Interview 3, p. 33.
65. Nadelhaft (1993).
66. Weis (1993); Southern Poverty Law Center (2000).
67. Interview 3, pp. 49–50.
68. Interview 3, pp. 50–51.
69. Interview 3, pp. 50.
70. Interview 3, p. 55.
71. Professor Linda Bensel-Meyers blew the whistle on unethical academic practices to keep athletes at the University of Tennessee eligible, and she has become a pariah. Meanwhile, two national groups of faculty, the Drake Group and the Rutgers 1000, have called big-time college athletics a corrupting influence on universities (Lipsyte, 2000).
72. M. Katz (1995); Miedzian (1991); Stein (1995).
73. Berlant & Freeman (1993, p. 195).

Chapter 7: When the Romance Is Gone . . .

1. Coles quoted in Stephens (1995, p. 1).
2. Baker (1998) and Katz, M. (1995).
3. Proposition 21 failed to pass in March 2000; for information on the initiative, see www.colorlines.com/waronyouth/.
4. Stephens (1995) is an excellent overview of children's conditions globally. My focus on schools as unhealthy environments owes a lot to my conversations with Mimi Orner, who suggested this direction.
5. Croddy (1997) and Zimring (1998) dispute the conventional wisdom of an epidemic of youth violence; see also Moore & Tonry (1998) for an overview of different sources of the "epidemic."
6. Bernstein (1975) and Foley (1990a).
7. Spring (1989); Graves (1998); Hargreaves (1967); Rees (1997, p. 202), emphasis added.
8. Eckert (1989, p. 3).
9. Eckert (1989, pp. 135–136, 12–13).
10. Wexler (1992).
11. Eckert (1989, p. 12); Lefkowitz (1996); Keddie (1971); Fordham (1997).
12. Connell (1997); Mac an Ghaill (1994); Bissell Brown (1990); Graves (1998); Krug (1969, p. 172); Tyack & Hansot (1992); Kliebard (1995).
13. Rousmaniere (1997, p. 119); Anderson (1988).
14. Wehlage et al. (1989) examine students at risk and school communities; see Powell et al. (1985) for schools as shopping malls; Kenway & Fitzclarence (1997) discuss violence and poisonous pedagogy. Davis (1999) utilizes the term "compassion" in her analysis of youth in crisis. Although I believe that to talk of youth in crisis recirculates the same turn-of-the-century arguments that I try to work against, her term "compassion" for what is lacking is very helpful.
15. Harvey (1990).
16. M. Katz (1995).
17. Ennew (1994, p. 134).
18. Field (1995, p. 52); Postman (1982).
19. Ennew (1994, p. 133).
20. Weiler (1998).
21. McClintock (1995); Hargreaves (1986).
22. On zero tolerance, see Ayers & Dohrn (2000).
23. Southern Poverty Law Center (2000, p. 1); Weis (1993) described this dynamic in a Rust Belt city in the late 1980s.
24. S. Hall (1993); see Gibson (1994) and Jeffords (1989) on social remasculinization; Davies (1992, p. 135); Rees (forthcoming, p. 10).

25. Mac an Ghaill (1994).
26. Shank (2000) for a feminist analysis of rigor; Apple (1996).
27. Solomon (1997) for some of these operations in higher education; also Mohanty (1997); Roman & Eyre (1997).
28. Kenway & Fitzclarence (1997); see also Stein (1995).

Chapter 8: Cutting Free from the Great Chain of Being

1. Nietzsche quoted in Rose (1999, p. 13).
2. I refer to the title of a recent book on adolescence, *A Tribe Apart* (Hersch, 1998).
3. For examples of what I, following Sedgwick (1990), call minoritizing discourses, see Gilligan (1982) and Gay (1994). See Talburt (2000) for minority and universal discourses around lesbian and gay identities and needs.
4. See Walkerdine (1984), Moss (1996), and Burman (1994) for examples of the difficulty in adding context onto conceptions of children.
5. Henriques et al. (1984) and Broughton (1987) are two useful sources for problematizing conceptions of the individual as outside of society. For additional critiques of problems with "development," see Buckingham (2000), Burman (1994), and Walkerdine (1990).
6. See Buckingham's (2000) excellent discussion of the passivity of children that haunts both conservative and radical scholarship on children and technology.
7. Connell (1990, 1995) and Mac an Ghaill (1994); Davies (1989); Walkerdine (1984, 1990, 1997); Hollway (1984).
8. Serres & Latour (1990, pp. 48–49).
9. Serres & Latour (1990, p. 50).
10. Wyn (2000); Buchmann (1989). Novelists capture this simultaneous age and youthfulness, for example, Kincaid's *Annie John* (1985) and Duras's *The Lover* (1985).
11. Serres & Latour (1990, p. 58).
12. Popkewitz (1998a).
13. See Gusfield's work on the making of public problems (1963; 1981).
14. Shafir (1998); Urry (2000) argues that sociologists must develop theories and methods to examine social life beyond stable societies, as flows, nodes, and mobilities.
15. Stephens (1995); Cohen (1997).
16. Hultqvist (1998); Wyn (2000).
17. For an insightful analysis of the call for student voice in scholarship on teaching, see Orner (1992).
18. Fraser (1989).

references

Acland, C. R. (1995). *Youth, murder, spectacle: The cultural politics of "youth in crisis."* Boulder, CO: Westview Press.

Aksoy, A., & Robins, K. (1991). Exterminating angels: Morality, violence and technology in the Gulf War. *Science as Culture, 12,* 322–337.

Alexander, R. M. (1995). *The "girl problem:" Female sexual delinquency in New York, 1900–1930.* Ithaca & London: Cornell University Press.

Anderson, B. (1983). *Imagined communities: Reflections on the origin and spread of nationalism.* London & New York: Verso.

Anderson, J. D. (1988). *The education of blacks in the South, 1860–1935.* Chapel Hill & London: University of North Carolina Press.

Apple, M. W. (1996). *Cultural politics and education.* New York: Teachers College Press.

Asad, T. (Ed.). (1983). *Anthropology and the colonial encounter.*

Ashcroft, B., Griffiths, G., & Tiffin, H. (1995). Introduction. In B. Ashcroft, G. Griffiths, & H. Tiffin (Eds.), *The post-colonial studies reader* (pp. 1–20). London & New York: Routledge.

Austin, R. (1989). Sapphire Bound! *Wisconsin Law Review,* 539–578.

Ayers, W. (1997). I walk with delinquents. *Educational Leadership, October,* 48–51.

Ayers, W., & Dohrn, B. (2000). Resisting zero tolerance. *Rethinking Schools, 14*(3), 14.

Ayres, L. P. (1909). *Laggards in our schools: A study of retardation and elimination in city school systems.* New York: Charities Publication Commitee.

Bakan, D. (1972). Adolescence in America: From idea to social fact. In J. Kagan & R. Coles (Eds.), *Twelve to sixteen: Early adolescence* (pp. 73–89). New York: W. W. Norton & Co.

Baker, B. (1998). "Childhood" in the emergence and spread of U.S. public schools. In T. S. Popkewtiz & M. Brennan (Eds.), *Foucault's challenge: Discourse, knowledge and power in education* (pp. 117–143). New York: Routledge.

Bakhtin, M. M. (1981). *The dialogical imagination*. M. Holquist (Ed.). (Emerson, C. & Holquist, M., Trans.). Austin, TX: University of Texas Press.

Barthes, R. (1972). *Mythologies* (Cape, Jonathan, Trans.). New York: Hill & Wang.

Beard, G. M. (1881). *American nervousness: Its causes and consequences*. New York: G. P. Putnam's Sons.

Bederman, G. (1995). *Manliness and civilization: A cultural history of gender and race in the united states, 1880–1917*. Chicago: University of Chicago Press.

Bender, J. (1992). A new history of the Enlightenment? In L. Damrosch (Ed.), *The profession of eighteenth century literature: Reflection on an institution* (pp. 62–84). Madison, WI: University of Wisconsin Press.

Bender, J., & Wellbery, D. E. (Eds.). (1991a). *Chronotypes: The construction of time*. Stanford, CA: Stanford University Press.

Bender, J., & Wellbery, D. E. (1991b). Introduction. In J. Bender & D. E. Wellbery (Eds.), *Chronotypes: The construction of time* (pp. 1–19). Stanford, CA: Stanford University Press.

Berk, L. (1992). The extracurriculum. In P. Jackson (Ed.), *Handbook of research on curriculum* (pp. 1002–1044). New York: Macmillan.

Berlant, L., & Freeman, E. (1993). Queer nationality. In M. Warner (Ed.), *Fear of a queer planet: Queer politics and social theory* (pp. 193–229). Minneapolis, MN: University of Minnesota Press.

Bernstein, B. (1975). *Class, codes and control* (Vol. III). London: Routledge and Kegan Paul.

Bhabha, H. (1995a). *The location of culture*. New York & London: Routledge.

Bhabha, H. K. (1995b). Freedom's basis in the indeterminate. In J. Rajchman (Ed.), *The identity in question* (pp. 47–62). New York: Routledge.

Bissell Brown, V. (1990). The fear of feminization: Los Angeles high schools in the Progressive Era. *Feminist Studies, 16*(3), 493–518.

Bissinger, H. G. (1990). *Friday night lights: A town, a team, a dream*. New York: Harper Collins.

Blacker, D. (1998). Intellectuals at work and in power: Toward a Foucaultian research ethic. In T. S. Popkewitz & M. Brennan (Eds.), *Foucault's challenge: Discourse, knowledge, and power in education* (pp. 348–368). New York: Teachers College Press.

Boler, M. (1997). Disciplined emotions: Philosophies of educated feelings. *Educational Theory, 47*(2), 203–227.

Boler, M. (1999). *Feeling power: Emotions and education*. New York: Routledge.

Breines, W. (1992). *Young, white, and miserable: Growing up female in the fifties*. Boston: Beacon Press.

Broughton, J. M. (Ed.). (1987). *Critical theories of psychological development*. New York & London: Plenum Press.

Brown, B. B. (1990). Peer groups and peer cultures. In S. S. Feldman & G. R. Elliott (Eds.), *At the threshold: The developing adolescent* (pp. 171–196). Cambridge, MA: Harvard University Press.

Brumberg, J. J. (1988). *Fasting girls: The emergence of anorexia nervosa as a modern disease*. Cambridge, MA: Harvard University Press.

Buchmann, M. (1989). *The script of life in modern society*. Chicago: University of Chicago Press.

Buckingham, D. (2000). *After the death of childhood: Growing up in the age of electronic media*. Cambridge: Polity Press.

Burdell, P. (1995/1996). Teen mothers in high school: Tracking the curriculum. In M. Apple (Ed.), *Review of Research in Education*, Vol. 21 (pp. 163–208). Washington, D.C.: Aera.

Burman, E. (1994). *Deconstructing developmental psychology*. London & New York: Routledge.

Butler, J. (1990). *Gender trouble: Feminism and the subversion of identity*. New York: Routledge.

Callahan, R. E. (1962). *Education and the cult of efficiency*. Chicago & London: University of Chicago Press.

Cavallo, D. (1981). *Muscles and morals: Organized playgrounds and urban reform, 1880–1920*. Philadelphia: University of Pennsylvania Press.

Carnegie Council on Adolescent Development. (1989). *Turning points: Preparing American youth for the twenty-first century*. Washington, D.C.: Carnegie Corporation of New York.

Carnegie Council on Adolescent Development. (1995). *Great transitions: Preparing adolescents for a new century*. New York: Carnegie Corporation of New York.

Cesaire, A. (1972). *Discourse on colonialism* (Joan Pinkham, Trans.). New York: Monthly Review Press.

Chamberlain, J. E., & Gilman, S. L. (Eds.). (1985). *Degeneration: The dark side of progress*. New York: Columbia University Press.

Chauncey, G. (1994). *Gay New York: Gender, urban culture, and the making of the gay male world, 1890–1940*. New York: Basic Books.

Children's Defense Fund. (1985). *Preventing children having children*. Washington, D.C.: Children's Defense Fund.

Childs, M. J. (1992). *Labour's apprentices: Working-class lads in late Victorian and Edwardian England*. Montreal & Kingston: McGill-Queen's University Press.

Chudacoff, H. P. (1989). *How old are you? Age consciousness in American culture*. Princeton, NJ: Princeton University Press.

Cohen, P. (1997). *Rethinking the youth question: Education, labour and cultural studies*. London: Macmillan.

Cole, T. R. (1984). The prophecy of *Senescence*: G. Stanley Hall and the reconstruction of old age in America. *The Gerontologist, 24*(4), 360–366.

Coleman, J. S. (1961). *The adolescent society*. New York: Free Press.

Collins, R. (1979). *The credential society: An historical sociology of education and stratification*. New York: Academic Press, Inc.

Connell, R. W. (1990). An iron man: The body and some contradictions of hegemonic masculinity. In M. A. Messner & D. F. Sabo (Eds.), *Sport, men, and the gender order* (pp. 72–90). Champaign, IL: Human Kinetics Books.

Connell, R. W. (1995). *Masculinities*. Berkeley & Los Angeles: University of California Press.

Connell, R. W. (1996). Teaching the boys: New research on masculinity, and gender strategies for schools. *Teachers College Record, 98*(2), 206–235.

Conrad, J. (1907/1998). *The secret agent*. New York: The Modern Library.

Coontz, S. (1992). *The way we never were: American families and the nostalgia trap*. New York: Basic Books.

Coté, J. E., & Allahar, A. L. (1996). *Generation on hold: Coming of age in the late twentieth century*. New York & London: New York University Press.

Cravens, H. (1978). *The triumph of evolution: American scientists and the heredity-environment controversy, 1900–1941*. Philadelphia: University of Pennsylvania Press.

Croddy, M. (1997). Violence redux: A brief legal and historical perspective on youth violence. *Social Education, 61*(5), 258–264.

Csikszentmihalyi, M., & Schmidt, J. (1998). Stress and resilience in adolescence: An evolutionary perspective. In K. Borman & B. Schneider (Eds.), *The adolescent years: Social influences and educational challenges* (97th Yearbook of the National Society for the Study of Education, pp. 1–17). Chicago: University of Chicago Press.

Cuban, L. (1993a, Summer). Are schools to blame? *Rethinking Schools*, 11.

Cuban, L. (1993b). *How teachers taught: Constancy and change in American classrooms, 1880–1990* (2nd ed.). New York: Teachers College Press.

Curti, M. (1959). *The social ideas of American educators*. Paterson, NJ: Littlefield, Adams & Co.

Cusick, P. (1962). *Inside high school*. New York: Holt Rinehart & Winston.

Dash, L. (1989). *When children want children: An inside look at the crisis of teenage parenthood*. New York: Penguin.

Davies, B. (1989). The discursive production of male/female dualism in school settings. *Oxford Review of Education, 15*(3), 229–241.

Davies, L. (1992). School power cultures under economic constraint. *Educational Review, 43*(2), 127–136.

Davis, N. J. (1999). *Youth crisis: Growing up in the high risk society*. Westpoint, CT, & London: Prager.

Dawson, G. E. (1896). A study in youthful degeneracy. *The Pedagogical Seminary, 4*(2), 221–258.

DeBord, G. (1977). *The society of the spectacle*. Detroit: Red and Black Press.

Dewey, J. (1896). Interpretation of the culture-epoch theory. *The Public School Journal, XV*(5), 233–236.

Deyhle, D., & LeCompte, M. (1994). Cultural differences in child development: Navaho adolescents in middle schools. *Theory into Practice, 33*(3), 156–166.

Dohrn, B. (1997). Youth violence: False fears and hard truths. *Educational Leadership, October*, 45–47.

Douglas, A. (1995). *Terrible honesty: Mongrel Manhattan in the 1920s*. New York: Noonday Press.

Duras, M. (1985). *The lover*. New York: Pantheon.

Dyhouse, C. (1981). *Girls growing up in late Victorian and Edwardian England*. London: Routledge and Kegan Paul.

Eckert, P. (1989). *Jocks and Burnouts: Social categories and identity in the high school*. New York: Teachers College Press.

Ecksteins, M. (1985). Anthropology and degeneration. In J. E. Chamberlain & S. L. Gilman (Eds.), *Degneration: The dark side of progress* (pp. 3–20). New York: Columbian University Press.

Education Week. (1986, May 14). Here they come, ready or not. Special issue.

Education Week. (1996, November 6, 1996). Teen birthrates down in nearly every state, survey shows, 8.

Eisenstein, Z. (1994). *The color of gender: Reimaging democracy*. Berkeley: University of California Press.

Ennew, J. (1994). Time for children or time for adults. In J. Qvortrup, M. Bardy, G. Sgritta, & H. Wintersberger (Eds.), *Childhood matters: Social theory, practice and politics* (pp. 125–144). Aldershot, UK: Avebury.

Erikson, E. H. (1950/1985). *Childhood and society*. New York & London: W. W. Norton & Co.

Erikson, E. H. (1968). *Identity: Youth and crisis*. New York: W. W. Norton & Co.

Fabian, J. (1983). *Time and the other: How anthropology makes its object*. New York: Columbia University Press.

Fabian, J. (1991). Of dogs alive, birds dead, and time to tell a story. In J. Bender & D. E. Wellbery (Eds.), *Chronotypes: The construction of time* (pp. 185–204). Stanford, CA: Stanford University Press.

Fanon, F. (1952/1986). *Black skin, white masks* (Markmann, Charles Lam, Trans.) (2nd ed.). London: Pluto Press.

Fanon, F. (1963). *The wretched of the earth* (Farrington, Constance, Trans.). New York: Grove Press.

Fausto-Sterling, A. (1995a). Gender, race, and nation: The comparative anatomy of "Hottentot" women in Europe, 1815–1817. In J. Urla & J. Terry (Eds.), *Deviant bodies: critical perspectives on difference in science and popular culture* (pp. 19–48). Bloomington, IN: Indiana University Press.

Fausto-Sterling, A. (1995b). *Myths of gender: Biological theories about women and men* (2nd ed.). New York: Basic Books.

Feldman, S. S., & Elliott, G. R. (Eds.). (1990). *At the threshold: The developing adolescent.* Cambridge, MA: Harvard University Press.

Fendler, L. (1998). What is it impossible to think? A genealogy of the educated subject. In T. S. Popkewitz & M. Brennan (Eds.), *Foucault's challenge: Discourse, knowledge, and power in education* (pp. 39–63). New York: Teachers College Press.

Fernandez, R., Geary, P. A., Lesko, N., Rutter, R. A., Smith, G. A., & Wehlage, G. G. (1987). *Dropout prevention and recovery: Fourteen case studies.* Madison, WI: National Center on Effective Secondary Schools.

Field, N. (1995). The child as laborer and consumer: The disappearance of childhood in contemporary Japan. In S. Stephens (Ed.), *Children and the politics of culture* (pp. 51–78). Princeton, NJ: Princeton University Press.

Figlio, K. (1976). The metaphor of organization: An historiographical perspective on the bio-medical sciences of the early 19th century. *History of Science 14*, 17–53.

Fine, G. A., & Mechling, J. (1993). Child saving and children's cultures at century's end. In S. B. Heath & M. W. McLaughlin (Eds.), *Identity and inner-city youth: Beyond ethnicity and gender* (pp. 120–146). New York: Teachers College Press.

Fine, M. (1988). Sexuality, schooling, and adolescent females: The missing discourse of desire. *Harvard Educational Review, 58*(1), 29–53.

Fine, M. (1993). Making controversy: Who's "at risk?" In R. Wollons (Ed.), *Children at risk in America: History, concepts, and public policy* (pp. 91–110). Albany, NY: State University of New York Press.

Fine, M., & Weis, L. (1998). *The unknown city: The lives of poor and working-class young adults.* Boston: Beacon Press.

Foley, D. (1990a). The great American football ritual: Reproducing race, class, and gender inequality. *Sociology of Sport Journal, 7*, 111–135.

Foley, D. E. (1990b). *Learning capitalist culture: Deep in the heart of Tejas.* Philadelphia: University of Pennsylvania Press.

Fordham, S. (1997). *Blacked out.* New Brunswick, NJ: Rutgers University Press.

Foucault, M. (1973). *The order of things: An archaeology of the human sciences.* New York: Vintage Books.

Foucault, M. (1978). *The history of sexuality, Volume 1: An introduction* (Hurley, Robert, Trans.). New York: Vintage Books.

Foucault, M. (1979). *Discipline and punish: The birth of the prison* (Sheridan, A., Trans.). New York: Vintage Books.

Foucault, M. (1991). Governmentality. In G. Burchell, C. Gordon, & P. Miller (Eds.), *The Foucault effect: Studies in governmentality* (pp. 87–104). Chicago: University of Chicago Press.

Franklin, B. (1986). *The struggle for the American community.* London: Falmer Press.

Franklin, B. (1990). "Something old, something new, something borrowed ...": A historical commentary on the Carnegie Council's Turning Points. *Journal of Education Policy, 5* (3), 265–72.

Fraser, N. (1989). *Unruly practices: Power, discourse and gender in contemporary social theory.* Minneapolis, MN: University of Minnesota Press.

Fraser, N., & Gordon, L. (1994). A genealogy of dependency: A keyword of the U.S. welfare state. *Signs: Journal of Women in Culture and Society, 19*(2), 309–336.

Frazier, E. F. (1957). *Black bourgeoisie: Rise of a new middle class.* New York: Free Press.

Freeman, M. (1997, April 13). Painkillers, and addiction, are prevalent in N.F.L. *New York Times,* 19, 22.

Friedenberg, E. Z. (1980). The changing role of homoerotic fantasy in spectator sports. In D. F. Sabo & R. Runfola (Eds.), *Jock: Sports and male identity* (pp. 177–192). Englewood Cliffs, NJ: Prentice-Hall.

Garrahy, D. (1998). *It depends where you lead them: Gender in the elementary school.* Bloomington, IN: Indiana University.

Gay, G. (1994). Coming of age ethnically. *Theory Into Practice, 33* (3), 149–155.

Gay, P. (1984). *The bourgeois experience, Vol. I: Education of the senses.* New York: Oxford University Press.

Gibson, J. W. (1994). *Warrior dreams: Violence and manhood in post-Vietnam America.* New York: Hill & Wang.

Gilbert, J. (1986). *A cycle of outrage: America's reaction to the juvenile delinquent in the 1950s.* New York & Oxford: Oxford University Press.

Gilligan, C. (1982). *In a different voice: Psychological theory and women's development.* Cambridge, MA: Harvard University Press.

Gillis, J. (1981). *Youth and history: Tradition and change in European age relations, 1770-present.* New York: Academic Press.

Gilman, S. L. (1985). *Difference and pathology: Stereotypes of sexuality, race, and madness.* Ithaca & London: Cornell University Press.

Gilroy, P. (1987). *"There ain't no black in the Union Jack": The cultural politics of race and nation*. Chicago: University of Chicago Press.

Giroux, H. A. (1996). Hollywood, race, and the demonization of youth: The "kids" are not "alright." *Educational Researcher, 25*(2), 31–35.

Goleman, D. (1995). *Emotional intelligence: Why it can matter more than IQ*. New York: Bantam.

Goldstein, R. (2000, February). We've got game. How sports took over American culture. *Village Voice*, 40–46.

Gould, S. J. (1977). *Ontogeny and phylogeny*. Cambridge, MA: Belknap Press.

Gould, S. J. (1981). *The mismeasure of man*. New York: W. W. Norton.

Gould, S. J. (1991). *Bully for the brontosaurus*. New York: Basic Books.

Graebner, W. (1990). *Coming of age in Buffalo: Youth and authority in the post war era*. Philadelphia: Temple University Press.

Graff, H. J. (1995). *Conflicting paths: Growing up in America*. Cambridge, MA: Harvard University Press.

Graves, K. (1998). *Girls' schooling in the Progressive Era: From female scholar to domesticated citizen*. New York & London: Garland.

Greider, W. (1997). *One world, ready or not: The manic logic of global capitalism*. New York: Touchstone Books.

Griffin, C. (1993). *Representations of youth: The study of youth and adolescence in Britain and America*. Cambridge, UK: Polity Press.

Grinder, R. E., & Strickland, C. E. (1963). G. Stanley Hall and the social significance of adolescence. *Teachers College Record, 64*, 390–399.

Grumet, M. (1981). Pedagogy for patriarchy: The feminization of teaching. *Interchange, 12*(2–3), 165–184.

Gruneau, R., & Whitson, D. (1993). *Hockey night in Canada: Sport, identities and cultural politics*. Toronto: Garamond.

Gusfield, J. R. (1981). *The culture of public problems: Drinking-driving and the symbolic order*. Chicago: University of Press.

Gusfield, J. R. (1963). *Symbolic crusade: Status politics and the American temperance movement*. Urbana, IL: University of Illinois Press.

Guthrie, R. V. (1976/1998). *Even the rat was white: A historical view of psychology*. Boston: Allyn & Bacon.

Hacking, I. (1991). How should we do the history of statistics? In G. Burchell, C. Gordon, & P. Miller (Eds.), *The Foucault effect: Studies in governmentality* (pp. 181–196). Chicago: University of Chicago Press.

Hale, G. E. (1998). *Making whiteness: The culture of segregation in the south, 1890–1940*. New York: Pantheon.

Hale, N. G., Jr. (1971). *Freud and the Americans: The beginnings of psychoanalysis in the United States, 1867–1917*. New York: Oxford University Press.

Hall, G. S. (1881). Editorial. *The Pedagogical Seminary, I*(2), 119–125.

Hall, G. S. (1883). The contents of children's minds. *Princeton Review, 11*, 249–72.

Hall, G. S. (1900). Child study and its relation to education. *Forum, 29*, 688–693, 696–702.

Hall, G. S. (1903). Coeducation in the high school. *National Education Association Journal of Proceedings and Addresses, 42*, 442–455.

Hall, G. S. (1904). *Adolescence: Its psychology and its relations to physiology, anthropology, sociology, sex, crime, religion, and education* (2 vols.). New York: D. Appleton.

Hall, G. S. (1911). The budding girl, *Educational Problems*. New York: D. Appleton.

Hall, G. S. (1914). Education and the social hygiene movement. *Social Hygiene, 1*, 29–35.

Hall, G. S. (1923/1977). *Life and confessions of a psychologist*. New York: Arno.

Hall, G. S., & Saunders, F. H. (1900). Pity. *American Journal of Psychology, 11*, 534–591.

Hall, S. (1993). Culture, community, nation. *Cultural Studies, 7*(3), 352–360.

Hall, S. (no date). *Race: The floating signifier* [video]. Northampton, MA: Media Education Foundation.

Haraway, D. (1989). *Primate visions: Gender, race, and nature in the world of modern science*. New York & London: Routledge.

Haraway, D. J. (1991). *Simians, cyborgs, and women: The reinvention of nature*. New York: Routledge.

Haraway, D. J. (1997). *Modest_witness@second_millenium*. New York: Routledge.

Hargreaves, D. H. (1967). *Social relations in a secondary school*. London: Routledge & Kegan Paul.

Hargreaves, J. (1986). *Sport, power and culture: A social and historical analysis of popular sports in Britain*. New York: St. Martin's Press.

Harvey, D. (1990). *The condition of postmodernity*. Cambridge & Oxford: Blackwell.

Haug, F. *Female sexualization: A collective work of memory*. London: Verso.

Hawes, J. M., & Hiner, N. R. (Eds.). (1985). *American childhood: A research guide and historical handbook*. Westport, CT: Greenwood Press.

Heath, S. B., & Mangiola, L. (1991). *Children of promise*. Washington, D.C.: National Education Association.

Heath, S. B., & McLaughlin, M. (Eds.). (1993). *Identity and inner-city youth: Beyond ethnicity and gender*. New York: Teachers College Press.

Henriques, J., Hollway, W., Unwin, C., Venn, C., & Walkerdine, V. (1984). *Changing the subject: Psychology, social regulation, and subjectivity*. London & New York: Methuen.

Henry, J. (1963). *Culture against man*. New York: Vintage.

Hirsch, E. D. (1987). *Cultural literacy*. Boston: Houghton Mifflin.

Holland, P. (1992). *What is a child? Popular images of childhood*. London: Virago Press.

Holloway, W., & Jefferson, T. (1997). The risk society in an age of anxiety: Situating fear of crime. *British Journal of Sociology of Education, 48*(2), 255–265.

Hollway, W. (1984). Gender difference and the production of subjectivity. In J. Henriques et al., *Changing the subject* (pp. 227–263). London & New York: Methuen.

Holquist, M. (1990). *Dialogism: Bakhtin and his world*. London & New York: Routledge.

hooks, b. (1981). *Ain't I a woman: Black women and feminism*. Boston: South End Press.

Horn, D. G. (1995). This norm which is not one: Reading the female body in Lombroso's anthropology. In J. Terry & J. Urla (Eds.), *Deviant bodies: Critical perspectives on difference in science and popular culture* (pp. 109–128). Bloomington, IN: Indiana University Press.

Hultqvist, K. (1998). A history of the present on children's welfare in Sweden: From Froebel to present-day decentralization projects. In T. S. Popkewitz & M. Brennan (Eds.), *Foucault's challenge: Discourse, knowledge, and power in education* (pp. 91–116). New York: Teachers College Press.

James, A., & Prout, A. (Eds.). (1990a). *Constructing and reconstructing childhood: Contemporary issues in the sociological study of childhood*. London & New York: Falmer Press.

James, A., & Prout, A. (1990b). Re-presenting childhood: Time and transition in the study of childhood. In A. James & A. Prout (Eds.), *Constructing and reconstructing childhood: Contemporary issues in the sociological study of childhood* (pp. 216–238). London & New York: Falmer Press.

Jansen, S. C., & Sabo, D. (1994). The sport/war metaphor: Hegemonic masculinity, the Persian Gulf War, and the new world order. *Sociology of Sport Journal, 11*, 1–17.

Jeal, T. (1990). *The boy-man: The life of Lord Baden-Powell*. New York: Morrow.

Jeffords, S. (1989). *The remasculinization of America: Gender and the Vietnam War*. Bloomington, IN: Indiana University Press.

Jenks, C. (forthcoming). The pacing and timing of children's bodies. In G. Dahlberg & K. Hultqvist (Eds.), *The changing child in a changing world*. New York: Routledge.

Jones, E. F., Forrest, J. D., Goldman, N., Henshaw, S., Lincoln, R., Rosoff, J. E., Westoff, C. F., & Wulf, D. (1986). *Teenage pregnancy in industrialized countries*. New Haven, CT: Yale University Press.

Jones, E. F., Forrest, J. D., Henshaw, S., Silverman, J., & Torres, A. (1989). *Pregnancy, contraception, and family planning services in industrialized countries*. New Haven, CT: Yale University Press.

Katchadourian, H. (1990). Sexuality. In S. S. Feldman & G. R. Elliott (Eds.), *At the threshold: The developing adolescent* (pp. 330–351). Cambridge, MA: Harvard University Press.

Katz, J. (1995). Reconstructing masculinity in the locker room: The Mentors in Violence Prevention Project. *Harvard Educational Review, 65*(2), 163–170.

Katz, J. N. (1995). *The invention of heterosexuality*. New York: Dutton.

Katz, M. (1995). *Improving poor people: The welfare state, the "underclass" and urban schools as history*. Princeton, NJ: Princeton University Press.

Keddie, N. (1971). Classroom knowledge. In M. F. D. Young (Ed.), *Knowledge and control: New directions for the sociology of education* (pp. 133–160). London: Cassell & Collier Macmillan.

Kenway, J., & Fitzclarence, L. (1997). Masculinity, violence and schooling: Challenging "poisonous pedagogies." *Gender and Education, 9*(1), 117–133.

Kern, S. (1983). *The culture of time and space, 1880–1918*. Cambridge, MA: Harvard University Press.

Kessen, W. (1990). *The rise and fall of development*. Worcester, MA: Clare University Press.

Kett, J. F. (1974). History of age grouping in America. In J. S. Coleman (Ed.), *Youth: Transition to adulthood* (pp. 9–28). Chicago: University of Chicago Press.

Kett, J. F. (1977). *Rites of passage: Adolescence in America 1790 to the present*. New York: Basic Books.

Kimmel, M. (1996). *Manhood in America: A cultural history*. New York: Free Press.

Kincaid, J. (1985). *Annie John*. New York: Farrar, Strauss, Giroux.

Kincaid, J. R. (1992). *Child-loving: The erotic child and Victorian culture*. New York: Routledge.

Kliebard, H. M. (1995). *The struggle for the American curriculum, 1893–1958* (2nd ed.). New York: Routledge.

Koselleck, R. (1985). *Futures past: On the semantics of historical time* (Tribe, Keith, Trans.). Cambridge & London: MIT Press.

Koven, S. (1992). From rough lads to hooligans: Boy life, national culture, and social reform. In A. Parker, M. Russo, D. Sommer, & P. Yaeger (Eds.), *Nationalisms and sexualities* (pp. 365–394). New York & London: Routledge.

Krug, E. A. (1969). *The shaping of the American high school, 1920–1941.* Vol. 2. Madison: University of Wisconsin Press.

Kunzel, R. G. (1993). *Fallen women, problem girls: Unmarried mothers and the professionalization of social work, 1890–1945.* New Haven, CT: Yale University Press.

Landes, D. (1983). *Revolution in time: Clocks and the making of the modern world.* Cambridge, MA: Belknap Press.

Laqueur, W. Z. (1962). *Young Germany: A history of the German Youth Movement.* New York: Basic Books.

Lawson, A. (1993). Multiple fractures: The cultural construction of teenage sexuality and pregnancy. In A. Lawson & D. Rhode (Eds.), *The politics of pregnancy: Adolescent sexuality and public policy* (pp. 101–125). New Haven, CT: Yale University Press.

Lears, T. J. J. (1981). *No place of grace: Antimodernism and the transformation of American culture, 1880–1920.* Chicago & London: University of Chicago Press.

Lefkowitz, B. (1997). *Our guys: The Glen Ridge rape and the secret life of the perfect suburb.* Berkeley, CA: University of California Press.

Lesko, N. (1990). Curriculum differentiation as social redemption: The case of school-aged mothers. In R. Page & L. Valli (Eds.), *Curriculum differentiation: Interpretive studies in U.S. secondary schools* (pp. 113–136). Albany, NY: State University of New York Press.

Lesko, N. (1991). Implausible endings: Teenage mothers and fictions of school success. In N. Wyner (Ed.), *Current perspectives on the cultures of schools* (pp. 45–63). Cambridge, MA: Brookline Books.

Lesko, N. (1994a). Back to the future: Middle schools and the *Turning Points* report. *Theory into Practice, 33*(3), 143–148.

Lesko, N. (1994b). The social construction of "the problem of teenage pregnancy." In R. Martusewicz & W. M. Reynolds (Eds.), *Inside/out: Contemporary critical perspectives in education* (pp. 139–150). New York: St. Martin's Press.

Lesko, N. (1995). The "leaky needs" of school-aged mothers: An examination of U.S. policies and programs. *Curriculum Inquiry, 25*(2), 25–40.

Lesko, N. (1996a). Denaturalizing adolescence: The politics of contemporary representations. *Youth and Society, 28*(2), 139–161.

Lesko, N. (1996b). Past, present, and future conceptions of adolescence. *Educational Theory, 46*(4), 453–472.

Lesko, N. (1997). Before their time: Social age, reproductive rights, and school-aged mothers. In S. Books (Ed.), *Neither seen nor heard: Invisible children in the society and its schools* (pp. 101–131). Mahwah, NJ: Lawrence Erlbaum Publishers.

Lesko, N. (1998). Feeling the teacher: A phenomenological reflection of Maxine Greene's pedagogy. In W. Pinar (Ed.), *The passionate mind of Maxine Greene: "I am . . . not yet"* (pp. 238–246). London & Bristol, PA: Falmer Press.

Lesko, N. (2000). Preparing to [teach] coach: Tracking the gendered relations of dominance on and off the football field. In N. Lesko (Ed.), *Masculinities at school* (pp. 187–212). Thousand Oaks, CA: Sage.

Lesko, N., & Bloom, L. (1998). Close encounters: Truth, experience, and interpretation in multicultural teacher education. *Journal of Curriculum Studies, 30*(4), 375–395.

Levidow, L. (1995). Castrating the other: The paranoid rationality of the Gulf War. *Psychoculture: Review of Psychology & Cultural Studies, 1*(1), 9–16.

Levine, R. (1997). *A geography of time*. New York: Basic Books.

Lewis, M., & Karen, B. (1994). Queer stories/straight talk: Tales from the school playground. *Theory Into Practice, 33*(3), 199–205.

Lipsitz, J. (1991). Public policy and young adolescents: A 1990s context for researchers. *Journal of Early Adolescence, 11*(1), 20–37.

Lipsyte, R. (2000, July 20). What happens after the whistle blows? *The New York Times*, D1–D2.

Lomawaima, K. T. (1995). Domesticity in Federal Indian Schools: The power of authority over mind and body. In J. Terry & J. Urla (Eds.), *Deviant bodies: Critical perspectives on difference in science and popular culture* (pp. 197–218). Bloomington, IN: Indiana University Press.

Lovejoy, A. O. (1936). *The Great Chain of Being: A study of the history an idea*. Cambridge, MA: Harvard University Press.

Lowe, D. M. (1982). *History of bourgeois perception*. Chicago: University of Chicago Press.

Luke, A, (1995/1996). Text and discourse in education: An introduction to critical discourse analysis. In M. Apple (Ed.), *Review of Research in Education*, Vol. 21 (pp. 3–48). Washington, D.C.: AERA.

Luker, K. (1996). *Dubious conceptions: The politics of teenage pregnancy*. Cambridge, MA: Harvard University Press.

Lutz, C. (1988). *Unnatural emotions: Everyday sentiments on a Micronesian atoll and their challenge to Western theory*. Chicago & London: University of Chicago Press.

Lutz, C. (1997). Epistemology of the bunker: The brainwashed and other new subjects of permanent war. In J. Pfister & N. Schnog (Eds.), *Inventing the psychological: Toward a cultural history of emotional life in America* (pp. 245–267). New Haven, CT, & London: Yale University Press.

Lutz, T. (1991). *American nervousness: An anecdotal history*. Ithaca & London: Cornell University Press.

Lyall, S. (2000, March 5). Oh, thank you. That hurt. *New York Times*, 4–3.

Mac an Ghaill, M. (1994). *The making of men: Masculinities, sexualities, and schooling*. Buckingham, UK, & Philadelphia: Open University Press.

Macleod, D. I. (1983). *Building character in the American boy: The Boy Scouts, YMCA, and their forerunners, 1870–1920*. Madison, WI: University of Wisconsin Press.

MacNaughton, G. (1998). Improving gender equity "tools": A case for discourse analysis. In N. Yelland (Ed.), *Gender in early childhood* (pp. 149–174). London & New York: Routledge.

Mandel, L., & Shakeshaft, C. (2000). Heterosexism in middle schools. In N. Lesko (Ed.), *Masculinities at school* (pp. 75–104). Thousand Oaks, CA: Sage.

Martin, J. R. (1985). *Reclaiming a conversation: The ideal of the educated woman*. New Haven, CT: Yale University Press.

McClintock, A. (1993). Family feuds: Gender, nationalism and the family. *Feminist Review, 44*, 61–80.

McClintock, A. (1995). *Imperial leather: Race, gender and sexuality in the colonial context*. New York: Routledge.

McMurry, C. A. (1925). *Elements of a general method based on the principles of Herbart*. New York & London: Macmillan.

McQuire, K. (1990). Business involvement in education in the 1990s. In D. Mitchell & M. Goertz (Eds.), *Education politics for the new century* (pp. 110–122). New York: Falmer Press.

Memmi, A. (1965). *The colonizer and the colonized* (Greenfield, Howard, Trans.). New York: Beacon Press.

Messner, M. A. (1992). *Power at play: Sports and the problem of masculinity*. Boston: Beacon Press.

Miedzian, M. (1991). *Boys will be boys: Breaking the link between masculinity and violence*. New York: Anchor Books.

Mohanty, C. (1997). Dangerous territories, territorial power, and education. In L. G. Roman & L. Eyre (Eds.), *Dangerous territories: Struggles for difference and equality in education* (pp. ix–xvii). New York & London: Routledge.

Moore, M. H. & Tonny, M. (1998). Youth violence in America. In M. Tonny & M. H. Mooore (Eds.), *Youth violence: Crime and justice, Vol. 24* (pp. 1–26). Chicago: University of Chicago Press.

Morrison, T. (1992). *Playing in the dark: Whiteness and the literary imagination*. Cambridge, MA: Harvard University Press.

Morss, J. (1996). *Growing critical: Alternatives to developmental psychology*. London & New York: Routledge.

Mosse, G. L. (1985). *Nationalism and sexuality: Middle class morality and sexual norms in modern Europe*. Madison, WI: University of Wisconsin Press.

Mosse, G. L. (1996). *The image of man: The creation of modern masculinity.* New York & Oxford: Oxford University Press.

Murcott, A. (1980). The social construction of teenage pregnancy: A problem in the ideologies of childhood and reproduction. *Sociology of Health and Illness, 2*(1), 1–23.

Nadelhaft, M. (1993). Metawar: Sports and the Persian Gulf War. *Journal of American Culture, 16*(4), 25–33.

Neubauer, J. (1992). *The fin-de-siècle culture of adolescence.* New Haven, CT, & London: Yale University Press.

Newmann, F. (1993). Beyond common sense in education restructuring. *Educational Researcher, 22*(2), 4–22.

Nicholson, L. (1998). I am modern hear me roar. Presentation to the society for Women in Philosophy, Hunter College, New York, NY, May.

Nieto, S. (1992). *Affirming diversity: The sociopolitical context of multicultural education.* White Plains, NY: Longman.

Nye, R. A. (1985). Sociology and degeneration: The irony of progress. In J. E. Chamberlin & S. L. Gilman (Eds.), *Degeneration: The dark side of progress* (pp. 49–71). New York: Columbia University Press.

Odem, M. E. (1995). *Delinquent daughters: Protecting and policing adolescent female sexuality in the United States 1885–1920.* Chapel Hill, NC, & London: University of North Carolina Press.

Orner, M. (1992). Interrupting the calls for student voice in "liberatory" education. In C. Luke and J. Gore (Eds.), *Feminisms and critical pedagogies* (pp. 74–89). New York: Routledge.

Parker, A., Russo, M., Sommer, D., & Yaeger, P. (Eds.). (1992). *Nationalisms and sexualities.* New York & London: Routledge.

Passerini, L. (1997). Youth as a metaphor for social change: Fascist Italy and America in the 1950s. In G. Levi & J. Schmitt (Eds.), *A history of young people in the West* (Vol. 2, pp. 281–342). Cambridge, MA: Belknap Press.

Peiss, K. (1986). *Cheap amusements: Working women and leisure in turn-of-the-century New York.* Philadelphia: Temple University Press.

Perry, T., & Fraser, J. W. (Eds.). (1993). *Freedom's plow: Teaching in the multicultural classroom.* New York: Routledge.

Peters, M. (1998). Introduction. In M. Peters (Ed.), *Naming the multiple: Poststructuralism and Education* (pp. 1–24). Westport, CT: Bergin & Garvey.

Pinar, W. F., Reynolds, W. M. Slattery, P., & Taubman, P. M. (1995). *Understanding curriculum.* New York: Peter Lang.

Platt, A. (1977). *The child savers: The invention of delinquency.* Chicago: University of Chicago Press.

Popkewitz, T. S. (1997). A changing terrain of knowledge and power: A social epistemology of educational research. *Educational Researcher, 26*(9), 18–29.

Popkewitz, T. S. (1998a). Dewey, Vygotsky, and the social administration of the individual: Constructivist pedagogy as systems of ideas in historical spaces. *American Educational Research Journal, 35*(4), 535–570.

Popkewitz, T. S. (1998b). *Struggling for the soul: The politics of schooling and the construction of the teacher.* New York: Teachers College Press.

Popkewitz, T. S. & Bloch, M. (forthcoming). "Bringing the parent in": A history of the present social administration of the parent to rescue the child for society. In G. Dahlberg & K. Lundquist (Eds.), *The changing child in a changing world.* New York: Routledge.

Popkewitz, T. S., & Brennan, M. (1998). Restructuring of social and political theory in education: Foucault and a social epistemology of school practices. In T. S. Popkewitz & M. Brennan (Eds.), *Foucault's challenge: Discourse, knowledge and power in education* (pp. 3–38). New York: Teachers College Press.

Popkewitz, T. S., & Pitman, A. (1986). The idea of progress and the legitimation of state agendas: American proposals for school reform. *Curriculum & Teaching, 1* (1 & 2), 11–23.

Popkewitz, T. S., Pittman, A., & Barry, A. (1986). Education reform and its millennial quality: The 1980s. *Journal of Curriculum Studies, 18*(3), 267–284.

Postman, N. (1982). *The disappearance of childhood.* New York: Delacorte.

Powell, A., Farrar, E., & Cohen, M. (1985). *The shopping mall high school.* Boston: Houghton Mifflin.

Prout, A., & James, A. (1990). A new paradigm for the sociology of childhood? In A. James & A. Prout (Eds.), *Constructing and reconstructing childhood: Contemporary issues in the sociological study of childhood* (pp. 7–34). London & New York: Falmer Press.

Qvortrup, J., Bardy, M., Sgritta, G., & Wintersberger, H. (Eds.). (1990). *Childhood matters: Social theory, practice and politics.* Aldershot, UK: Avebury.

Rajchman, J. (1985). *Michel Foucault: The freedom of philosophy.* New York: Columbia University Press.

Rains, P. M. (1971). *Becoming an unwed mother.* Chicago: Aldine.

Rees, C. R. (1997). Still building American character: Sport and the physical education curriculum. *The Curriculum Journal, 8*(2), 199–212.

Rees, C. R. (forthcoming). School sports in America: The production of "winners" and "losers." In S. Bailey (Ed.), *School sport and competition.* Aachen: Meyer & Meyer.

Richardson, T. (1989). *Century of the child: The mental hygiene movement and social policy in the U.S. and Canada*. Albany, NY: State University of New York Press.

Rifkin, J. (1987). *Time wars*. New York: Henry Holt.

Robins, D., & Cohen, P. (1978). *Knuckle sandwich: Growing up in the working-class city*. Harmondsworth: Penguin.

Rodgers, D. T. (1998). *Atlantic crossings: Social politics in a progressive age*. Cambridge, MA: Belknap Press of Harvard University Press.

Roman, L. (1996). Spectacle in the dark: Youth as transgression, display, and repression. *Educational Theory, 46*(1), 1–22.

Roman, L. G., & Eyre, L. (Eds.). (1997). *Dangerous territories: Struggles for difference and equality in education*. New York & London: Routledge.

Rosario, J. R. (1990). Guiding principles are not enough: On thinking, folly, & middle school reform. *Journal of Education Policy, 5* (3), 273–81.

Rose, N. (1989). *Governing the soul*. New York: Routledge.

Rose, N. (1999). *Powers of freedom: Reframing political thought*. Cambridge, UK: Cambridge University Press.

Rosenthal, M. (1984). *The character factory: Baden-Powell and the origins of the Boy Scout movement*. New York: Pantheon Books.

Ross, A. (1988). *Universal abandon?* New York: Routledge.

Ross, D. (1972). *G. Stanley Hall: The psychologist as prophet*. Chicago: University of Chicago Press.

Ross, D. (1984). American social science and the idea of progress. In T. L. Haskell (Ed.), *The authority of experts: Studies in history and theory* (pp. 157–179). Bloomington, IN: Indiana University Press.

Rousmaniere, K. (1997). *City teachers: Teaching and school reform in historical perspective*. New York & London: Teachers College Press.

Russett, C. E. (1989). *Sexual science: The Victorian construction of womanhood*. Cambridge, MA: Harvard University Press.

Ryan, M. P. (1981). *Cradle of the middle class: The family in Oneida County, New York, 1790–1865*. New York: Cambridge University Press.

Rydell, R. W. (1984). *All the world's a fair: Visions of empire at the American International Expositions, 1876–1916*. Chicago: University of Chicago Press.

Sabo, D. (1994). Pigskin, patriarchy and pain. In M. A. Messner & D. Sabo (Eds.), *Sex, violence and power in sports: Rethinking masculinity* (pp. 82–88). Freedom, CA: Cross Press.

Said, E. W. (1978). *Orientalism: Western representations of the Orient*. London: Routledge & Kegan Paul.

Said, E. W. (1993). *Culture and imperialism*. New York: Routledge.

Sander, J. (1991). *Before their time: Four generations of teenage mothers*. New York: Harcourt Brace Jovanovich.

Sapon-Shevin, M. (1989). Selling cooperative learning without selling it short. *Educational Leadership, 47*(4), 63–65.

Scheiner, S. M. (1965). *Negro mecca: A history of the Negro in New York City, 1865–1920*. New York: New York University Press.

Schlesinger, A. M. (1992). *The disuniting of America*. New York: W. W. Norton & Co.

Schlossman, S. (1977). *Love and the American delinquent: The theory and practice of "progressive" juvenile justice, 1825–1920*. Chicago: University of Chicago Press.

Schlossman, S., & Wallach, S. (1978). The crime of precocious sexuality: Female juvenile delinquency in the Progressive Era. *Harvard Educational Review, 48*(1), 65–94.

Schwartz, G. (1987). *Beyond conformity or rebellion: Youth and authority in America*. Chicago: University of Chicago Press.

Sedgwick, E. K. (1990). *The epistemology of the closet*. Berkeley, CA: University of California Press.

Sedgwick, E. K. (1993). How to bring your kids up gay. In M. Warner (Ed.), *Fear of a queer planet: Queer politics and social theory* (pp. 69–81). Minneapolis, MN: University of Minnesota Press.

Serres, M., & Latour, M. (1990). *Conversations on science, culture, and time* (Lapidus, Roxanne, Trans.). Ann Arbor, MI: University of Michigan Press.

Shafir, G. (Ed.). (1998). *The citizenship debates*. Minneapolis, MN: University of Minnesota Press.

Shank, M. J. (2000). Striving for educational rigor: Acceptance of masculine privilege. In N. Lesko (Ed.), *Masculinities at school* (pp. 213–230). Thousand Oaks, CA: Sage.

Siegel, S. (1985). Art and degeneration. In J. E. Chamberlin & S. L. Gilman (Eds.), *Degeneration: The dark side of progress* (pp. 210–230).

Sizer, T. R. (1984). *Horace's compromise: The dilemma of the American high school*. Boston: Houghton Mifflin.

Smith, D. E. (1990). *The conceptual practices of power: A feminist sociology of knowledge*. Boston: Northeastern University Press.

Smith-Rosenberg, C. (1985). *Disorderly conduct: Visions of gender in Victorian America*. New York: Oxford University Press.

Solberg, A. (1990). Negotiating childhood: Changing constructions of age for Norwegian children. In A. James & A. Prout (Eds.), *Constructing and reconstructing childhood: Contemporary issues in the sociological study of childhood* (pp. 118–137). London & New York: Falmer Press.

Solinger, R. (1992). *Wake up Little Susie: Single pregnancy and race before Roe v. Wade*. New York: Routledge.

Solomon, H. M. (1997). "What a shame you don't publish": Crossing the boundaries as a public intellectual activist. In L. G. Roman & L. Eyre (Eds.), *Dangerous territories: Struggles for difference and equality* (pp. 179–190). New York & London: Routledge.

Southern Poverty Law Center. (2000). *Youth at the edge*. Montgomery, AL: Southern Poverty Law Center.

Spacks, P. M. (1981). *The adolescent idea: Myths of youth and the adult imagination*. New York: Basic Books.

Spear, A. H. (1967). *Black Chicago: The making of a Negro ghetto 1890–1920*. Chicago: University of Chicago Press.

Spring, J. (1989). *American education: An introduction to social and political aspects*. 4th ed. New York: Longman.

Springhall, J. (1977). *Youth, empire and society: British youth movements, 1883–1940*. London: Croom Helm.

Springhall, J. (1986). *Coming of age: Adolescence in Britain, 1860–1960*. Dublin: Gill & Macmillan.

Stafseng, O. (1994). Autobiography or ethnography in youth theories? Unpublished manuscript, Oslo, Norway.

Stafseng, O. (no date). A critique of slippery theories on postmodernity and youth. Unpublished manuscript, Oslo, Norway.

Stecopoulos, H. (1997). The world according to Normal Bean: Edgar Rice Burrough's popular culture. In H. Stecopoulos & M. Uebel (Eds.), *Race and the subject of masculinities* (pp. 170–191). Durham, NC, & London: Duke University Press.

Stein, N. (1995). Sexual harassment in school: The public performance of gendered violence. *Harvard Educational Review, 65*(2), 145–162.

Stepan, N. (1982). *The idea of race in science: Great Britain 1800–1960*. London: Macmillan.

Stepan, N. L., & Gilman, S. L. (1993). Appropriating the idioms of science: The rejection of scientific racism. In S. Harding (Ed.), *The "racial" economy of science*. Bloomington, IN: Indiana University Press.

Stephens, S. (Ed.). (1995). *Children and the politics of culture*. Princeton, NJ: Princeton University Press.

Stewart, I. (1998). *Life's other secret: The new mathematics of the living world*. New York: John Wiley & Sons.

Stocking, G. W. (1968). *Race, culture, and evolution: Essays in the history of anthropology*. Chicago: University of Chicago Press.

Stoler, A. L. (1995). *Race and the education of desire: Foucault's history of sexuality and the colonial order of things*. Durham, NC, & London: Duke University Press.

Strickland, C., & Burgess, C. (Eds.). (1965). *Health, growth, and heredity: G. Stanley Hall on natural education*. New York: Teachers College Press.

Talburt, S. (2000). *Subject to identity: Knowledge, sexuality, and academic practices in higher education*. Albany, NY: State University of New York Press.

Tchudi, S. (1991). *Travels across the curriculum*. New York: Scholastic.

Terry, J. (1995). Anxious slippages between "us" and "them": A brief history of the scientific search for homosexual bodies. In J. Terry & J. Urla (Eds.), *Deviant bodies: Critical perspectives on difference in science and popular culture* (pp. 129–169). Bloomington, IN: Indiana University Press.

Thistlethwaite, F. (1963). *America and the Atlantic community*. New York: Harper & Row.

Thompson, A. (1995). Not the color purple: Black feminist lessons for educational caring. *Harvard Educational Review 68* (4), 522–554.

Thompson, E. P. (1993). *Customs in common*. New York: The Free Press.

Thompson, W. I. (1996). *Coming into being: Artifacts and texts in the evolution of consciousness*. New York: St. Martin's Press.

Thurow, L. (1996). *The future of capitalism*. New York: William Morrow & Co.

Time. (1985, December 9). Children having children. 16–20.

Tolen, R. J. (1995). Colonizing and transforming the criminal tribesman: The Salvation Army in British India. In J. Terry & J. Urla (Eds.), *Deviant bodies: Critical perspectives on difference in science and popular culture* (pp. 78–108). Bloomington, IN: Indiana University Press.

Toulmin, S., & Goodfield, J. (1965). *The discovery of time*. New York: Harper & Row.

Treichler, P. (1988). AIDS, homophobia, and biomedical discourse: An epidemic of signification. *October, 43*, 31–70.

Trinh, T. M. (1989). *Woman, native, other*. Bloomington, IN: Indiana University Press.

Tyack, D., & Hansot, E. (1992). *Learning together: A history of coeducation in American public schools*. New York: Russell Sage Foundation.

Urry, J. (2000). *Sociology beyond societies: Mobilities for the twenty-first century*. London & New York: Routledge.

Usher, R., & Edwards, R. (1994). *Postmodernism and education*. London & New York: Routledge.

Van Liew, C. C. (1895). The educational theory of culture epochs viewed historically and critically. In C. A. McMurry (Ed.), *The first yearbook of the Herbart Society* (pp. 70–121). Bloomington, IL: Public-School Publishing Co.

Varenne, H. (1982). Jocks and freaks: The symbolic structure of the expression of social interaction among American senior high school students. In G. Spindler (Ed.), *Doing the ethnography of schooling* (pp. 210–235). New York: Holt Rinehart & Winston.

Wakefield, W. (1996). *Playing to win*. Albany, NY: State University of New York Press.

Waksler, F. C. (1991). The hard times of childhood and children's strategies for dealing with them. In F. C. Waksler (Ed.), *Studying the social worlds of children: Sociological readings* (pp. 216–234). London: Falmer Press.

Walker, J. C. (1988). *Louts and legends: Male youth culture in an inner-city school*. Sydney: Allen & Unwin.

Walkerdine, V. (1984). Developmental psychology and the child-centred pedagogy: The insertion of Piaget into early education. In J. Henriques, W. Hollway, C. Urwin, C. Venn, & V. Walkerdine (Eds.), *Changing the subject: Psychology, social regulation, and subjectivity* (pp. 153–202). London & New York: Methuen.

Walkerdine, V. (1990). *Schoolgirl fictions*. London & New York: Verso.

Walkerdine, V. (1997). *Daddy's girl: Young girls and popular culture*. Cambridge, MA: Harvard University Press.

Weatherley, R. A., & Cartoof, V. G. (1988). Helping single adolescent parents. In C. S. Chilman, E. W. Nunnally, & F. M. Cox (Eds.), *Variant family forms* (pp. 39–55). Newbury Park, CA: Sage.

Weber, M. (1958). *The Protestant ethic and the spirit of capitalism*. New York: Scribner.

Weedon, C. (1987/1997). *Feminist practice and poststructuralist theory*. London: Blackwell.

Wehlage, G., Rutter, R., Smith, G., Lesko, N., & Fernandez, R. (1989). *Reducing the risk: Schools as communities of support*. London: Falmer Press.

Weiler, J. (1998). *The athletic experiences of ethnically diverse girls* (131). New York: ERIC Clearinghouse on Urban Education Digest.

Weis, L. (1993). White male working-class youth: An exploration of relative privilege and loss. In L. Weis & M. Fine (Eds.), *Beyond silenced voices: Class, race, and gender in United States schools* (pp. 237–258). Albany, NY: State University of New York Press.

Weiss, N. J. (1974). *The National Urban League 1910–1940*. New York: Oxford University Press.

Wexler, P. (1976). *The sociology of education: Beyond equality*. Indianapolis, IN: Bobbs-Merrill.

Wexler, P. (1992). *Becoming somebody*. London: Falmer Press.

Whitson, J. A. (1991). Post-structuralist pedagogy as counter-hegemonic praxis (Can we find the baby in the bathwater?). *Education and Society*, 9(1), 73–86.

Whyte, W. F. (1943/1955). *Street corner society: The social organization of a slum*. Chicago: University of Chicago Press.

Wiebe, R. (1967). *The search for order, 1877–1920*. Westport, CT: Greenwood Press.

Willinsky, J. (2000). Tempering the masculinities of technology. In N. Lesko (Ed.), *Masculinities at school* (pp. 253–282). Thousand Oaks, CA: Sage.

Wishy, B. (1968). *The child and the republic*. Philadelphia: University of Pennsylvania Press.

Wood, J. (1984). Groping towards sexism: Boys' sex talk. In A. McRobbie & M. Nava (Eds.), *Gender and generation* (pp. 105–129). London: Macmillan.

Wyn, J. (2000). Education for the new adulthood: Implications of youth research for education. Paper presented at American Educational Research Association annual meeting, New Orleans, LA, April.

Young, R. M. (1985). *Darwin's metaphor: Nature's place in Victorian culture*. Cambridge, UK: Cambridge University Press.

Young, R. (1990). *White mythologies: Writing history and the West*. New York: Routledge.

Young, R. (1995). *Colonial desire: Hybridity in theory, culture and race*. New York: Routledge.

Young-Bruehl, E. (1996). *The anatomy of prejudices*. Cambridge, MA: Harvard University Press.

Zimring, F. (1998). The youth violence epidemic: Myth or reality? *Wake Forest Law Review, 33*, 727–744.

Zinn, H. (1980/1995). *A people's history of the United States: 1492 to present*. New York: HarperPerennial.

author index

subject index

Lightning Source UK Ltd.
Milton Keynes UK

174425UK00012B/47/P